Empowerment of Tribal Women in South India

Empowerment of Tribal Women in South India: Gender Perspectives

Editors

Dr. Sukumaran M
Dr. Anji. A

ISBN: 978-93-5324-258-9 (HB)

First Published, 2020

Published by

Kalpaz Publications
C-30, Satyawati Nagar,
Delhi – 110052
Ph.: 011-47034999, 9811692060
www.kalpazpublications.com
E-mail: kalpaz@hotmail.com

Printed at: G. Print Process, Delhi

Contents

Introduction 7
Acknowledgment 11

1. Land Holdings of Tribal Women: Evidence from Agricultural Census 13
   Dr. J. V. Arun and A. Premkumar
2. A Rationalised Analysis on Tribal Women Participation in Sports 21
   Dr. Ajesh.C.R
   Savitha. V.
3. A Study on Practice of Child Marriage in Tribal Communities in Karnataka: A Gender Lens 27
   Dr. Anji A
4. Tribal Women as a Pillar When Disaster Strikes: A Case from Wayanad District 41
   Athira K
5. Financial Discipline Among Women in Paniya Community of Township Colony of Kannur District-kerala 47
   Dr. Bindu M. P.
6. Problems and Challenges of Empowering Schedule Tribe Women-with Special Refrence of Haveri District In Karanataka 63
   Channappa Lamani,
   Dr, Thimmaiah T. D
7. Economic Status of Women: A Case Study of Sc & St Women of Kozhikode District 73
   Deepa. E & Jeni B. S.
8. Issues and Challenges of Tribal Women in India: A Socio Economic Perspective 81
   Dr. Indira P M
9. Tribal Women's Health in India: Issues, Challenges and Strategies 95
   Dr. Shilpa M. Sangam
10. Empowerment of Tribal Women and Education as a Tool 101
    Dr. Naseema. P K
11. Social Exclusion of Paliyar Tribal Women In Dindigul District of Tamil Nadu 111
    Dr.T. S. Bala Gomala & V. Ariya Nathu

12. Kudumbashree and Empowerment of Tribal Women: Evidence from Wayanad, Kerala 123
Fathima Fidha & Dr. Sukumaran M

13. Economic Status of Scheduled Tribal Workers Working in Leather Tanneries in Vellore District Tamil Nadu 133
Mr. S. John Sundar

14. Social Exclusion and Tribal Women 141
Kavi Mozhi. M Dr. P. S. Sreedevi Nandini. P

15. Importance of personal hygiene among adolescent women's in rural India 147
Lukkumanul Hakkim S

16. Status of Tribal Women in Karnataka: Reference to Policies and programmes 153
Dr. M. H. Hullur

17. Contemporary Stigmatisation of Devadasi Women of South India 169
Popy Devi Nath
Ms. Bastobee Borsaikia

18. An Anthropological analysis of Patelia Tribal women in Karnataka state 175
Dr. Prabudha S. Kamble

19. Tribal Women in their Traditional Social Settings: An Anthropological Appraisal 181
Dr. K. S Pradeep Kumar

20. Problems and Challenges of Kalvarayan Malai Tribal People 189
Dr. K. Pushpam, and K. Manivasakam,

21. A Critical Appraisal on the Issues and Challenges of Tribal Education in Kerala 195
Dr. Remmiya Rajan P & Ms. Anjana

22. Status of Malapandaram Women in Kerala 203
Salini. R & Dr. PK. Muthukumar

23. Educational Status of Scheduled Tribes-A Gender Perspective 213
Dr. Sivasankar, V and Premkumar, A

25. Health Status of Paliyan Tribal Women in Sirumalai Hills: A Sociological Perspective 217
Dr. K. Seenivasan

25. Education and Empowerment of Tribal Women: Empirical and Theoretical Dialogues 227
Vinayakan S B, & Dr. Sukumaran M

Index 235

Introduction

Empowering the Adivasi Women: Old Dynamics, New Dialectics.

M. Kunhaman

Empowering women is not just a question of protecting women from various types of atrocities, iniquities and discriminations, but, more importantly, of creating and maintaining a just and healthy society. Such empowerment is, needless to say, is a multi-dimensional process. Empowering Adivasi Women, unquestionably the weakest social group is an arduous task considering the multiple vulnerabilities faced by them and the formidable hostilities and resistances posed by the state, political parties and the church, all in cahoot with the pillaging, deprading non-tribal settlers.

The Indian Constitution putatively proclaims the highest degree of protection to the Adivasis. It has two Schedules(Fifth and Sixth) and nearly 20 Articles directly and indirectly benefiting them. Article 46 enjoins the state to protect them from various sorts of exploitation and oppression and promote their development. But the state has singularly failed in these two duties. It may be observed, en passant, that the tribal problems can be solved and the adivasis are seeking solutions within the Constitutional framework.

The Focal Point

As the adivasis are not a homogeneous and undifferentiated group, we should decide on the category of adivasi women to be empowered. Needless to say, it is the deprived, pauperized Adivasi women who should be empowered,thus treating them as a part of the precariat. And bestowing on them ownership of and control over resources must be the starting point. As Hegel said in 1820, property is freedom; it is this freedom, i.e., real freedom that members of the precariat badly need. Property enriches and empowers. It enhances the access to resources, enjoyment of life and, hence, happiness. Property title can be used to access institutional finance for taking up entrepreneurial activities.Health and education are the next vital areas in empowering the precariously perched Adivasi women. Studies show that nutrition and prenatal and post-natal care are not available, affecting the health, employability and productivity of future generations.

Empowerment crucially hinges upon the level and quality of education. Here, the state can play a significant role. Admission, retention and completion rates must be raised, The question of quality should be combined with cognitive, retentive, reproductive and application abilities. Wherever necessary, adivasi students(of both the sexes) must be given remedial learning facilities/opportunities.Every family should have a T.V set. Students' attention should be fully turned into creative channels, As Abhijit Banerjee and Esther Duflo, Nobel laureates, unambiguously drive home, miracles can be achieved by taking care of small things at the ground level (Banerjee and Duflo, 2011 , 2019). Life at community and society levels is, of course, important. But perhaps more important is the functioning of the family. Alcoholism and domestic violence ruin life not only of the present generation but also, more ominously, that of the future. All successful persons come from well-organized, disciplined families. Making family life infernal and ruining the adivasis are in the interest of their oppressors. Such machinations must be exposed and defeated.

In thinking about empowering Adivasi women, a few basic questions are apposite. Is there an Adivasi question? If yes, what is it? Is it a political, administrative, or Constitutional question?

The weak position of the Adivasi women is the cumulative outcome of a long, dialectical process. Understanding the present dynamics requires an examination of the past dialectics. In the typical Adivasi society, there was bride price, an amount given to the bride's family as a compensation for taking away earning family member through marriage. Gender equality,along with society-environment symbiosis, was an in situ venerated, parametric value carried forward through generations. When the adivasis lost their control over their life situation, adivasi women's marginalization and subordination began. They came to be subject to the exploitation and oppression by the non-tribal settlers who, by grabbing Adivasi land, depeasantised and pauperized a whole indigenous population. Adivasis'sdestiny came to be determinedby 'the others'. Everything is now decided 'for them' by 'the others'. The tribal-non-tribal divide is stark today. The tribals are the borrowers; the non-tribals are the money-lenders; tribals are labourers and non-tribal settlers are the employers.Tribals, bonded labourers, non-tribals, the masters. Tribal unwed mothers, non-tribal settlers are the perpetrators. In tribal land alienation, land flows from the tribals to the non-tribals. And in these unavailing processes, the state, political parties and the church invariably support the non-tribal settlers.

The Adivasis have been excluded through development; their inclusion has been sought through welfare programs, inculcating in them a dependency syndrome. Welfare programs have been used to silence them and prevent them from seeking their own solutions.Of course, innumerable Constitutional,legal and administrative provisions and safeguards are there, purportedly to help adivasis. But these without any exception help the oppressors. After all,the state is to protect the rich and powerful, of course, from the poor and the weak. As the noted lawyer and human rights activist, K.G.Kannabhiran, famously said, crime is defined by law, but the criminal is determined by the state. Social iniquities get reflected in state policies, programs and actions. In an egregiously unequal system, rule of law is a sham. Some persons are subjected to the rule of law; some are above law, and some are ruled without law. Tribal women's lack of empowerment is, however, not due to functional reasons but due to structural reasons.In a system characterized by graded inequality, graded injustice is immanent and natural.

The focus in the foregoing paragraphs has been on the poor, pauperized Adivasi women. Empowering such an impoverished social group is chasing a chimera. One cannot empower the poor and the destitute. They cannot be empowered because they are poor. Beggars cannot be empowered unless begging stops. Making them non-poor through the establishment of a regime of universal property right is inescapably the necessary first step. Empowering a vulnerable social group is unarguably a desideratum. But who will empower and through what means are the most basic questions. The studies included in this volume will, without doubt, throw critical and analytical light on these and other related issues. They have been written from various perspectives but the unifying theme is the same. I place on record my sincere appreciation for Dr. Sukumaran Mavilan and Dr. Anji A for bringing together such a large number of studies on a very important theme. I also congratulate the paper writers for their original insights and unremitting scholarly commitment.

References

Banerjee.Abhijit.V,(2014): Poor Economics. Rethinking Poverty and the Ways to End It.Random House India.Seventh Impression.First published in 2011.

-— (2019)GoodEcob\nomics for Hard Times. BJuggernaut.

Hegel (1820): Elements of the Philosophy of Right. Trans.T. M.Knox.Oxford.1942.

Standing, Guy.(2011): The Precariat.The New Dangerous Class.Bloomsbury.

Dr. M.Kunhaman was Professor at Tata Institute of Social Sciences, Tuljapur Campus, Maharashtra.

Acknowledgment

Our sincere gratitude to the National Commission for Women (NCW) New Delhi for the Financial Assistance made to organize Two Days National Seminar on "Gender and Domestic Violence: Problems and Prospects of Empowering Tribal Women in South India" held on 28th & 29th February 2020. This edited volume is focused various issues and challenges about tribal women in south India in different aspect. This include all the research papers and articles received from different authors to present in the seminar. The seminar Organised by the Department of Development Economics Dr. B. R. Ambedkar Memorial Govt. Arts & Science College Balussery, Kozhikode by the Seminar Directors Dr. Sukumaran M, Assistant Professor of Economics, Dr.B.R. Ambedkar Memorial Govt. Arts & Science College Balussery, and Dr. Anji A Teaching Faculty (Ad-hoc) Department and Research Centre for Women's Studies, Karnatak University, Dharwad.

Dr. Sukumaran and Dr. Anji A are extent our gratitude to Prof. (Dr) M. Kunhaman(Rtd), Tata Institute of Social Sciences, Tuljapur Campus, Maharashtra, Dr. C.J. George, Principal, Dr.B.R. Ambedkar Memorial Govt. Arts and Science College Balussery and Prof. Shakuntala C shatter, Chairperson of Sociology and Hon. Director of Research Centre for Women, Karnarna University, for supporting and guidance.

Our extent warm thank full to all colleagues, non teaching faculties and friend those who are directly or indirectly help to successfully achieving the academic out come from

Chapter - 1

Land Holdings of Tribal Women: Evidence from Agricultural Census

Dr. J. V. Arun and A. Premkumar

Abstract

Land distribution among marginalized groups is very low which often leads to their perpetual poverty, exploitation and social injustice. Research reveals that landlessness is more in India and in this set-up; the paper makes an attempt to study gender differences among tribes in the distribution of land holdings by major size groups. The study has utilized the Agriculture Census (2015-16) report to understand the anomalies in gender wise operational holdings for all social groups and SC/STs exclusively. The results for operational holdings and area operated carried out between different size groups show that there exists poor gender equality in the tribal community. The study also examines distribution of average size per holding by major size groups and gender. Effective implementation of the already existing policies on property entitlement and creating awareness among the stakeholders will go a long way in bridging the gender gap in land holdings.

Keywords: *land, operational, holdings, gender, tribes, social groups*

1. Introduction

Asymmetrical distribution of land is an appalling feature of Indian agricultural system which is largely due to inherent socio-economic disparities (Mungekar, 1999; Thorat, 2002). Land holdings and property rights governed by law of inheritance discriminates women and thereby curtails their economic independence. Land inequality leads to low agricultural productivity, low growth, high rates of poverty, and oppressive social relations (Mohanty, 2001; Faguet *et al.*, 2016). And, above all it curtails economic independence of the landless and leads to concentration of political power (Cinnirella and Hornung, 2016). As far as equity in land holdings is concerned, it can not only reduce women's but her whole family's poverty and increase in livelihood options and thereby enhance women empowerment (Agarwal, 1994). Ninth Plan (1997-2002) envisaged efforts to give land titles to women even then all the efforts and measures of the constitution to remain non – discriminatory has not met with desired results. Even National Agricultural Policy (2000) which aimed to streamline gender concerns in agriculture could not bring out significant change (Planning Commission, 2007).

Work force participation is one of the important parameters to measure gender inequalities along with health, education and political empowerment (Gender Inequality Index, 2016). According to 2011 Census, distribution of female workers in India comprises 32.9 % cultivators, 38.9 % agricultural labourers, 6.5 % workers in household industries and 21.7 % other marginal workers. Significantly, the percentage of female cultivators, agricultural labourers and workers in household industries is more than their male counterparts except in the case of marginal workers. This can be attributed to the poor land holding pattern of the female population. Land is the only resource for tribal people (Prabhakar, 1989) and in spite of that percentage of tribal cultivators declined by more than 10 % in 2011 when compared with 2001 census data whereas percentage of ST agricultural labourers increased by about 9 % (Statistical profile of scheduled tribes in India, 2013). Further, there exist major gender differences in the operational holdings of tribes even after more than 60 years of planned initiatives and policy actions (Arun, 2019). However, there is a scanty of studies related to land distribution among tribal women. At this backdrop, the paper makes an attempt to study gender differences in land holdings among STs for all land holding size with the help of Agriculture Census (2015-16) report.

2. Gender wise distribution of operational holdings

Land which is used wholly or partly for agricultural production and is operated as one technical unit without regard to the title, legal form, size or location is referred as operational holdings (Agriculture Census, 2019). NSS report on operational land holdings, 2002–03 highlighted the fact about mounting population pressure on the limited land base and it got reflected in the changes in the absolute numbers of operational land holdings in different size classes. This particular aspect of land holdings justifies a study on the trends in number and area of operational holdings. The total number of operational holdings has increased from 138.34 million in 2010–11 to 146.45 million in 2015–16, indicating an increase of 5.8 %. In line with the Agricultural Census report, operational holdings are analyzed for different size categories which includes Marginal, Small, Semi-medium, Medium and Large.

Table – 1.1 : Gender wise distribution of number of operational holdings by major size groups

(Number in '000)

Size of Land Holding	*SC*			*STs*			*All Social Groups*		
	Male	*Female*	*Total*	*Male*	*Female*	*Total*	*Male*	*Female*	*Total*
2010-11									
Marginal	11556	1691	13247	5698	772	6470	80032	12656	92826
Small	2187	277	2464	2552	325	2877	21736	3010	24779
Semi – Medium	905	100	1005	1601	186	1787	12418	1451	13896
Medium	303	27	330	693	67	760	5355	499	5875
Large	49	3	52	102	8	111	887	66	973
All Size Classes	15000	2099	17099	10646	1359	12005	120427	17683	138348
2015-16									
Marginal	11686	1872	13559	6168	959	7127	85383	14716	100251
Small	2142	310	2452	2598	374	2972	22303	3469	25809
Semi – Medium	861	113	974	1568	203	1771	12318	1645	13993
Medium	279	30	309	634	69	704	4995	543	5561
Large	44	4	48	88	7	95	753	66	838
All Size Classes	15013	2329	17341	11057	1612	12669	125751	20439	146454

Source: Compiled from Agricultural Census 2015-16, Government of India

In Table – 1.1, gender wise (Male / Female) break-up of number of operational holdings by its size for each social category (SC / STs / All Social Groups) is presented for the nation. It can be observed that distribution of operational holdings in 2015 – 16 among female population for 'all social groups' is only 13.95 % whereas for SCs and STs it is 13.43 % and 12.72 % respectively. Thus it can be inferred that gender bias is slightly higher among STs than other social groups for 'All Size Classes'. It has also to be noticed that gender gap in terms of share of land holdings between male and female population is higher in 'large' holdings and lowest in 'marginal' land holding size for all social groups. From 2010–11 to 2015–16, it can be noticed that operational holdings for 'all social groups' has increased by 15.59 % whereas the increase among STs is 18.62 % and for SCs it is only 10.96 %. Thus it can be presumed that rate of change in operational land holdings of SCs are slower and needs policy intervention. It is also seen percentage variation of number of operational holdings for their different sizes decrease as the holding size increases.

3. Gender wise distribution of area operated

Operated area includes both cultivated and uncultivated area, provided part of it is put to agricultural production during the reference period (Agriculture Census, 2019). Between 2010–11 and 2015–16, there is an increase of 12.01 % in the operated area among females whereas percentage variation for SC/ST women is 10.77 % and 8.65 % respectively. A further analysis shows that for 'marginal' holdings of operated area, the percentage variation is higher for tribal women (22.63 %) followed by the females of 'all social groups' (14.62 %) and SCs (9.62 %).

Table – 1.2: Gender wise distribution of area operated by major size groups

(Area in '000 ha)

Size of Land Holding	*SC*			*STs*			*All Social Groups*		
	Male	*Female*	*Total*	*Male*	*Female*	*Total*	*Male*	*Female*	*Total*
2010-11									
Marginal	4285	582	4867	2786	358	3144	31315	4549	35908
Small	3074	382	3455	3662	457	4119	30979	4218	35244
Semi – Medium	2417	260	2678	4335	496	4831	33767	3864	37705
Medium	1732	153	1885	3984	380	4363	30863	2834	33828
Large	782	54	836	1628	135	1763	14617	1045	16907
All Size Classes	12291	1430	13721	16395	1826	18221	141540	16510	159592
2015-16									
Marginal	4316	638	4955	2974	439	3413	32659	5214	37923
Small	3005	426	3431	3681	521	4202	31286	4813	36151
Semi – Medium	2294	294	2588	4215	537	4752	33182	4353	37619
Medium	1584	167	1752	3595	390	3984	28586	3078	31810
Large	697	59	756	1336	98	1434	12071	1035	14314
All Size Classes	11897	1584	13481	15801	1984	17784	137784	18493	157817

Source: Compiled from Agricultural Census 2015-16, Government of India

Note: Total may not tally due to rounding off & institutional holdings are added under 'total'

As expected, when the size of land holdings of operated area increases percentage variation goes on declining for the women folk of all three social groups with the exception of 'medium' and 'large' size holdings in the SC category (Table – 1. 2). In absolute terms, area of operational holdings of males is higher than their counterparts for all sizes of land holdings. On the contrary, area of operational holdings of males dropped by 2.65 % between 2010–11 and 2015–16 and same is the case for SCs (-3.21 %) and STs (-3.62 %). Also, it is heartening to note that the percentage variation between two census periods among female STs is showing an increasing tendency except for 'large' holdings of operated area.

4. Gender wise distribution of average size per holding

Any significant change in agrarian structure will have some kind of impact on the size distribution of land holdings (NSS 59th Round). Considering the changes that have happened in the last few decades particularly after the advent of state intervention in land distribution, it becomes all the more important to study percentage distribution of average size per holding (Selvaraj and Arun, 2017). However, the average size per holding has been steadily declining in the country in successive census (Agriculture Census, 2011). The following section deals with the gender wise distribution of average size per holding in India for SC/STs and 'all social groups' by different size of land holdings (Table – 1. 3).

Table – 1. 3: Gender wise distribution of average size per holding by major size groups

(Area in '000 ha.)

Size of Land Holding	*SC*			*STs*			*All Social Groups*		
	Male	*Female*	*Total*	*Male*	*Female*	*Total*	*Male*	*Female*	*Total*
2010-11									
Marginal	0.37	0.34	0.37	0.49	0.46	0.49	0.39	0.36	0.39
Small	1.41	1.38	1.40	1.43	1.41	1.43	1.43	1.40	1.42
Semi – Medium	2.67	2.60	2.66	2.71	2.67	2.70	2.72	2.66	2.71
Medium	5.71	5.62	5.70	5.75	5.66	5.74	5.76	5.68	5.76
Large	16.01	15.72	15.99	15.96	15.88	15.95	16.48	15.83	17.38
All Size Classes	0.82	0.68	0.80	1.54	1.34	1.52	1.18	0.93	1.15
2015-16									
Marginal	0.37	0.34	0.37	0.48	0.46	0.48	0.38	0.35	0.38
Small	1.40	1.38	1.40	1.42	1.39	1.41	1.40	1.39	1.40
Semi – Medium	2.66	2.60	2.66	2.69	2.64	2.68	2.69	2.65	2.69
Medium	5.68	5.62	5.67	5.67	5.62	5.66	5.72	5.67	5.72
Large	15.75	15.14	15.70	15.16	14.47	15.11	16.03	15.77	17.07
All Size Classes	0.79	0.68	0.78	1.43	1.23	1.40	1.10	0.90	1.08

Source: Compiled from Agricultural Census 2015-16, Government of India

Average size per holdings of female STs outweighs other two social categories under consideration but the level has come down by 8.21 % between 2010–11 and 2015–16. In both the study periods, average size per holding of female STs is better than the males of SCs and 'all social groups' but not more than male STs. This clearly highlights the presence of gender inequality irrespective of their socio-economic status. It is also seen that in marginal sized land holdings, average size per holding of female STs has an edge over the male SCs and also against the males of 'all social groups'. Moreover, for all social categories and importantly for both the genders average size per holding increases with the increase in land holding sizes.

5. Conclusion

The study reveals about the existence of gender inequities among tribes in all the three parameters under consideration which includes distribution of number and area of operational holdings and average size per holdings during the study period. In particular, under 'medium' and 'large' categories of land holdings, gender disparities are higher for both operational holdings and operated area. Another important outcome of the study is that average size per holdings of female STs is higher than male SCs and 'all social groups' males but not than male STs. By and large, women have to go a long way to claim their legal rights on land ownership. The major reason for the poor land holding pattern among tribal women is probably due to poor implementation of the already existing policies on property entitlement and this warrants a pressing need for correcting implementation anomalies. Failure to do so will force the tribal community to remain in subsistence agricultural economy. ST-women specific policy intervention and conducting special campaigns to create awareness among the stakeholders are the two important ways and means by which the gender gap in land holdings can be set right.

References

Agarwal, B. (1994). "A Field of one's own: Gender and Land Rights in South Asia". Cambridge University Press. Cambridge.

Agriculture Census Division. (2019). "All India Report on Number and Area of Operational Holdings". Agricultural Census 2015-16. Government of India, New Delhi.

Cinnirella, F. and Homung, E. (2016). "Land ownership concentration and the expansion of education". Journal of Developmental Economics, 121, 135-152

Faguet, Jean-Paul, Sanches, Fabio and Villaveces, Marta-Juanita (2016). "The paradox of land reform, inequality and local development in Colombia". The London School of Economics and Political Science, London, UK.

Mohanty, B.B. (2001). "Land Distribution among Scheduled Castes and Tribes". Economic and Political Weekly, 36(40), 3857-3868.

Mungekar, N. (1999). "State, Market and the Dalits: Analytics of New Economic Policy" in S.Michael (ed), Dalits in Modem India, Vistaar Publications, New Delhi.

National Sample Survey Organization. (2006). "Some Aspects of Operational Land Holdings in India, 2002-03". National Sample Survey 59th Round. Government of India, New Delhi.

Planning Commission. (2007). "Gender Issues, Panchayat Raj Institutions, Public Private Partnership, Innovative Finance and Micro Finance in Agriculture for the Eleventh Five Year Plan". Report of Sub Group on Land Related Issues, Government of India, New Delhi.

Prabhakar Reddy, T. (1989). "Tribal land alienation in Andhra Pradesh". Economic and Political Weekly, 24 (28), 1571-1573.

Selvaraj, N., and Arun, J. V. (2017). "Land Holdings in Tamil Nadu: Issues and Challenges". The Voice, 4 (1), 79 – 89.

Sharma, H. R. (2007). "Land Reforms: Status and Opportunities". In Agricultural Paradigm for the Ninth Five Year Plan under New Economic Environment. Oxford & IBH, New Delhi.

Shivashankara, B. Somashekhar, J. (2018). "Social Inequality and Land Holding for Dalit in India". The International Journal of Business Management and Technology, 2(1), 34-36.

Statistical Division. (2013). "Statistical profile of scheduled tribes in India, 2013". Ministry of Tribal Affairs, Government of India, New Delhi.

Thorat, S. (2002). "Oppression and Denial: Dalit Discrimination in the 1990s". Economic and Political Weekly, 39(6), 572-578.

Chapter - 2

A Rationalised Analysis on Tribal Women Participation in Sports

Dr. Ajesh.C.R
Savitha. V.

Sports as a Social Tool

Sport is considered as one of the most sustainable way to bring out productive and remarkable changes in a society. It is being accepted and put in practices under varied canvases all over the world. The development of sports and its influence in the socioeconomic conditions among humans were critically analysed by many researchers and proved even in the era before. The transformation of sports was utilized to cartelize the socio-economic balances among humans. Sports at its wider scope illustrate the nature of it to be deform to any shape for having a better outlook and social acceptability and practicability as well. There for as the evidences showed in the world history it was one among driving force in many countries which had an upper hand in determining the social integrity. In a larger contest we can say that the active participation in sports improves society health and efficiency, reduces medical expenses, take in discipline in character and enhances social structure. The implementation of a mega sporting event helps in developing infrastructure, generates employment and thus contributes significantly to the economic development of a country. Therefore, it can be said that the impact of sports on the society is multi-dimensional. When we address the influence of sports to every social unit the role that it played in the tribal community is still in its infant stage in many countries. The scenario still exists like that in the world where many countries have produced their excellent in sports from the tribal community. The existing world records and awards in their accounts in international as well as national level are ever lasting evidences for the same.

When we address the tribal community in India, initially the focus was more oriented towards their existence and later on bringing out them towards the world of equality in all sense. Indian sports history is also have an account of many elite, international sports personals from tribal community. But when we critically analyse the role that they have put on had made any change in the socialization of the community that they belong to, still asks many questions to us. The sports policies executed in our country obviously doesn't so pin pointed to any class of society in it. But at the same time the practicability of them were assured in the socio economic group who were all set to access it. The cases that the history showed are some exceptional cases under the same category. When the socio economic and civilization factors influences the utility of any policies, programs, or even an organization the question of chances of execution to some will be extremely imperative. When sports and recreation activities provides a platform for generation an immense amount of joy, happiness, energy, and productivity, its extensiveness among tribal people leads to thoughts which always have apositive direction.

For very many the need of anything will be based on the hierarchy in life. It will not have a different dimension to any social group. But at the same time once the fruitfulness of any positively marked activity come in practice man will try to make it in habit. The activities of tribes make the difference in priority of sports in their life. The lack of knowledge, system, policies, and many more can make much bigger impact in the non practice of sports activities among tribal people. The secondary need of to be happy was satisfies with many other means that might have historians listed down as the back pulling causes of the entire community. They were never tried to be re-prioritised. The reason may not be physical ill-literacy, rather the canvases in which the policies were applied was too small to even reach them. Due to a better civilization the percentage of knowledge, skill and attitude might have changed, but still it does not attained its full form. The sports in it bigger context, one of the biggest tool for socialization and empowerment is still need to addressed to tribal community in a better way. The joy and happiness that sports and related recreational activities can provide is need to be performed among them in a popular manner. When the daily need itself imposes too much physical needs to their life people may ignore the active participation in a way. But if we are able to convey the fruitfulness of the same, the transformation of talent to champion the result that we can produce will change the life of them ceaselessly.

The Language of Sports

Whenever we address the tribal community the practicability of any thing leads to the gap in the levels of many learning factors. But in the case of movements the language remains the same. Rather it can be put up in such way that they may be characteristically efficient in many things due to biological, physical and life style reasons. As they learn a proficiency in it through the medium of physical activities, they will try to exhibit their talents. The hand to hand, shoulder to shoulder efforts with them can bring out glory to the life of tribe.The strength, stamina and the psychological characteristics of tribes are of more suitable for many activities in sports, where their proficiency can be converted in to medals that can bring glory to the country. As we do in every part of our country the hunt for talents must cover the geographical areas where tribes are civilized. The Indian sports history is the evidence of such results made before in our country. For a tribal child as we promote basic and higher education with an attempt to bring out a social competency among them, education on sports and games can also be provide to them in a systematic ways so that we can dream for more Olympic gold in the medal tally of our country. The children generally try to be within their own social set up as they were brought up under such circumstances, the language of sports can share the feeling of social inclusiveness of talents everywhere in the world. The effort taken up by others form their own community, who walked before them should be narrated, and conveyed to them in such way that the in born fire in then can be used to lighten the talents in them. If it does so the language of sports can do wonders in their life. The canvases may be changes for a number of times to make them realise that the fruit of the activity with add many dimensions to their life and it leads to a better civilization. The well again focus from the policy makers and administrators that run different systems and policies can bring out the change that we address for them. When we teach the language of sports to them we guarantee the mobilization, motivation, training and development of young people to liberate them from social ills such as crime, poverty, prostitution, drugs abuse, and violence. The sports can use its power to bring out peace and conflict management also.

Empowering Tribal Women through Sports

As in many any field sports were also not having much acceptability in the society when it comes to women participation. That even reflected in the inclusion of women in Olympics also. But the scenario has been changed. We have seen the productive and efficient sports carriers of many women after that. To its wider scope it extends the freedom of expressing and utilizing the energy in women and through they can bring out new altitude of life where there are no demarcations in the power of men and women. When we consider sports as the one of most effective tool for socialisation, we may understand the power in it to teach , practice, and experience different situations through which offers a hands on practice along with multidimensional benefits. Apart from the physical and physiological developments in human body, sports are empowering the women to adjust with many psychological variables. The life of tribal women was not that much complex, but it is still being a mixture of problems rather situation where it becomes difficult deal with it. There are several factors which influence the community. Even though we take an account of their cognitive skills of tribal women still they face many problems to have better choice in real life situation. The inability of being discriminating according to the situational conditions is exploited in some or others way. That can lead them to face difficulties in later life. A wise choice of what to do is very necessary as per the need and to have better output in life they need to be practised to take up decisions in real life situations. The question arises why sports and how it can make a change in the instinct the said change. Sports and games can address many issues of tribal women to make make the literate in day to day practice. Health and wellbeing practices, gender specific disorders, reproductive health, use of drugs, women and girls self esteem and self empowerment, social integration and social inclusion, an accesses to safe place, challenging and transforming gender norms, and opportunities of women and girls in leadership and achievement some of the pin points were we can address the community to strengthen them. Sport inculcates spirit of team-work. There is strength in number; therefore, the ability to strive within a team construct should be the hallmark of women's sport participation. Women could learn leadership practices, how to win and lose with grace, how to recognize strength and weaknesses in themselves and others, and get used to perform under pressure.

Sirsalkar (1988) has given some suggestions based on his study 'Evaluation of Ashram Schools in Maharashtra State'. This study has revealed various lacunas in implementing this scheme in true spirit. Various suggestions like building and library, common room for teachers, separate urinals and bathroom for boys and girls, availability of electricity, provision of annual maintenance to overcome infrastructure problems, arrangement of parent meetings, medical and physical checking organisation of educational tour, competitions of folk songs and folk dances, availability of play grounds and sports material, special coaching, debates, periodicals and lectures etc. has to be arranged to improve existing conditions. Santhosam and Samuel (2013) studied on the Health Status of elderly Irular Tribal Women in Kancheepuram District. The results of the study showed that there is a need for geriatric clinics that can take care of their physical and psychological needs. It further stressed accessibility of health services as a main reason for the elderly not availing the health care services. The study also suggested provision of mobile clinic to cater to the needs of the community every month on a selected date on a regular basis. Singh, et al (1995) writes in an article on Health status of trials in India. Eleven surveys, covering a total sample of 6051 cases, collected in Chota Nagpur and Santal Paragana region of Jharkhand, Bihar have reported very low level of knowledge, attitudes and practice in relation to physical and mental health, diet and nutrition, family planning and child care, health habits, and physical conditions of living.

Policies and programs developed and ran by governmental and nongovernmental organizations ultimately put its best to uplift the addressed community at its best. But in many situations the changes in positives outlook seems to be furnished in a healthier manner. When we try to incorporate all the tools of general population to the tribal community for a better socialization, the improvisations made in those practices gives a remarkable change in the output of the same programme. In the same sense considering the practices in sports related activities with in the tribal community the policies may improvised to create more suitable action plans to bring out changes in the society. The strength and weakness of the community may be assessed in a better manner, which is suitable for them to stream line them into a productive and economic manner to make them capable dream for the socialization through sports activities. Considering the energy and enthusiasm of the group there should be flexibility of action plans to make them beneficial from it one or another way. Sports is an area of human interaction where respect for rules, teamwork and fair play are the norm. Teamwork, cooperation, abiding by the rules, respect for opponents. Sports include all forms of physical exercise, whether local or imported, amateur or professional, casual or organized. Despite the importance of sports, it is an area which is underdeveloped and underfunded. Sporting activities have a wide range of benefits, from improved personal health, job creation and income-generation to the promotion of cultural values and national identity. These potential benefits have yet to be fully realized among tribes. Stronger partnership needs to be forged between sports associations and the private sector to promote sporting activities, particularly sports infrastructure. The organizations need to change their attitude to sports to ensure that they have realistic and up-to-date policies that are strengthened by strong legal frameworks to combat corruption and mismanagement. Association can be made with development projects in the health and education to create synergies beyond the fun of competition in sports. Together, we can do it.

References

Bhasin, Veena. (2007). Status of Tribal Women in India. Stud. Home Commun. Sci.. 1. 10.1080/09737189.2007.11885234.

Perry, Cynthia & Hoffman, Barbara. (2010). Assessing Tribal Youth Physical Activity and Programming Using a Community-Based Participatory Research Approach. Public health nursing (Boston, Mass.). 27. 104-14. 10.1111/j. 1525-1446. 2010. 00833.

Singh, P.K., Singh J., Mahanti S.C. and Modi S. (1995), Watershed approaches in improving the socio-economic status of tribal area: A case study, Journal of Rural Development. 14(2).

Sirsalkar, P.R. (1988), Primitive Tribes: Challenge for Development in Tribal Research Bulletin, Vol. 7, No.2, March, TRTI, Pune.

Chapter - 3

A Study on Practice of Child Marriage in Tribal Communities in Karnataka: A Gender Lens

Dr. Anji A

Abstract

Child marriage in India has been practiced for centuries, with children married off before their physical and mental maturity. The problem of child marriage in India remains rooted in a complex matrix of religious traditions, social practices, economic factors and deeply rooted prejudices. Regardless of its roots, child marriage constitutes a gross violation of human rights, leaving physical, psychological and emotional scars for life. Sexual activity starts soon after marriage, and pregnancy and childbirth at an early age can lead to maternal as well as infant mortality. Moreover, women who marry younger are more likely to experience domestic violence within the home. While regional disparities exist, child marriage has significantly decreased from 47 percent (2006) to 27 percent (2016) It also affects society as a whole since child marriage reinforces a cycle of poverty and perpetuates gender discrimination, illiteracy and malnutrition as well as high infant and maternal mortality rates. Tribes of Karnataka are represented with a blend of culture, religion and ethnicity. These tribes of Karnataka have built their settlements in several hilly and mountainous areas. Kannada language is the main language. Several other tribal communities of Karnataka possess their distinct tradition and ethnicity. Some of them are also reckoned as being originated from the warrior race. Fairs and festivals too are an integral part of the culture of and tradition of the state of Karnataka. The State is the home to 42,48,987 tribal people, of whom 50,870 belong to the primitive group. Although these people represent only 6.95 per cent of the population of the State, there are as many as 50 different tribes notified by the Government of India, living in Karnataka, of which 14 tribes including two primitive ones are primarily natives of this State. It is however, interesting to note that most of these tribes who had been original natives of the forests of the Western

Ghats have been privy to an enormous amount of knowledge about various medicinal plants and their use in traditional/folklore medicine and these practices have been the subject matter of various scientific studies. But still exciting social evils in our Indian. Hence, this research is based on the objective (1) To assess the prevalence and incidence of child marriages, especially in the selected areas,(2)To analyze the various socioeconomic and cultural factors leading to child marriage and (3)To analyze constitutional and legal measures against child marriage and their implementation. The used data from both primary and secondary sources. The study will use probability sampling method. Total sample to be selected for this study are 50 respondents. In this study from different age groups, geographical areas will be selected as respondents. The data analysis will be use qualitative and quantitative manner through gender lens. The researcher will be used for feminist research methods to this entire study. Field visits and discussions revealed a multitude of factors that help sustain and even endorse the custom of child marriage, despite legal barriers. First, social groups follow traditions from previous eras without questioning contemporary relevance. Early marriage allows parents to waiver 'responsibility' of settling their children. Secondly, economically weak and large families encourage the practice as it helps send off girl children early, while marriage of a boy brings an additional hand to assist in household and economic activities. This paper is an attempt to list and map the various tribes of the State of Karnataka and review the studies carried out on the child marriage of ethnic groups.

Keywords: *Child Marriage, Social Economic Factors. Traditions, Human Rights, Gender Discrimination*

1. Introduction

Child marriage is a violation of child rights, and has a negative impact on physical growth, health, mental and emotional development, and education opportunities. It also affects society as a whole since child marriage reinforces a cycle of poverty and perpetuates gender discrimination, illiteracy and malnutrition as well as high infant and maternal mortality rates. Both girls and boys are affected by child marriage, but girls are affected in much larger numbers and with greater intensity. Child marriage can be seen across the country but it is far higher in rural than in urban areas. Girls from poorer families, scheduled castes and tribes, and with lower education levels are more likely to marry at a younger age. Although child marriage is declining, the rate of decline is slow. Broad, multi-faceted strategies are needed to target different aspects of the problem, including deep-rooted social norms and behaviours, the perceived low value of girls, limited access to education, exposure to violence, restricted freedom of movement and economic vulnerability.

2. Profile of Scheduled Tribes in Karnataka

In Karnataka the tribal population has been enumerated in the census from the beginning of the century. According to 1981 census there are 49 notified tribes with a population of 18, 25,203 persons i.e., 4.91 per cent of the general population in the state and about 3.54 percent of the total tribal population in the country. The growth of tribal population from one census to another was more or less similar to that of general population till 1971. However, during 1971-81 the tribal population has substantially increased and has grown at an unprecedentedly high rate. This increase in the tribal population has been due to the fact that non-tribes like Naik, Mota Naik, Nana Naik, Parivara, Beda, Talwars and Valmikis have enumerated themselves as scheduled tribes in 1981 census (Nanjunda Rao, 1988). The Scheduled Tribe population is about 6.6 percent of the total population. The tribal population of Karnataka increased to 34.64 lakh in 2001 from 19.16 lakh in 1991. The decadal growth rate during this period is as high as 80.8 percent, caused not by a spurt in fertility rates but by the addition of several new tribes to the Scheduled Tribes (ST) category. Nayakas sub communities population contains 84.25% among tribes in Karnatak (Srikantha nayaka.G, 2007). Even though there are 49 tribes notified in Karnataka, about 6 to 8 tribes account for over 90 percent of the total scheduled tribal population in the state. The state population data show that Nayaka and Kadu Kuruba cover over 75 percent of the total tribal population and if Marathi, Jenu Kuruba, Gond, Koya and Koli Dhor are also included along with Nayaka and Kadu Kuruba, they account for over 95 percent of the total scheduled tribe population in the state. It may be relavant to mention here some of the anamolies in listing the people belonging to different tribal groups. The scheduled tribes being highly backward do not correctly report the name of their tribe. For instance, many times Marathi Nayakas declare themselves as Nayakas and Beda, Talwar and Valmikis also declare themselves as Nayakas. In some areas the Kurubas who are leading a settled life as Shepherds are reporting themselves as Kadu Kurubas and Jenu Kurubas. (Muthurayappa 2000).

As per details from Census 2011, Karnataka has population of 6.11 Crores, an increase from figure of 5.29 Crore in 2001 census. Total population of Karnataka as per 2011 census is 61,095,297 of which male and female are 30,966,657 and 30,128,640 respectively. In 2001, total population was 52,850,562 in which males were 26,898,918 while females were 25,951,644. The total population growth in this decade was 15.60 percent while in previous decade it was 17.25 percent. The population of Karnataka forms 5.05 percent of India in 2011. In 2001, the figure was

5.14 percent. Recently as per Karnataka census data, 74.25% houses are owned while 23.02% were rented. In all, 70.06% couples in Karnataka lived in single family. In 2011, 61.11% of Uttar Pradesh population had access to Banking and Non-Banking Finance Corporation. Only 4.84% of Uttar Pradesh population had internet facility which is likely to improve in 2021 due to Jio. 6.32% of family in Uttar Pradesh owned car while 25.60% owned two wheller. In few months we will also get details of election data for Karnataka.

3. Review of Literature

According to Saraswat (2006) Child Marriages exist in feudal societies where the Nagnika concept was prevalent. Parents were made to believe that if they did not get their daughters married off before puberty, they would go to hell. Indian tradition places a high premium on virginity before marriage. This applies to women and to some extent men too. In a culture where premarital chastity is valued, one of the easiest ways of achieving this is to get the young girls married in their childhood. A number of social, health and economic disadvantages are associated with early marriage. While existing data do not draw conclusions regarding whether early marriage alone causes these adverse outcomes, it is likely that the links between early marriage, poverty, low educational attainment and other variables in diverse settings have found that married girls are likely to have frequent unprotected sexual relationships.

According to Miller and Lester, (2003), Marriage dramatically increases the likelihood and pressures of childbearing. The first-time mothers below the age 16, in addition to the normal risks and responsibilities of child bearing, face an increased risk of maternal and infant mortality. Married girls typically have low levels of educational attainment, limited or even absent peer networks, restricted mobility and less access to mass media such as T.V., Radio and Newspapers as compared to boys or unmarried girls Haberland & Bracken, (2004).

4. Objective of the study

- To assess the prevalence and incidence of child marriages, especially in the selected areas,
- To analyze the various socio-economic and cultural factors leading to child marriage
- To analyze constitutional and legal measures against child marriage and their implementation

5. Research methodology

The data was collected from both primary and secondary sources. Research methodology of the study was used probability sampling method. The total sample size of this study is 50 respondents from different age groups; geographical areas have been selected as respondents. The participants were selected from the area of Hatti katti, Toni and Mahalingapur Soratur in, Koppal, Bagalkot and Gadag district. The data analysis was use qualitative and quantitative manner through gender lens. The researcher was used the feminist research methodology to this entire study.

The socio economic status of respondents is said to have a greater bearing on the performance in the activity selected. The indicators are age, sex, marital status, education level, and community groups, religion and occupation of family are presented in above table.

- More than fifty percent of the respondents from the age group of 31 to 50 years.
- More than 30 percent of the respondent's not literate, which means they are illiterate.
- 100 percent of the respondents.
- 100 percent of the respondents from Social category of ST community.
- Nearly 85 percent of the respondents are married.
- More than 88 percent of working coolie.
- Nearly 70 percent respondent's income per monthly 2001 to 4000.

Table — 3.1 : Distribution of the Respondents on the Basis of Background Characteristics

P. S.N	*Variables*	*No. of women respondent*	*Percentage*
Pattern 1	Age (Years)		
	Below 30	16	32
	31-50	26	52
	Above 51	08	16
Pattern 2	Gender		
	Male	0	0
	Female	50	100
	Education		
	Not literate	15	30
	Primary	12	24

(*Contd...*)

Pattern 3	Middle	10	20
	High school	05	10
	Degree / Diploma	02	04
	Can read and write	06	12
Pattern 4	Religion		
	Hindu	50	100
	Christian	0	0
Pattern 5	Community groups		
	Scheduled caste / Scheduled Tribes	50	100
	Others	0	0
Pattern 6	Marital Status		
	Unmarried	02	04
	Married	42	84
	Widow/ Separated	06	12
Pattern 7	Occupational Background of Family		
	Government	02	04
	Private	04	08
	Coolie	44	88
Pattern 8	Monthly income		
	less than 2000	09	18
	2001 - 4000	33	66
	4001 - 6000	06	12
	Above 6001	02	04

***Sources:-** from primary data*

- More than fifty percent of the respondents don't have awareness about legal age of marriage.
- Nearly 22 respondents getting child marriage
- 32 percent of respondents are did not having awareness about child marriage violate human right
- 68 percent of respondents are did not aware about Child marriage restriction act.
- After early marriage of children 40 percent of the respondents going to deterioration of health and nutrition.
- 16 percent of respondents are said that nobody did not discuss about issue related to early marriage with their place

Challenges to eradicating the child marriage

There are many causes of child marriage in India and multiple barriers to the eradication this social evil. Poverty, weak enforcement of laws, patriarchal social norms intended to ensure family honour are significant factors that increase the risk of girls being married off while still a child. Also, girls from poor households are more likely to marry as children, since marriage becomes a solution to reduce the size of the family. The cost of marriage plays a big role in families sliding further into poverty, and these high costs contribute to girls being forced to marry when other ceremonies are taking place in the family or when older siblings are being married.

Table — 3.2: Awareness about the Child Marriage

S.N	*Particulars*	*Yes*	*Percent*	*No*	*Percent*
1	Did you know legal age of marriage –boys and girls	19	38	31	62
2	What are age of during your marriage a) Below 18 years b) Above 18 years	16 34		32 68	
2	Did you know main reasons for the early marriage: (a)Traditional system (b) Pressure from relatives (c) Pressure from family members (d) Safety and security problems of girls (e) Demand of dowry (f) Others	16 05 05 11 04 04		32 10 10 22 08 08	
3	Do you know that there is a Child Marriage Restraint Act :	16	32	34	68
4	Do you feel child marriage is violation of human rights	34	68	16	32
5	What are the changes after early marriage of children: (1) Increased household responsibility (2) Pressure to work in field (3) Deterioration of health and nutrition	16 14 20		32 28 40	
6	Did anybody discuss issue of early marriage with you or in your place (1) Govt (2) NGOs/CBOs (3) Others (4)No	04 22 16 08		08 44 32 16	
7	Age of respondents during first pregnancy (a) Below-18 years (b) Above 18	12 38		24 76	

Sources:- *from primary source*

Action from UNICEF

UNICEF is working alongside the Government of India in its efforts to prevent the child marriage, including the implementation of the convergent national strategy, which includes:

- **Law enforcement:** Capacity-building on laws, support mechanisms such as a child marriage telephone hotline.
- **Girls' empowerment:** Life skills, protection skills.
- **Community mobilization:** Working with influential leaders, oaths and pledges, counselling, folk and traditional media.
- **Promoting convergence** of sectors at all levels, in particular with education and social protection schemes and programmes.

UNICEF is also working with different and new sectors to ensure a comprehensive approach since child marriage is entrenched in structural problems such as poverty and limited education and vocational opportunities. Partnerships with civil society organizations and communities are key to supporting community mobilization efforts and mindset changes and partnerships with the media are very important for raising awareness for impact on social, economic, health due to child marriage.

Government strategy and action

The Ministry of Women and Child Development, as the nodal agency for women and children, has developed a convergent national strategy and is currently drafting a plan of action on child marriage to guide all states in the implementation of strategies to prevent the problem. Key components of the strategy and draft action plan include: law enforcement, quality education and other opportunities, changing mindsets and social norms, empowering adolescents, producing and sharing knowledge and data, and monitoring. The Government of India is also implementing national programmes aimed at protecting and promoting the development of children, while states are supporting these initiatives through state-level schemes. However, many of the programmes focus on addressing financial vulnerability through cash transfer schemes to keep girls in schools. At the same time, there is a legal framework to prevent child marriage and protect children like, the Prohibition of Child Marriage Act, 2006 makes it illegal for girls to marry under 18 years and for boys under 21 years. Child marriage can be made voidable by the child but within two years of becoming an adult. Child marriage is a punishable offence with a fine up to Rs. 1,00,000 or up to two years of imprisonment or both. It is a non-cognizable and non-bailable offence.

United Nations (2017), reveals that, India has the second highest number of child marriages. For a nation which is touted to be the next emerging superpower, it is a disturbing reality that evils like child marriages still persist not only in ST social category apart from other community in rural.

Marriage is considered to be a sacred union between two mature and consenting individuals who are ready to accept each other and share responsibilities for a lifetime. With respect to this context, child marriages happen to be an unsound institution. The fact that it is still prevalent in India explains that it is a Herculean task to devise measures to eradicate this social evil of child marriage.

6. Discussion

As might be expected, Bagalkot is among the 100 districts in the country with a high incidence of child marriage and teenage pregnancy. According to The National Family Health Survey (NFHS) 2016, one in every six marriages in the state is child marriage .

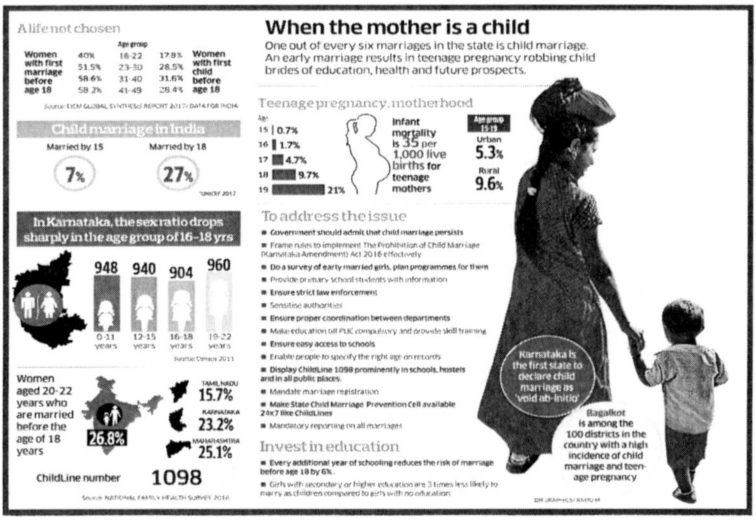

Source: NFHS - 2016

Though its prevalence is high in North Karnataka, particularly in the border districts, child marriage persists in all districts both in rural and urban areas. The practice is mostly found in socially and economically disadvantage communities in rural areas. Poverty, migration, illiteracy, tradition, family pressure and fear of sexual violence are the major causes of early marriages. In most marriages, the groom is in his early 20s and the parents get his married to ensure that he doesn't get into bad habits.

In a stark contrast to the claims of the led Congress government, Karnataka has the second-most number of child marriage cases in India from 2013 till now. Figures released by the Union Ministry of Women and Child Development during the on-going Parliament session show Karnataka has witnessed 130 cases of child marriages since 2013. Umashree, the lone woman representative in the State Cabinet, has been holding the portfolio despite several reshuffles in the Cabinet. Shockingly, Bagalkot the home turf of Umashree (she represents Teradal in Bagalkot) has been identified by the Centre as having the highest incidences of child marriages in Karnataka with Davanagere.

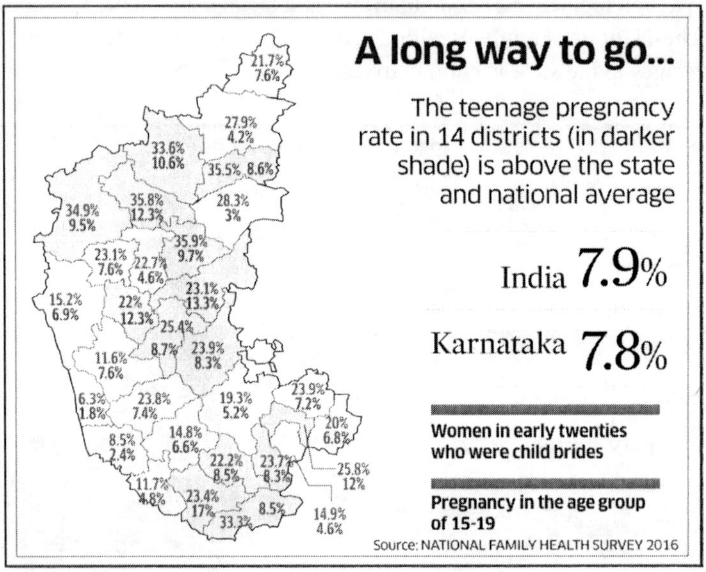

Source: NFHS-2016

The Centre's observation, according to Union Minister for State for Women and Child Development Krishna Raj, is based on the data collated by the National Crime Records Bureau (NCRB). Based on the NCRB figures, the ministry had also commissioned an independent survey 'A statistical analysis of Child Marriages in India based on Census 2011' to ascertain the districts with the highest incidence of child marriages in India. The minister said 70 districts have been identified with high incidence of child marriages. Experts say droughts have forced parents to resort to marrying off their children at an early age, the Centre has attributed it to the people's mindset. The problem has also triggered multiple troubles like early pregnancy, birth complication, delivery of low birth-weight babies and high incidence of infant and maternal mortality ratios. BM had reported about the spurt in the number of child marriage cases in its edition dated 22 November 2016.

The top five state of child marriage

Years	*2012*	*2014*	*2015*	*2016*	*2017*	*2018*
No. of Crime	09	41	34	48	67	75

Source: Karnataka Police reports 2019

Krishna Raj also revealed the cases of child marriages were the highest during Akshaya Tritya and other festivals. "Advisories are sent out to all the states during such occasions to initiate stringent steps to prevent child marriage cases," she said. Asked if the Centre would bring in any amendment to the Prohibition of Child Marriage Act 2006, Krishna Raj said, "The issues involved cannot be tackled by legislative interventions alone. There is no move to amend the Act." Oddly, the difference between data collected by the state women and child development department on child marriage and the Centre is huge. President Pranab Mukherjee has given his assent to the long-pending Prohibition of Child Marriage (Karnataka amendment) Bill, 2016, giving broader powers to the police and increasing the penalty for child marriage. Karnataka is among many states with a high percentage of child marriage cases in south India and according to a survey, 23.2 per cent of such cases are reported from the state, according to the Karnataka State Commission for

Protection of Child Rights

The Bill, according to home ministry officials, was delayed for the past several years. It was last amended in 2016 by the state Assembly and sent to the Centre for Presidential nod. The Home Ministry that acts as an administrative ministry for the state Bills and legislation, after consulting other central ministries, had forwarded the Bill to the Presidential secretariat, said a home ministry official. Chief Minister Siddaramaiah has been urging the Centre to pass the Bill, saying that his government wants to completely eradicate the social menace in the next few years. The percentage of child marriages has come down from 41.2 per cent in 2005 to 23.2 per cent in 2016, according to the state government. Officials said a majority of cases are reported from north Karnataka which includes Dharwad, Belagavi, Bagalkot and the surrounding districts.

The state government's amendment to the Karnataka Prohibition of Child Marriage Act, 2006, was based on recommendations made by a 2011 committee headed by former Supreme Court judge Shivaraj V Patil. It seeks to ensure zero tolerance towards any child marriage, granting powers to policemen and enhancing penalties for those attending marriage ceremonies of minors.

Problems to be addressed

- Low awareness
- Indifferent implementation
- Lack of competent human resource and inadequate infrastructure
- Cultural banded
- Low education

Conclusion and Suggestion

Elimination of early marriage is a clear starting point. The outcomes from this study suggest the following strategies to address this problem:

1. Challenge the traditions that surround early marriage. Inform parents, community members, and youth about the negative consequences of early marriage.
2. Create a supportive network of (religious) leaders and teachers who can empower girls tonegotiate with their parents.
3. Expand training for health and community workers on the dangers of early marriage, engaging them as advocates and change agents in their communities and institutions.
4. Strengthen and establish community networks and partnerships involving girls clubs, teachers, elders, localgovernment officials, women and youth groups, community and religious leaders, etc., that jointly work towards ending early marriage.
5. Strengthen the role of the judicial system particularly the police, judges and persecutors through training on enforcement of the law against early marriage.
6. Develop strong support systems to keep girls in school. Provide scholarships where necessary and encourage teachers to support girls.
7. Bring leading professional women to communities to talk to girls as role models and a source of inspiration.
8. Finally, given the factors motivating child marriages, all efforts should aim at change the gender biased attitudes of parents and society by imparting proper education on one hand and eradicating poverty on the other.

9. Increase awareness generation: All stakeholders should be sensitized and convinced about the negative impacts of child marriage.
10. Gender sensitization programs: Gender training programs should be spread throughout the district for police and NGOs. Primary and secondary education for girls should be promoted.
11. Training: Child Marriage Prevention Officers need to be trained for vigilance.
12. Special police cells: Task forces must be set up to focus on cases of child marriage.
13. Increased authority for NGOs: NGOs should be given the authority to report and intervene in cases of child marriage.

Though there is substantive work initiated to reduce the incidence of child marriages, yet a lot remains to be done to attain Zero Child Marriage. Each country has to set up its own mid-term and long term goals to bring about significant reduction in child marriages. The issue is not an isolated one rather it is intertwined with social norms, cultural taboos and traditions and economic conditions of the families. Partnerships with related Government agencies, NGOs, Media, Women's groups and the private sector will lead to a faster attainment of goals. The problem when addressed through a holistic approach with clearly defined indicators, milestones and responsibilities will help families, communities, nations and regions achieve Zero Child Marriages in a defined time period.

Reference

UNICEF. Child protection from violence, exploitation and abuse. Updated: 2014 October 22

United Nations Treaty Collection. Convention on the Rights of the Child. Retrieved 2015 October

Senderowitz, J. (1995). "Adolescent Health: Reassessing the Passage to Adulthood." World Bank Discussion Paper No. 272. World Bank: Washington, D.C.

Senediak, C. (1990). The value of premarital education. Australian and New Zealand Journal of Family Therapy, 11.

Seymour, S. C. (1999). Women, family, and child care in India: A world in transition. Cambridge University Press.

Anjala Kanesathasan, Laura J. Cardinal, Erin Pearson, Sreela Das Gupta, Sushmit Mukherjee, Anju Malhotra,*Catalyzing Change: Improving Youth Sexual and Reproductive Health through DISHA, an Integrated Program in India* (2008)

Shackelford, T.K., & Buss, D.M. (1997). Anticipation of marital dissolution as a consequence of spousal infidelity. Journal of Social and Personal Relationships, 14(6).

Agarwal, Deepti & Mehra, Sunil. (2004). Adolescent Health Determinants for Pregnancy and Child Health Outcomes among the Urban Poor, Indian Pediatrics – Environmental Health Project, Special Article Services, Volume 41, New Delhi.

Bhatt, A. Sen and U. Pradhan (2005) "Child Marriage & the Law in India", Human Rights Law Network, New Delhi. p. 259

Biswajit Ghosh, (2006): Trafficking in Women & Children, Child Marriage and Dowry: A Study for Action Plan in West Bengal, Dept of Women & Child Development & Social Welfare, Govt. of West Bengal & UNICEF.

International centre for research on women - motivation to prevent child

marriage- http://www.icrw.org/media/news/motivation-prevent-child-marriage,

The Balika Samridhi Yojna http://wcd.nic.in/BSY.htm.

Anjala Kanesathasan, Laura J. Cardinal, Erin Pearson, Sreela Das Gupta, Sushmita Mukherjee, Anju

Malhotra, *Catalyzing Change: Improving Youth Sexual and Reproductive Health through DISHA, an Integrated Program in India* (2008) http://www.icrw.org/publications/catalyzing-change

ICRW, *Improving the Reproductive Health of Married and Unmarried Youth in India*,

http://www.icrw.org/files/publications/Improving-the-Reproductive-Health-of-Married-and-Unmarried-Youth-in-India.pdf

http://www.csrindia.org/child-marriage-in-india

http://unicef.in/Whatwedo/30/Child-Marriage

http://unicef.in/Whatwedo/30/Child-Marriage

https://timesofindia.indiatimes.com/city/bengaluru/child-marriage-cases-in-karnataka-spike-in-6-years-but-only-1-conviction/articleshow/68028979.cms

https://www.deccanherald.com/state/though-outlawed-child-marriage-717642.html

Chapter - 4

Tribal Women as a Pillar When Disaster Strikes: A Case from Wayanad District

Athira K

Abstract

The marginalized communities are worst effected by natural disasters because of their high dependency on climate sensitive livelihood, limited resources & Capacity to adapt. Tribal Population is first in the firing line. Natural Disasters that effected Kerala during 2018 August has adversely affected the life and livelihood of Scheduled Tribes in Kerala. In Tribal Communities, the role of women is substantial and crucial. In Tribal society women are more important than in any other social groups because they work harder and the family economy and management depends on them. The role that women plays become more predominant when there is a natural calamity. This study tries to analyze the role tribal women had played in supporting their family in withstanding natural calamity that hit them in 2018.

Keywords: *Tribal Women, Female Headed Households, Natural Calamities, Tribal Economy*

Introduction

Wayanad derived from "Vayal Nadu" which means the land of paddy fields is a picturesque plateau situated at a height between 700 metres and 2100 metres above the mean sea level nested among the mountains of the Western Ghats on the eastern portion of North Kerala. The total area of the district is 2130 sq km with a total population of 817420 which is 2.45 percent of the total population of the state. The culture of Wayanad is mainly tribal oriented.

The population of Scheduled Tribes in the district in 2011 is 151443 consisting of 74476 males and 76967 females. This accounted for 31.24 percent of Scheduled Tribe population in the state. The major tribes in the district are Paniyan, Kurichian, Kurumans, Kattunayakan and Adiyan. In tribal communities, the role of women is substantial and crucial. In tribal society women are more important than in any other social groups because they work harder and the family economy and management depends on them. Even after industrialization and the resultant commercialization swamped the tribal economy, women continued to play a significant role. Mostly women do collection of minor forest produce. Many also work as labourers in industries, households and construction, contributing to their family income (Ali, S., & Akter, T. 2014). Apart from day to day chores, women also do play very important role at a time of catastrophe especially if it is a female headed household. This study focuses on how natural calamities have affected the tribal women and how they had managed through to have a proper livelihood after the same.

Significance of the study

Tribal women in India contribute positively to the local economy and participate along with men in subsistence activities. In reality, women do more work than men. They participate in all agricultural activities and other sectors .They share major responsibilities in the production process. In addition, they have to manage household chores, which is a stupendous task. Child rearing is also the responsibility of the women. The role and burden of women again changes when the family experiences some catastrophe. Women are especially hard-hit by the social impacts of environmental disasters. Existing inequalities are the root cause of women's disaster vulnerability. Global forces and social changes placing more people at greater risk of disaster also disproportionately impact women. Women are particularly vulnerable because they have fewer resources in their own right and under their own control. They have no permanent place in decision - making systems and they suffer traditional, routine and gratuitous gender-biased oppression. By virtue of their lower economic, social, and political status, women tend to be more vulnerable to disasters. Women's high rate of poverty as well as cultural constraints on their activities in some societies means they are more likely to suffer losses of life and property in the face of natural disasters. Their role in ensuring household food security, and their dependence on natural resources to do this, reinforces the impact of disasters. In search of supplemental income; this leaves women to fend for themselves and assume even greater responsibility for caring for their family. In post disaster situations women are often more vulnerable than men (Bhasin Veena 2007). Their care giving roles expand dramatically after a disaster. They have had to work harder than usual, and in defiance of their own safety imperatives, to gather fuel wood for cooking. Their special health needs, in fact especially those of pregnant and lactating women, are ignored. We always talk about the plight of women and when they are from marginalized communities especially from Scheduled Tribes they assume greater significance. We discuss about the discrimination they face, the day to day chores they handle etc. In this particular study we discuss about the role tribal women had played to withstand a natural catastrophe that had hit them.

Data Source and Methods

This is a qualitative study on the basis of primary survey. The primary data has been collected from Anamala Tribal colony of Wayanad District. Anamala Tribal Colony is a paniya colony located inside Kerala Veterinary and Animal Sciences University. Anamala is a small colony with 24 households and a total population of 98.

When Kerala witnessed the worst flood in August 2018, Wayanad was one of the most affected districts. The district experienced recurrent floods, severe landslides, erosion and siltation, which distressed the socio economic foundation and livelihood of the people. Anamala tribal settlemt is one of the most affected regions of Wayanad.

Women's Role in Disaster Manangement: through the Literature

Although women's social, economic and political position in society makes them more vulnerable to natural hazards, they are not helpless victims. Women are important agents for change and need to be further strengthened as such. Recognizing and mobilizing their skills and capacities as social force and channeling it to enhance efforts to protect their safety and that of their communities and dependants is a major task in any disaster reduction strategy.

Indian women are the backbone of the rural subsistence economy. Their respective role in family which is of productive nature to a large extent makes the family and society sustainable but it is not acknowledged by and large. Women's work in agriculture is often seen as an extension of their domestic responsibilities, rather than a separate economic activity. In rural areas which are more vulnerable to natural hazards since rural population depend more on the natural resource base for all aspects of life. Securing food, water and fuel are key community concerns, which are predominantly taken care of by women (Ghokale Vasudha 2008). There are many examples of women's informal community involvement in disaster reduction, but women are still largely excluded from formal planning and decision-making and need to be empowered to do so effectively. This is essential to ensure effective disaster reduction policies. If some decision-making is shifted Emergency relief and aid processes particularly disadvantage women who must organize food provision, shelter, and child and family care according to chaotic aid-delivery systems and entitlement procedures that rarely take their work or opinions into account. Although women commonly organize themselves to distribute supplies, establish shelter, and pool labor and resources to create community support services to meet basic family needs in the emergency period, their efforts are often invisible or go unacknowledged.

Indian women face a number of hurdles in applying and qualifying for aid after a disaster this primarily because of illiteracy or limited literacy, limited access to information on how to apply and navigate the bureaucracy in addition to the eligibility requirements. In majority of instances it has been found that relief and rehabilitation schemes favor men over women, where priority has been given to property owners, tenants of record, bank-account holders, and perceived heads of households. Women's economic condition becomes critical because in large number of cases employment assistance concentrates on workers in the formal economy and business aid is awarded to formal enterprises.

Post disaster aid and investments generally undermine women's collective capacity to surmount day-to-day problems adversely affecting the economic base of women. There is no consideration for women's productive and reproductive activities as far as conventional disaster response in India is concerned, It is not at all reflect how important housing and informally held resources and assets are to women's security. The impact of disaster on women's day to day work is great. In such a situation generally support systems such as child care, schools, clinics, public transportation and family networks are disrupted or destroyed, resulting in an increased domestic work. They have to face loss of workspace, tools, equipment, inventory, supplies and markets or even domestic violence.

Through the eyes of Tribal Women: Withstanding Natural Catastrophe (Case from Anamala)

In August 2018 the Anamala tribal colony were also severely affected by recurrent floods, severe landslides, erosion and siltation. Rather than flood, it was the landslide that had changed their life overnight. All the 24 families were shifted to rehabilitation camps set up at nearby school. They had stay in the camps for 60 days. It was reported that it was not at easy for them to spend days in camps. It was so congested and any of them had to sleep in floor. Major problem especially women faced was shortage of dresses rather than the shortage of food. One of the lady said that they were praying for not to have menstruation these days. After spending two months in the school, they were shifted to a temporary shed setup since their houses were unfit for settlement.

They have been staying in these shed since one year and six months. Even though the calamity has affected everyone irrespective of gender, the women had to adjust and manage efficiently since they are responsible for the household chores. The present shed in which they are staying is very congested and they have got a small kitchen where these women had to cook. Among 24 families, in six families there are small kids and these women tries to take care of their child the best they can do. At the time of field visit, I could see that some women were bringing grass in an auto. When I asked the purpose they said that they brought the grass to make broom so that they need not buy it. This show how economical they are and how they support their family even by taking care of small things.

In all 24 families women are working and are a source of income to their respective family. Some are working in Thozhiluruppu and few others in Kerala Veterinary and Animal Sciences University. Three of them are permanent staffs in Kerala Veterinary & Animal Sciences University. Among 24, 3 are female headed households. In the female headed households, they are not only responsible for households cores but the whole family are their responsibility. They go to do work, to ration shops, for oorukoottams likewise anything that is required.

Conclusion

Tribal women are always considered as a group who face double discrimination. They are at times portrayed as weak and helpless. But are they really? No they are not. This study had tried to study about the impact of natural calamities on tribal women. In the field the researcher has seen a group of women who has been a pillar of support to their family. They had withstood the worst natural calamity that they experienced. These are also a source of income. They had met their household expenses even after the catastrophe. Women have a definite role to play in disaster relief and reconstruction activities. Considering this a new approach to disaster needs to be developed out and disaster research, planning and practice should look into their vulnerabilities and requirements.

References

Ali, S., & Akter, T. (2014). Gender development and the status of tribal women: a study of Tripura. *A journal on tribal life & culture*, *28*(2), 86-91.

Bhasin, V. (2007). Status of tribal women in India. *Studies on Home and Community Science*, *1*(1), 1-16.

Gokhale, V. (2008, October). Role of women in disaster management: An analytical study with reference to Indian society. In *The 14th World Conference on Earthquake Engineering October* (pp. 12-17).

Chapter - 5

Financial Discipline Among Women in Paniya Community of Township Colony of Kannur District-Kerala

Dr. Bindu M. P.

Introduction

In the modern era of economic growth and development it is very essential for any nation that the citizens of the nation should be integrated with the banking and financial system of that country. Integration of everyone from different segment of the society with banking and financial system of the nation accelerates the economic as well as social growth and development of the nation. To achieve these goals nations across the world are focusing aggressively on effective implementation of financial inclusion. According to The Committee on Financial Inclusion headed by Rangrajan (2008), RBI, "Financial inclusion may be defined as the process of ensuring access to financial services and timely and adequate credit where needed by vulnerable groups such as weaker sections and low income groups at an affordable cost."

Now the Government of India has a flagship programme 'Digital India'. The tribes remained beyond governmental control for long due to their inaccessible and perilous location. Most of the tribal communities are at various stages of transition. Financial literacy is inevitable in the digitalization processes. Both the Information Literacy and Financial Education help the tribes to escape from the so called "middle man", who exploits the ignorance and innocence of tribes. Hence it is essential to empower them for future India. More over any policy and programme for tribes will be effective only when it is planed through Community sensitization programmes at grass root level rather than a centralised programme.

Financial inclusion is termed as the delivery of financial services at reasonable costs to sections of underprivileged and low-income segments of society, in contrast to financial exclusion where those services are not available or affordable. The concept financial inclusion refers to all types of financial services, including credit, savings and payments, from all types of formal financial institutions (Kanti Das and Kanti Das, 2003). The access to a transaction account is considered as a first step towards the broader financial inclusion since it allows people to store money, send and receive payments.

Financial inclusion is a concept of making available banking/financial services to a vast section of low income groups and weaker section at an affordable price. It means that individuals and businesses have access to useful and affordable financial products and services that meet their needs – transactions, payments, savings, credit and insurance – delivered in a responsible and sustainable way. Access to a transaction account is a first step toward broader financial inclusion since it allows people to store money, and send and receive payments. Financial access facilitates day-to-day living, and helps families and businesses plan for everything from long-term goals to unexpected emergencies. As accountholders, people are more likely to use other financial services, such as credit and insurance, to start and expand businesses, invest in education or health, manage risk, and weather financial shocks, which can improve the overall quality of their lives. Financial inclusion is important priority of the country in terms of economic growth of the society.

The success of financial inclusion is measured on the basis of the availability of various financial services to various sections of the society and its effective utilization by whatever means. In the recent years the Union Government has introduced the so called 'Digital India' initiative, which seeks to transform India into a digitally empowered, knowledge economy. Digital India initiative was taken by the central government on 1st July, 2015 to ensure that the governmental services are made available electronically to the citizens. The concept of digital banking under digital India initiatives will be very helpful in financial inclusion. Presently, India is on the path of "Digital Financial Inclusion", it can be defined as digital access to and use of formal financial services by excluded and underserved populations. (CGAP, 2017)

Research Problem

Tribal communities of India have been facing financial challenges for many years, and these have increased along with commercialisation led by industrialisation and technological bang. The major reason for this is that tribal communities are neglected by the state, which has a negative impact on their livelihood and financial status (Choudhury,1982). This situation is more critical in the state like Kerala where consumerism is the dominant way of applies among public, irrespective of socio-economic status. Compared to other state, Kerala has made some attempts to promote these communities, but due to many unwanted stigma, wrong political intervention and conventional bureaucracy all these have been unsuccessful. These communities suffer from poverty and are economically weak due to a lack of education and livelihood opportunities. Majority of the tribes lack financial discipline. This financial illiteracy and financial indiscipline act as a hindering agent to achieve inclusive financial growth towards digital economy(Das and Das,2003). Against this background, this article explores the financial practices of womenin Paniya communities of Township colony-Kannur. Good financial practices demands financial discipline and financial literacy.

Need and Significance of The Study

Financial inclusion is important and simple because it is obligatory provision available for obtaining an equitable growth especially for an economy transiting from an agrarian system to industrial modern society. Such access is especially powerful for the tribal groups as it provides those opportunities to build savings, make investments, deposit, loan, bank overdraft facilities, and awareness. (Shah, and Pathak (eds.).(2014). Most of the tribal societies are depending on informal sources of finance available locally. Various social factors have bearing on the financial inclusion of the tribal people in the banking activities. But when it comes to the implementation of the policies relating to the upliftment of the downtrodden poor, the sophisticated form of delivery of banking activities are not feasible from the point of view of banks as well as from the people side. Hence the banks are facing various problems to take up financial inclusion plan among the mass of people who do not even know about the basics of banking. The Indian financial services landscape is now undergoing a technology-driven shift. The traditional concept of branch banking is at the stage of its obsolescence, because every banking and financial facilities are now available at the customer's fingertips. The government has accelerated its approach to achieve financial inclusion with the help of digital innovations in banking services. In this context, digital platforms are likely to deliver financial services to both the unbanked and the under banked population, especially in rural/remote regions, at a low cost, and subsequently increase digital financial access to provide high quality, affordable financial services. The development and availability of these digital innovations made many changes in the socio-economic sphere of Indian citizens. The government is always arguing that the digitalization and new digital innovations are reaching at each and every corner of the nation and made a transformation in their lives. But, there is an apprehension that whether the bottom level and marginalized communities are having access to these digital innovations and do the yaw are of digital updates about financial innovations. In this context, the study raises a research question as an exploration of the financial practices of tribal communities in Township Colony of Kannur district, Kerala.

Scope of the Study

Financial inclusion is important because of the below mentioned reasons.

1. Financial inclusion is required to make available the necessities to the people.
2. Financial inclusion is helpful in raising the standard of living of the people.
3. Financial inclusion is required for the overall development of the economy.

Despite India boasting economic growth rates higher than most developed countries in recent years, a majority of the country's population still remains unbanked. Financial Inclusion is a relatively new socio-economic concept in India that aims to change this dynamic by providing financial services at affordable costs to the underprivileged, who might not otherwise be aware of or able to afford these services. Financial inclusion requires financial discipline and financial literacy. This Town ship colony which is situated in Irrity municipality where number of banks, post offices and educational institutions are situated within 5 to 10 kilometres away. More over this colony is in the just 500 meter away from Thalassery and Kannur- Mysore highway. The financial practices of a colony which is not in rural area or remote forest reflect the extent of financial inclusion among the tribes.

Significance of the Study

Despite India boasting economic growth rates higher than most developed countries in recent years, a majority of the country's population still remains unbanked (Kumar and Nanda,2018). Financial Inclusion of tribal people of rural area is comparatively low. Global trends have shown that in order to achieve inclusive development and growth, the expansion of financial services to all sections of society is of utmost importance. Empirical evidence shows that Financial Inclusion leads to Economic Growth. To have an inclusive growth we need to bring the under-developed regions of the country at par with the developed regions. The present study is useful to find the banking habit of tribal people and awareness level of tribal people towards various financial products and services. Further, researchers can use this paper in order to carry further studies which will bring into light of different new dimension.

Limitation of the Study

The study undertaken by the researcher suffers the following limitation:

1. The study has been conducted during a very short span of time
2. The study is restricted to Township colony of Irrity Muncipality Kannur district
3. Due to time constraints researcher could not conduct an interview with bank officials

Objectives of the study

1. To study the extend of financial inclusion and exclusion among women in Paniya community of Township colony of Kannur district
2. Financial Practices among women in Paniya Community of Township Colony in Kannur District
3. To find out the financial products and services awareness of women in Paniya community in Township colony of Kannur district.
4. To study the socio-familial problems faced by the Paniya community of Township colony of Kannur district

Definition of Key Terms

Financial Practices

In the present study financial practices means all forms of financial behaviour related to financial dealings by each households in their day to day life.

Financial Inclusion

Financial inclusion is defined as the availability and equality of opportunities to access financial services.

Financial Exclusion

Financial exclusion can be defined as the unavailability of banking services to people with low or non-income

Financial discipline

Financial refers to how well an individual be able to conform spending and saving to the plans that he or she have set to achieve your monetary goals.

Review of Related Study

The following studies were reviewed to identify the extent of work done in the field and to examine the knowledge gaps, if any

Study conducted by Pramod (2017), Brahamanandan and Babu (2016), Vinesh Kumar (2016), Suresh (2015), Mohammed and Haseena (2014) were reviewed. The findings reported the various factors that impacted tribal education in Kerala. They were Economic Factors - Poverty and Indebtedness of the Family; Cultural Factors - Nature of Habitation and Difference in Dialect and Medium of Instruction; Social Factors - Illiteracy of Parents, Lack of Motivation from Parents, Unfavourable Family Environment and Familial Help by the Students; Institutional Factors - Accessibility to School and Lack of Sufficient Grants and Schemes. With regard to the employment pattern of tribal communities 19.9 % are engaged in work under agriculture and allied sectors, 61.9 % in a casual non-agriculture labour,6.9 % work in forest areas, 6.7 % engaged in collection of forest products and only 1.6 % engaged in the government employment category.Kumar (2015) examined status of financial inclusion in India and study its determinants. Cull, Robert, Ehrbeck, and Holle (2014) explained that how financial inclusion can help poor households to improve their lives and spur economic activity. Ranparia (2013) discussed about various financial inclusion initiatives taken by the banking fraternity . Barik (2013) analyzed the relationship between financial inclusion and acceleration of agricultural development.

Research Methodology

The study was carried out as a descriptive one. Both primary and secondary data were used for the study. In order to collect the primary data random sampling method was used. Primary data are collected from a sample of 188 respondents belonging to Paniya community of Township colony in Kannur district. Data were collected by administering a questionnaire and interview. Secondary data which are used for the purpose of exploring the socio familial and economic aspects of financial practices are taken from various published sources of books, journals, newspapers, various websites and other related publications and interaction with ST promoters, students from tribal and non-tribal community and ward member.

Sample

Total population of Township colony is 683. Sampling procedure consists of two phases. First phase consists of stratified sampling techniques. By using stratified random techniques total women in tribal population were divided into four strata based on their age group such as age between 13-25, 26-40,41-60 and 61 above. In the second phase random sampling techniques was adopted for selecting the sample. A total of 188 samples were selected for the study. Sample were selected by giving due representation to all the four age groups.

Analysis and Interpretations of Data

1. Extent of Financial Exclusion and Inclusion among Paniya Community of Township colony

Here attempted to examine the extent of financial exclusion among the tribe communities with regard to banking, credit, insurance, and pension services. With regard to access to banking services, the study enquired into whether the tribe households have any type of accounts with the formal banks. The study has found that ninety-five percent of tribe households are 'banked', showing that the extent of exclusion from bank accounts is negligible among the tribe households in Township colony. Regarding the type of accounts, the influence of MGNREGS in compelling the households to open accounts is very evident. More than 70 % the tribe households have opened MGNREGS account. The study has found that most of the tribe households have opened accounts with the nationalized banks, with RRBs coming in the second position. As far as the reason for exclusion from having bank accounts is concerned, self-exclusion has come out to be the prominent reason. Unsurprisingly, it is among the Paniya tribe that most have suggested self-exclusion to be the reason for them being 'unbanked'. To find out the importance of MGNREGS in making tribes banking included, the study has analyzed the extent of banking inclusion MGNREGS account, and has found that more than half of the tribe household has become 'unbanked' in the absence of MGNREGS account. Tribes, it has been found, do not consider savings bank account as a saving tool, which is evident from the small sum of money recorded in their passbook as the current balance. Tribes, it appears, have not benefited from the banking technologies. More than ninety percent have ATM Card. 95 % do not have chequebooks. 100 % of the senior citizen didn't use ATM card. From youth; only male use ATM. With regard to the alternative mode of savings, most of tribes prefer to keep money in liquid form.

Unlike exclusion from having bank accounts, exclusion from credit market, both formal and informal, has been found to be high among the tribe households, which is evident from the fact that around half of the tribes households have been excluded from the credit market. The study has revealed that an overwhelming percent of tribe are indebted to informal sector, and informal indebtedness is high among the Paniya. Private Moneylender is the preferred choice of many households in the case of informal sources of credit. It is interesting to note that most of the households take credit to meet household current expenditure, a reason for the persistent debt trap. Fear of refusal by banking people and being insulted by bank officialsare the main reason discouraging households to seek credit from the formal sources.

Insurance, another financial instrument, appears to have eluded tribes largely. The study has found that nearly forty percent do not have any type of insurance. LIC and government are the main insurance service providers in the study area. Government supplies mainly health insurance to tribes, which they find most helpful. Regarding access to pension schemes, the study has observed that nearly seventy percent of tribe households have some form of pension.

Determinants of Financial Inclusion in the Study Villages

The financial inclusion status of a household is expected to be influenced by various socio-economic factors, such as household income, educational background, land holding status and involvement with employment generation programmes. It may be due to more opportunity of educated household head towards knowing about availability of financial facilities and their importance in present society. The results state that the higher the possession of land, the higher will be the probability of that household being financially included. Moreover, households with a large size of land are more likely to use banking services, such as agricultural loan for cultivation purposes. Besides, the results state that the higher the household annual income, the higher will be the probability of the household being financially included. The employment guarantee scheme, such as

MGNREGS, has a significant positive impact towards achieving financial inclusion. It is found that household possessing job card under MGNREGS scheme are having more probability of being financially included.

2. Financial Practices among Paniya Community of Township Colony in Kannur District

(A) Reasons for Taking Bank Accounts

(I) In the preceding section, it was observed that an overwhelming number of tribe households in the study area are in a position of having received at least one bank account, and most of them hold an MGNREGS account. Perhaps, owing to the wide popularity that MGNREGS has received, it is observed that the tribe households, regardless of the gender, hold bank account and the NREGS account. This being the picture of the status of holding bank accounts among the tribe households, now it would be of interest to investigate into the reasons that influenced the tribes to open accounts with banks. Tribes are not fully aware of the schemes launched by the government. The tribes look at the schemes in a prejudiced manner. Language problems and Personal and social problems act as obstacles to have bank account

(B) Respondents having Bank account

Table:- 5.1

Sl.No	*Bank A/C*	*No of Respondents*	*Percentage*
1	Having bank A/C	145	77.12
2	Not having Bank A/c	43	22.88
3	Total	188	100

Source: Primary data

The table shows that out of 188 respondents 145 (77.12%) have bank account. And only 43 do not have bank account

(C) Type of Bank Account Preferred by the Respondents

Table:- 5.2

Sl. No.	*Bank A/C*	*No of respondents*	*Percentage*
1	Saving	128	88.27
2	Recurring	10	6.89
3	Time/fixed deposit	7	4.82
4	Total	145	100

Note: *12 respondents having more than one account at atime*

It is clear from the table that majority of the respondents 88.27 % prefer saving bank account because of easy conveninece. Followed by 6.89% of the respeondents prefer recurring deposit 4.82% of the respondents like to invest their money in time deposit.

(D) Saving habits of the respondents

Table:- 5.3

Sl.No	*Category*	*No of respondents*	*Percentage*
1	Yes	10	5.31
2	No	178	95.72
3	Total	188	100

Source: Primary data

It was found that 5.31 % respondents save money, 95.72 % of the respondents said that they don't have enough money that can be saved.

(E) Reasons for opening bank account

Table:- 5.4

Sl. No.	*Reasons*	*No. of respondents*	*Percentage*
1	For receiving remuneration of MGREGA programme	163	86.70 (Total adults)
2	For making deposits and availing loans	0	0
3	For getting any subsidies from government	10	5.31
4	For receiving scholarship	15	7.97
5	Others	0	0
6	Total	188	100

Source: Primary data

From above table it was found that 86.70% of the respondent have opened their bank account for receiving remuneration of MGNREGA programme. 7.97 % receiving scholarship and 5.31 % getting subsidies and no respondents for other reasons opened their bank accounts.

(F) Tribes holding ATM/Credit Cards

Tribes do have ATM cards, no matter whether they use it or not. Today, banks issue ATM cum debit cards simultaneously with the opening up of accounts, especially savings bank accounts. Nevertheless, unlike ATM cards, normally banks issue Credit Cards on demand and that too after having been satisfied with the eligibility of the customer.

In this study, we have never observed any household having both ATM and Credit cards. Nor have we found any household possessing Credit Card alone. This implies that technical financial exclusion is rampant among the tribes perhaps because tribes are averse to using such services. Banks, on the other hand, hardly find any use in offering high-end services to tribes based on the presumption that tribes never use it. It is evident from the data that among tribe group, ATM cards are widely held by the youth, which is quite natural considering the economic backwardness of these tribes. The low number of tribe households holding ATM cards clearly shows that tribes are inclined not to use ATM cards and the banking services that have been offered to tribes are limited to just opening an account in the name of the tribes. Although holding of ATM card shows a remarkable improvement in the financial behaviours of tribes, the use of ATM/Credit card matters a lot.

3. Financial Products and Services Awareness of People of Paniya Community in Township colony in Kannur district.

(a) Financial products and services awareness among respondents

Table:- 5.5

Sl.No.	*Options*	*No. of respondents*	*Percentage*
1	Very high	0	0
2	High	6	3.19
3	Average	13	6.91
4	Low	36	19.14
5	Very Low	133	70.74
6	Total	188	100

Source: Primary data

It is evident from Table 5.5, that majority of the respondents are not highly aware of the financial products and services offered through banking system. No respondent have above average level of awareness. Majority of the respondents (70.74%) belonging to very low category.

(b) Sources of information about Financial Products and Services

Table:- 5.6

Sl.No.	*Sources*	*No of Respondent*	*Percentage*
1	News paper	0	0
2	Television	2	1.06
3	Friends and relatives	20	10.63
4	Mobile	0	0

(Contd...)

5	Radio	18	9.57
6	Promoter	102	54.25
7	Gramasabha/ Orrukutam	46	24.46
8	Total	188	100

Source: Primary data

Table shows that friends, relatives ST promoters are the major source of information about financial products and services.

Following types of socio-familial problems are faced by the scheduled tribes (secondary data)

In tribal areas parents send their daughter in schools only up to secondary level. After that parents have two options regarding their daughters either to educate them further or get them married, so they prefer to marriage than education. Hence drop out ratio of girls is quite high in secondary level. It is observed that 70 % mothers marry before they attain 15 years of their life. As a result of early marriages there is decreases in school attainment, experience more frequent reproductive health complications, have higher fertility and lower level of gender equality. It is really pathetic that in this small age physical and mental growth of girls is yet to achieve in such immaturity condition burden of marriage creates vulnerable condition for girls. Such adolescent girls become mother, most of them are not physically ready for motherhood and so new born babies are undernourished.

(II) Most of the houses are one-room houses or huts. They need repair in every season and they don't get protection against the seasonal variation in temperature.

(III) Land and agriculture: I) Scheduled tribe's people have a very small size of landholding. Most of the households have one acre of land. It could not be used for agriculture purpose, because of its nature. It is a dry area with rocks. When the land is divided among brothers it is not recorded legally. Thus the statistics of land holdings are quite misleading.

(IV) There is no proper method for giving open forestland for cultivation to the tribals.

(V) The agriculture is carried on the most primitive way. The agricultural implements are also very traditional. They do not use improved variety of seeds.

(VI) No irrigation facilities

(VII) The administrative hurdles are too much for the illiterate tribals.

(VIII) In the tribal community the number of dependents is more than the number of earning members.

(IX) Health problems: I) Health depends upon the quality of the food and as tribes suffer from poverty they cannot afford sufficient and balanced diet.

(X) Tribes are working hard they do not earn enough and so they cannot get sufficient food and they take alcohol. This has an adverse effect on their health.

(XI) Because of mal-nutrition they become victims of many life style diseases

(XII) No attention has been paid to the environmental aspects and hygiene are responsible for several diseases.

(XIII) Exploitation by the outside communities: - Exploitation of Scheduled Tribes by non-tribals. Like non-tribal merchants, big farmers and moneylenders etc.

(XIV) Tribals are not fully aware of the schemes launched by the government. The tribes look at the schemes in a prejudiced manner. N) Language problems. O) Personal and social problems.

(XV) Lack of knowledge about the law and rights.

(XVI) Difficulties in better implementation of various schemes. For better implementation of various schemes' identification of beneficiaries should be done in accordance with the stipulated guidelines. Family survey of income and assets position, beneficiaries' capability and zeal to handle the schemes effectively, availability of infrastructure and marketing facilities, and above all beneficiaries' social character need to be assessed carefully by efficient technical staff fully conversant with the rural development programmes.

Findings

1. The study reveals that the majority of the respondents have bank account.
2. Through the analysis the majority of the respondents prefer Savings Bank Account because of easy convenience..
3. Study found that majority of the respondents said that they don't have enough money that can be saved.

4. Majority depend money lenders for financial assistance.
5. Technology, language, paper works, procedure and time lag etc. act as barrier to reach into bank.
6. From the study it is found that majority of the respondents prefer Life insurance as an avenue of savings other than banks. Some of the respondents prefer Life insurance as an investment. Post office savings are also preferred by the respondents as savings other than banks. No one respondent prefer Mutual funds as avenues of savings as they don't aware about Mutual fund.
7. The analysis found that friends & relatives and ST promoters are the major source of information about financial products and services. Newspaper and radio also provides information about financial products and services to a certain extent.
8. Majority of the respondents are not highly aware about financial products and services.
9. Majority of the respondents are opened bank account for making deposits and availing loans and use of zero balance accounts for getting MGNREGA wages.
10. It is noted that tribals have great interest for smoking and drinking. Majority of them are addicted to pan chewing.
11. It is observed that majority of the tribals do not have any interest towards saving. A small proportion of them do save for tomorrow. Among them small post office savings are often used as the mode of saving.
12. Age at marriage is an important demographic factor which is responsible for several social and economic issues.

Implications and Conclusion

Financial inclusion is a fundamental cornerstone of economic and social development. Still half of the tribal people are not getting awareness of banking services. It is observed that there are many financially excluded people in the study area that must have to be bought under the purview of financial services for the upliftment of these people. The Government, financial regulator and bank is performing well in reducing financial exclusion and at the same time promoting financial inclusion in many regions. However it has to cover as many areas as possible. It has been able to provide banking services to the unreachable in the rural areas which is an achievement in the area of financial inclusion. If every person of the society takes advantage of the financial services than only the society can become economically strong and independent. A financially independent society can be possible only if every section of the society can be provided with the benefits of financial services.

The present study concluded that there is need to educate and take more steps to make tribal community a part of financial inclusion.To increase the awareness of no Frills saving account benefits, because more than half of the account holders are still no saving behaviour to them. Some customers only gotten the bank loan it's not enough them to develop the life style, so all types of banks must advice the loan benefits especially no or low level educates. To increase the awareness, there is a good scope of having financial literacy cell or credit counselling centre in every place so that it can take care of uneducated and illiterate peoples. At the present time well awareness of bank service scheme but still illiterate primary and poor people are not good aware of more bank schemes. The financial inclusion awareness of tribal community region after its implementation, though the scheme had a strong social mission of financial inclusion, the mission had not been fully translated into satisfactory action on the ground that the scheme was not fully included. Still half of the tribal citizen not getting awareness of banking services especially. The study results of financial inclusion initiatives, benefits, and awareness of these society people, so that the main objectives of improving their awareness and standard of living can be aimed.

Reference

Ajaya Kumar Nanda, Sasmita Samanta, (2018) "Mainstreaming tribals through financial *and Political Weakly*.

Barik (2013), 'Financial Inclusion And Acceleration Of Agricultural Development – An Empirical Analysis',www.naspublishers.com/particle/download/854

Bidhan Kanti Das and Rajat Kanti Das.(2003). Rethinking the Tribes.Rawat Publication.

Business Today, 'Whose Dhan Is It Anyway', September, 2014, pg: 26-27

Census of India. (2011). Ministry of Home Affairs: Government of India.

Choudhury, B. (1982). Tribal Development in India. New Delhi: Inter India Publications

Cull, Robert, Tilman Ehrbeck, and Nina Holle. (2014), "Financial Inclusion and

Development: Recent Impact Evidence." Focus Note 92. Washington, D.C.: CGAP., ISBN 978-1-62696-036-7

Government of Kerala (GoK). (2005). Selected Educational Statistics 2004-2005.

In What is Indigenous knowledge? Voices from the Academy, ed.

Hannig and Jansen (2010), "Financial Inclusion and Financial Stability: Current Policy Issues", ADBI Working Paper Series 259, Tokyo, ADBI.

Kumar (2015),'Financial inclusion and its determinants: evidence from India', Journal of Financial Economic Policy , Vol. 5, No. 1, pp:4-19, ISSN: 1757-6385

Ladislaus M. Semali., and Joe L. Kincheloe. New York: Falmer Press.

Jayapur.India literacy – a review of literature", International Journal of Social Economics, Vol. 45 Issue: 2, pp.437-444, https://doi.org/10.1108/IJSE-12-2016-0371

Nathan, D and Virginiusn Xaxa(eds.) 2012. Social Exclusion and adverse Inclusion: Development and Deprivation of Adivasies in India.Oxford,UK: Oxford University Press.

N. K.Thingalaya,M.S.Moodithaya and N.S. Shetty.(2010). Financial Inclusion and Beyond. Issues and Challenges. Academic Foundation, New Delhi

Ranparia N (2013), "Financial Inclusion in Gujarat: A Study on Banker's Initiatives", Research Scholar (commerce), Singhania University, Volume: 2, Issue: 2, ISSN No 2277 – 8179

Rath, G. C. (Ed).2006. Tribal Development in India: The Contemporary Debate. New Delhi: Sage Publications.

Semali, L.M. (1999). "Community as Class Room: (Re) Valuing Indigenous Literacy." www.cdit.org.www.stdd.kerala.gov.in

Shah, A., and J. Pathak (eds.).(2014). Tribal Development in Western India. London: Roatledge

Srivastava, L.R.N(2012). "The problem of integration of the tribal people", 'The Indian Journal. Thiruvananthapuram: Directorate of Public Instruction (Statistics Unit).

Xaxa,V., (2005).Politics of Language , Religion and Identity: The Tribes in India. *Economic and Political Weakly.*

Chapter - 6

Problems and Challenges of Empowering Scheduled Tribe Women-with Special Refrence of Haveri District In Karanataka

Channappa Lamani,
Dr, Thimmaiah T.D

Abstract

The empowerment of scheduled tribe women is the challenging issue in India. This study reveal the importance of scheduled tribe women in Haveri District in Karnataka. A study covers total 300 scheduled tribe women respondents as sample size were selected as sample using stratified random sampling technique on Haveri District of Karnataka and data was collected through face to face interview by using survey method. The study reveals that, It has opened many opportunities to them in terms of participation and to fight against negative impact of patriarchy, Though scheduled tribe women are facing many problems like domestic violence, physical and mental torture, wife beating, sexual abuse etc. It is also realized that women face resistance in participating in training programmes due to sharing of responsibilities at family level. They also face barriers due to bias and discriminatory behavior common in society. Arrangements are made by the government and NGO'S to encourage scheduled tribe women to form self help groups and seek answers to their own problems. The paper brings out the cases of under represented women who are successful in empowering themselves by making use of education and training, Still she has so many opportunities to grow, So, here in participatory democracy has great significance in the process of schedule tribe women empowerment.

Key Words: *Tribal women, Problems, Governance, Skills development*

Introduction

India is a country of villages as the majority of its population lives in villages and far flung remote areas. The interesting aspect is that every region of the country though connected with the cities now however, Tribal women are still devoid of modern facilities like education, electricity, proper drinking water, health care and transportation, etc. But the lack of education in many of the rural belts of Haveri district is proving fatal and acting as the breeding ground for social vices, evils and Education enhances ones competence level to cope up better in physical and social environments, It can transform the tribal women of Haveri district by Ensuring the upward social mobility among people, by liberating them though slowly from the shackles of casteism, groupism and superstitious life ways. Further education will ensure opportunities for functional employment thereby empowering rural folk for more economic opportunities, growth and development and can thus lead to the change in the whole map of poor and downtrodden rural landscape,

Objectives of the Study

The general objective of the study was to evaluate the "Problems and challenges of empowering scheduled tribe women with special reference of Haveri district in Karnataka" However, specifically, the study tried to attain the following objectives.

(1) To know the schedule tribe Women Empowerment in the study area.

(2) To examined the scheduled tribe women's social, economic and political empowerment, fulfillment of their rights, of the district.

(3) To find out the problems faced by the Scheduled tribe women's and to suggest the suitable policy measures.

Statement of The Problem

Earlier schedule tribe women were restricted to take part in any social, Political and education etc. activities have not given roles in decision making in her family. The situation was, even more, critical in rural areas. Now the situation has been changed. She is given the freedom to do what she wishes. In today's scenario more, still also schedule tribe women's are engaged in income-generating activities. This is because of NGO and other financial institution came forward to provide microfinance to poor scheduled tribe women. They believe that a schedule tribe woman is the small credit risk and often benefits the whole family. The main aim of scheduled tribe women empowerment. This induced the researcher to focus more on the empowerment of scheduled tribe women.

Methodology

The study has been designed under the framework of the both primary and secondary sources. The secondary data have been collected from books, journals, newspapers, and reports, etc. Primary data have been collected by survey method through face to face interview on well structured and pretested schedule tribe women empowerment women's through micro finance collected to know the Economic background, Social background, Cultural background, Political awareness etc. Various officials from the Department of Child and welfare office, Government of Karnataka interviewed during the collection of information for the study.

Selection of the Sample

The present study conducted in Haveri district of Karnataka State, The study basically pertains to the sample from Scheduled Tribe women's of 7 taluks of Haveri district.

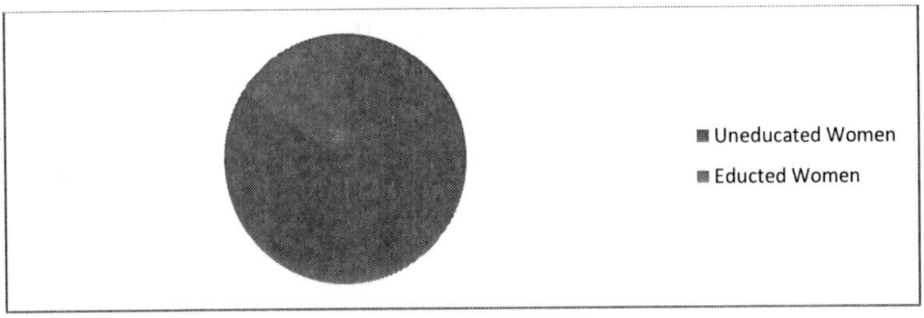

(Source: Personal survey) Chart 1.0

Selection of the Sample blocks

Hence the samples are selected in 7 taluks of the Haveri district namely Haveri, Byadaghi, Shiggaon, Ranibennur and Savanur, Hanagal, and Hirekerur, scheduled tribe women's are the main parameters which are located in the 7 taluks of Haveri.

Selection of Sample respondents

Selection of the sample respondents has been on the basis of scheduled tribe women's in the 7 taluks of Haveri district and how many scheduled tribe women are facing challenges for leading poor condition life and facing unemployment problems in the district, with this parameters 300 Samples were selected from 7 taluks of Haveri district. In this study scheduled tribe women problems and their education and financial, employment, Political involvement status were studied.

Limitations

The researchers surveyed only 300 rural scheduled tribe women's in Haveri district, which may not sufficient. The majority of this work is to provide a set of state of art information.

Review of Literature

The review of literature is an important stage of research it helps to identify the research gaps. This exercise is very useful in formulating the objectives and hypotheses of the research study. In this study the literature review is broadly classified into two heads.

1. Theoretical review of Literature
2. Empirical review of Literature

Theoretical review of Literature

In the theoretical literature review, theories, policies, plans are reviewed relating to women in empowerment with different perspective.

Economic Survey of Karnataka 2010-11

The Stree Shakthi Programme launched in 2000-01, aiming at empowering rural women through the formation of self-help groups (SHGs). Since the inception of the programme 76,952 groups have taken up income generating activities like sheep rearing, poultry rearing, readymade garments, papad preparation etc., with an investment of Rs.821.81 crores. So far 1.40 lakh groups have been formed with 20.73 lakh women members. Out of which, 3.83 lakhs are SC members, 1.52 lakhs are ST members and 1.42 lakhs belong to minority communities. Karnataka State Women s Development Corporation has been implementing various schemes such as Udyogini, Women Skill Training Programme, Devadasis Rehabilitation Programme, Marketing Assistance Scheme for the upliftment of the women. The Integrated Child Development Services Scheme was started in Karnataka on 2nd October 1975. Since then, the programme has been expanded to all the revenue taluks in the state. Karnataka is the first state in the country to introduce "Karnataka Mahila Abhivrudhi Yojane" scheme for the empowerment of women. The scheme is to earmark 1/3rd of resources for women in individual beneficiary oriented schemes and labour intensive schemes of the various departments of the Government. Under this programme, 25 departments have identified 238 schemes in Central, State and District Sector.

Welfare Programmes for Scheduled Tribe

The Department of STs Welfare has implemented various programmes for the development and empowerment of the ST community in the state. For the welfare of Primitive Tribal Groups (PTGs), the budgetary allocation for comprehensive development of these groups in the tribal concentrated districts has declined and its utilization needs improvement during 2010-11. In the case of the programmes meant for economic advancement of STs such as Self-employment Scheme, Land Purchase Scheme and Special Development Programmes mainly implemented in the backward taluks, the budgetary allocation has come down during 2010-11 over the previous year, but under the Ganga Kalyana Scheme largely implemented in the backward taluks (as identified by the High Power Committee headed by the late Dr. D. M. Nanjundappa), it has gone up during the same period.

Reecha Upadhyay women's Empowerment in India an Analytical Overview: Womens empowerment in India is heavily dependent on many different variables that include geographical location, educational status, social status and age. Policies on womens empowerment exist at the national, state, and local levels in many sectors, including health, education, economic opportunities, gender-based violence, and political participation. The impact of the patriarchal structure can be seen in rural and urban India, although womens empowerment in rural India is much less visible than in urban areas.

Heggade (1984) with special reference to India has identified the socio-economic and politicocultural obstacles for women participation in economic development and also identified different institutional mechanisms and policy measures to promote women empowerment in India. This is one of the early studies on women in economics development in India. It has analyzed the empowerment level, malnutrition, and absence of property rights, lack of access to bank credit absence of skill formation programmes for women, low parental investment in women HRD or capabilities as the factors responsible for women low participation.

Review of Literature on Empirical studies

In the Empirical literature review consists of articles, survey, research, and working paper published with primary and secondary data sources reviewed about issues and difficulties women empowerment with different perspective.

Gurulingaiah (2002) this has attempted to analyze the role of NGOs in the empowerment of tribal women in Tumkur District of Karnataka. It also has been conducting social and health awareness campaigns to eliminate superstitious customs, attitude and thinking related to puberty and child birth which are blocking the progress of tribal women. They suggest that women should be encouraged to take active part in spreading social awareness and literacy campus. The Government has vital role in empowerment kadu golla socially and bringing them into the mainstream of the society.

Rao (2002) has analyzed the determinants of social economic status of tribal woman in Arunachal Pradesh. This study analyzed in education and economic empowerment of tribal women of Arunachal Pradesh. Since 1985 some of the findings are A large majority of women in Arunachal Pradesh participate in wage employment activity. They are also involved in household chores. This on an average of women in Arunachal Pradesh work for over 12 hours a day and hence like elsewhere are confronted with double cay work problem. A good number of NGos have been established for the emancipation of women and girl children of Arunachal Pradesh. These NGOs are working towards educational empowerment, social empowerment and improving the women status.

Scheduled Tribe women's Empowerment Programs: The role of Scheduled tribe women in development is most intimately related to the goal of comprehensive socio-economic development and it is a strategic for the development of all societies. Yatra Naryantu Poojanthe, Tatra Ramanthe Devatha, says a famous Sanskrit verse. It means where the Women is venerated there the Gods Rejoice. It also means where the woman is free, respected and given her due place there in that land the people live in peace and happiness. (Lalita and Prasad, 2009)

Department of Women and Child Development of Karnataka is implementing various schemes, programmes, Social welfare schemes, Health and Nutrition, scholarship for Scheduled tribe women empowerment the rural widows, Old age women, Women self-help group (SHG), Women Entrepreneurs and Adolescent Girls. Also special assistance is given to the rural scheduled tribe women and Socially and Educationally Backward Classes(SEBC) Minority Category and below poverty line(BPL) rural women empowerment purpose the respective of State and Central Government have been implemented several policies and programmes for better improvement for the rural scheduled tribe Women as we can see below.

Some of the important schemes with the collaboration of Central and State Governments are:

(1) Bhagyalaxmi scheme for girls of below poverty line (BPL)

(2) Namma Magalu Namma Shakthi for girls insurance facility, Karnataka

(3) Beti Bachao Beti Padhao Scheme

(4) Indira Gandhi Matritva Sahyog Yojana (IGMSY) for the pregnant and lactating women. etc

The Scheduled Tribe Women empowerment Sub-Plan was first introduced in 1976-77 when it was implemented in select districts of Karnataka state. This project was extended to all districts in the state in 1992. The Protection of tribal culture, education, healthcare and providing basic minimum infrastructure. The state has emphasized the need and importance of tribal development in the post-independence period. Series of STs Women empowerment programmes are implemented across the state for the welfare and progress of tribal people. The government has also formulated a policy on tribal development and implemented Tribal's Sub-Plan (TSP) which is the Special 107 Component Plan (SCP) of national Fifth Five-Year Plan. In particular, the Department of Tribal Welfare was formed specifically to address the needs of STs in Karnataka. Its budget is part of the budget of the Department of Social Welfare. The Department of Tribal Welfare was formed specifically to address the needs of STs in Karnataka. The concept of the Tribal Sub-Plan (TSP) and its counterpart the Special Component Plan (SCP) emerged in the National Fifth Five Year Plan.

Taluk	***Total Population of ST women***	***Illiterates***	***In Percentage***
Shiggaon	5098	2508	49%
Savanur	5762	2917	51%
Hanagal	10167	4657	46%
Haveri	10504	5257	50%
Byadagi	7632	3652	48%
Hirekerur	11468	4892	43%
Ranibennur	11038	4884	44%

(*Source:* District Census Handbook, Haveri 2011) Table 1.1

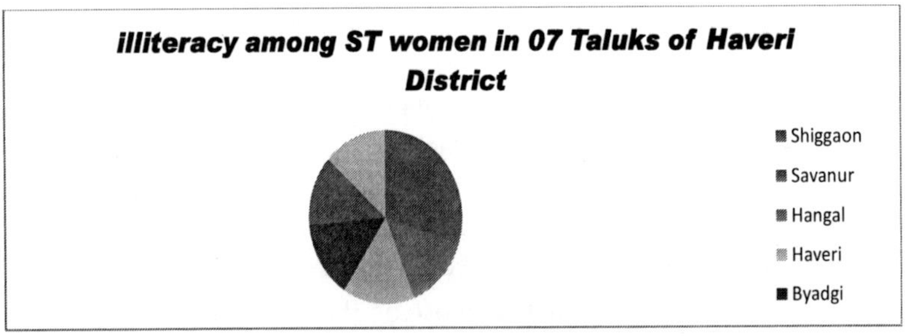

(*Source:* 2011) Chart 1.2

From the data given above we can clearly understand that the illiteracy among schedule tribe women in Haveri District is comparatively more and they are leading poor standard of life. Micro finance is helping them in making their life in a better way by providing financial assistance.

Microfinance is emerging as a powerful instrument for poverty alleviation in the new economy. In India, Microfinance scene is dominated by Self Help Group, Bank Linkage Programmes as a effective mechanism for providing financial services to the Un -reached Poor Scheduled Tribe women. This has been successful not only in meeting financial needs of the rural poor Scheduled Tribe women but also strengthen collective self-help capacities of the poor scheduled Tribe women, leading to their empowerment. Economic empowerment results in women ability to influence or make decision, increased self confidence, better status and role in household etc. This paper attempts to place forward how micro finance has received extensive recognition as a strategy for economic empowerment of schedule tribe women. This research examined the role of Micro finance institutions with respect to economic schedule tribe empowerment and poverty alleviation of rural schedule tribe women. An effort is also made to suggest the ways to increase schedule tribe women empowerment.

Findings

The conditions of schedule tribe women in 07 Taluks of Haveri district are discussed as below: (Source: Personal Survey)

- Most of the respondents who indulged in the agriculture activities are illiterate and at least not completed their Primary education. It clearly shows that, in rural areas of Haveri district scheduled Tribe women empowerment in still remain as a challenge.
- 89 percent of the total respondents are in the age of 17 to 30 years. Gender equality still not achieved so far and gender and caste discrimination still continued. It is identified that Government policies are not reached every corner of society.
- While considering the percentage of respondents 60 percent of them are having less than 5 lack income, 35 percent are more than 5 Lack income, and only 5 percent are with more than 20 lack income people who are living in rural areas. It clearly throws light on the existence of poverty in rural areas of the district.
- We can understand that most of the rural families are doing agriculture and farming, the Central and State Government should

have to provide scientific agriculture training to rural farmers and mainly focus on rural scheduled Tribe women empowerment by proving them basic training and support.

- Micro financing NGOs and other institutions are able to reach the corners of rural society and schedule tribe women and these are indirectly helping them to make better standard of living through financial assistance.
- Scheduled Tribe women are highly interested in participating in Micro financing activities which would help them in a greater way.

Suggestions

- Scheduled Tribe women should be encouraged and given education, employment training status and other uplifting programs effectively and which would contribute to increase the independency and the standard of living of the rural society.
- Government should concentrate more on schedule tribe women empowerment, especially in regions like Haveri District, where more women are living in rural areas. Giving financial assistance in terms of loans, concessions will help these community women to develop their living life of standard in a broad range.
- In this digital and technologically transforming world it is vital to create awareness among Schedule tribe women on leading their self dependent life for alone and encouraging them to use these training programmes should be initiated by the local Government like Village Panchayats in an effective way.
- Bringing all the schedule tribe women related to unemployment and illiterate women on a single platform by establishing a separate organization or society in district level will enable them to explore more in the same training business oriented field.
- Encouraging schedule tribe women to indulge in business activities by providing them financial support through Micro financing.
- Haveri is known for the agriculture crop growing area which is a potential product for Export business. Majority of the producers are not aware about the export business procedures for their product in the District. Export business is a major source of income to them as well as to the whole economy. If they are trained well to export their products, definitely there is no doubt that large number of scheduled Tribe women's will come forward to take up the same business.

- Creating a market for producers to sell their products directly to the customers and avoiding retailers in business may help them to earn more and expand the current business.

Conclusion

Haveri district is one of the major agriculture growing crop seeds in the State and we can see on more people are staying in rural areas, In the district more number of scheduled Tribe women are facing very critical condition like illiteracy, low income, depending on family members or husband, poor quality of life leading. Remarriage is not allowed in rural areas as a part of customs and women with low income and poor family background are forcefully leading difficult life after being widowed and are struggling to lead their life without support and education. Most of the schedule tribe families are still suffering with a high degree of superstitious beliefs like, not taking proper treatment at the time of illness and blindly following blind beliefs. Scheduled Tribe women life expectancy is in very poor and most of the families in rural areas are exploited both financially and socially from their rights. Government policies are not reaching them as expected and there is a necessity for uplifting them socially and economically with serious efforts.

References

1. **Mohammad Awais Tosib Alam Mohd. Asif** Socio-Economic Empowerment of Tribal Women: An Indian Perspective International Journal Of Rural Studies (Ijrs) Vol. 16 No. 1 October 2009 Issn 1023–2001 Www.Ivcs.Org.Uk/Ijrs Article 5 Page 1 Of 11.
2. **Puttaraja and O. D. Heggade Economic Empowerment of Tribal Women in Karnataka:** A Case Study in Mysore and Chamarajanagara Districts © Kamla-Raj 2012 Stud Tribes Tribals, 10(2): 173-181 (2012).
3. **D. Pulla Rao Socioeconomic Status of Scheduled Tribes MERC Globals International Journal of Management** ISSN 2321-7278 (Print) and ISSN 2321-7286 (Online) Vol. 1, Issue 1: July-2013, pp. 36-50 URL: http://www.mercglobal.org/ijm-vol1-issue1- july2013.html © MERC Global.
4. **Young Kate' (2000)** "WID,GAD and WAD", In Vandana Desai and Robert B. Potters (Ed) The development studies compendium, pp 321-325.
5. **Odeyar D Heggade (1984)** women and economic development ,Ramya roopeprakashana , Bangalore. 6. N.K Gowda.
6. **Karnataka Survey report 2011.**

Chapter - 7

Economic Status of Women: A Case Study of SC & ST Women of Kozhikode District

Deepa. E & Jeni B. S.

Abstract

This study tries to find out the economic status of women: SC and ST women in urban areas of Kozhikode districts. Specific objectives of the study are Educational Awareness, the job aspects of the SC ST of Kozhikode district and the problems of SC ST Women of Kozhikode districts. The present study is based on both primary and secondary data. In this study the primary data is collecting from 50 household in, Kozhikode district with the help of interview schedule. Random sampling method is used to collect primary data. As a part of the study interview schedule was distributed to 50 household in Kozhikode district. Although the numbers are improving, scheduled castes, which comprise 16.6% of the population, and scheduled tribes, who make up 8.6% of the population, have lower literacy rates than the Indian average. The literacy rate for female STs is still under 50% and just 57% for SC women, while the numbers are slightly higher for men. Through this study it is revealed that the empowerment of SC women through education is greater than that of ST women .But comparing to the past situations the ST women also shows improvement in all areas. It is concluded that Education is the most powerful weapon to make changes especially among women. Though education marginalised women's are able to realize the evils in the society and education gave them not only a secure life but also the courage to react and attain justice.

Keywords*: Economic Status, SC ST Women, Education, Problems*

1. Introduction: Women's economic empowerment refers to the ability for women to enjoy their rights to control and benefit from resources, assets, income and their own time, as well as the ability to manage risk and improve their economic status and wellbeing. The Scheduled Castes (SCs) and Scheduled Tribes (STs) are various officially designated groups of historically disadvantaged indigenous people in India. The terms are recognised in the constitution of India and the various groups are designated in one another of the categories. During the period of British rule in the Indian sub-continent, they were known as the depressed classes.

Education is the milestone of women empowerment because it enables them to responds to the challenges, to confront their traditional role and change their life. It helps in reducing inequalities and functions as a means for improving their status within the family. Education is the key factor for women empowerment, prosperity, development and welfare. There is continued inequality and vulnerability of women in all sectors-economic, social political, healthcare, nutrition, right legal etc. Women oppressed in all spheres of life, they need to be empower din all walk of life. In order to fight against the socially constructed gender biases, women have to swim against the system that requires more strength. Such strength comes from the process of empowerment and empowerment come from education.

So many studies have been conducted on the topic impact of education in women empowerment including SC ST women. Like impact of education in women empowerment: A case study of SC & ST women of Sonipur district, assume by Mukut Kr. Sonawal (2013) impact of education in women empowerment of in Begalkot district Karnataka by Sandhya (2015).in our state usually women have a higher literacy rate, freedom & decants standard of living. Even in this situation a small group of women are facing discrimination and other inequalities. Even through government has introduced many development measures for them. Our study is focusing on the life of this small group of women. In this context our study is differs from other studies.

In modern society women face so many problems. Education is the most powerful way to empower women. Most of the women are unaware of the rights. Only through education they will be aware of the discriminations in their life. On account to improve their situation government has introduced many programmes. But only minor part of women has received the advantages of these programmes. Another reason for women to not to get education is because of their financial problems. Some of the illiterate parents also do not encourage education of women. The women's are backward in education, economic, social, decision making, political aspect, etc. Moreover they are lagging behind in general awareness, communication skill& health and family welfare aspect. These are the major problems due to which SC, ST women are not getting proper education.

This study tries to find out the effect of education on SC and ST women in urban areas of Kozhikode districts.

2. Major Objectives of the Study

(1) To study on the economic empowerment through education of SC ST Women of Kozhikode districts.

Specific objectives

(a) To study the Educational Awareness of SC ST of the Kozhikode district.

(b) To analyse the job aspects of the SC/ST of Kozhikode district.

(c) To study the problems of SC ST Women of Kozhikode districts.

3. Methodology

The methodology is the general research strategy that outlines the way in which research is to be undertaken and, among other things, identifies the methods to be used in it. Methodology, define the means or modes of data collection or, sometimes, how a specific result is to be calculated. The present study is based on both primary and secondary data. In this study the primary data is collecting from 50 household in, Kozhikode district with the help of interview schedule which helped in getting more accurate data.Stratified random sampling is used to collect primary data. As a part of the study interview schedule was distributed to 50 household in Kozhikode district.

4. Data Analysis

4.1. Educational Awareness of SC ST of the Kozhikode district

Education is one of the most important characteristics of the respondents because the perception, awareness and behaviour of the respondents depend largely on his/her educational qualifications. Among the selected respondents, a majority (30%) were graduates. Kerala ranks first among the Indian States in respect of both male and female literacy among the STs. The overall literacy rate among the Scheduled Tribes has increased from 57.2 percent in the 1991 Census to 64.4 percent in the 2001 Census. This is higher than the national average of 47 percent.

4.2. The job aspects of the SC/ST of Kozhikode district

Only about 4 per cent each of rural Scheduled Tribe and Scheduled Caste households have a member in a government job, according to the findings of the Socio Economic and Caste Census 2011. The highest proportion of the tribal workers in the state is 'Agricultural Labourers'. Tribals are undergoing a massive occupational change. While there has been a fall in the proportion of people working as cultivators and a rise in agricultural labour across the country, this shift is most marked in the case of STs. Nearly 10 lakh fewer tribals reported being cultivators in 2011 as compared to ten years ago, while there were 73 lakh more tribal agricultural labourers. It is observed that the ST population lags far behind in the changing occupational structure of the Kerala economy.

4.3. Problems of SC ST women

They suffered from many economic problems. They had to face many economic hardships and they were not given proper reward for their service. Women are discriminated against in all walks of life..Women are subjugated, dominated and exploited both at work places and home. In modern society women faces so many problems. Education is the most powerful way to empower women. Most of the women are unaware of the rights. Only through education they will be aware of the discriminations in their life. On account to improve their situation government has introduced many programmes. But only minor part of women has received the advantages of these programmes. Another reason for women to not to get education is because of their financial problems. Some of the illiterate parents also do not encourage education of women. The women's are backward in education, economic, social, decision making, political aspect, etc. Moreover they are lagging behind in general awareness, communication skill & health and family welfare aspect. These are the major problems due to which SC, ST women are not getting proper education.

5. Data

Table. 7. 1. Educational Qualification of the Respondents

Educational Qualification	*SC*	*ST*
Illiterate	27	51
Below 7	34	26
SSLC	28	14
Plus two	11	9
Graduation	0	0

Source: Primary Data

Table. 7. 2: Respondents on the basic of Occupation

Types of job	*SC(%)*	*ST(%)*
Koolie	20	30
Government Job	10	10

(Contd...)

Private Job	30	30
None of these	40	30
Total	100	100

Source: Primary Data

Table. 7.3: Respondents Awareness about Education facilities

	Percentage(sc)	***(ST) Percentage***
Awareness of facilities	59.9	57.09
Lack of awareness of facilities	40.1	42.91
Total	100	100

Source: Primary Data

Table. 7.4: freedom of Opinion and Expression among Respondents

Freedom of opinion and expression	***SC(%)***	***S T(%)***
Yes	62.5	30
No	37.5	70
Total	100	100

Source: Primary Data

Table. 7.5: Problems faced by the Respondents

Types of Problems	***SC(%)***	***ST(%)***
Caste	2.5	20
Gender	42.5	20
Atrocities	15	20
Both 2 & 3	40	40
Total	100	100

Source: Primary Data

6. Findings and Conclusion

The study analysis The Economic status of Women: a Case Study of SC & ST Women of Kozhikode district" gives almost a clear idea about the SC ST women. The major conclusions of the data analysis are given below

- Comparing to ST women, SC women have more educational qualification in graduate level.
- More SC women are jobless than ST women. This is because the fact that ST woman is ready to do any kind of job.

- Most of the ST women are doing coolie and private jobs. Some educated women in SC group do not get job according to their educational qualifications.
- As they are educated women they are not willing to do coolie works.
- Even though ST woman's gets a little more reservations than SC woman, ST woman's with government jobs are less than SC woman with government job.
- Among ST, most of the working women are getting monthly income below 2000 and also most of the women in ST group get 3000 to 5000 and 6000 to 10000 income which is higher than that of SC.
- Income which is higher than 10,000 is only earned by a very few among both of these groups.
- More SC women have regular job than ST women. Women who are able to satisfy their needs with their income are more in SC group than in ST groups.
- On the basis of gender, there still exists a large scale discrimination of income. In the case of SC women the wage wise discrimination is mostly seen in the private job and coolie jobs. Most of SC women have economic contribution to the society than ST women.
- SC women have more awareness for proper education than ST women.
- More members among ST women are not aware of facilities provided to them because of
- Lack of proper knowledge or education.
- Gender based discrimination exist largely among SC/ST women.
- There also exist both atrocities against women and gender based discriminations. Caste based discriminations is very few in urban area.
- In the case of SC more women have freedom of opinion and expression in their life than ST women.
- Most of the ST women have no freedom of opinion and expression ie their decisions depends on the head of the family or men.
- Health problem is very less among both SC and ST women.
- The availability of hospitals in urban areas, transportation facilities, awareness and education helped to reduce health problems.

- Although the numbers are improving, scheduled castes, who comprises 16.6% of the population, and scheduled tribes, who make up 8.6% of the population, have lower literacy rates than the Indian average. The literacy rate for female STs is still under 50% and just 57% for SC women, while the numbers are slightly higher for men.
- Through this study it is revealed that the empowerment of SC women through education is greater than that of ST women .But comparing to the past situations the ST women also shows improvement in all areas. It is concluded that Education is the most powerful weapon to make changes especially among women. Though education marginalised women's are able to realize the evils in the society and education gave them not only a secure life but also the courage to react and attain justice.

References

Anand and Yadav (2006) "The Inclusion of SC Girls in Education : A Long path Ahead".

Amar Kumar Singh and Rajyalakshmi (1993) "Status of Tribal Women in India".

Despande Savita P (2001) "Status of educated Scheduled caste in their Local Socio Cultural Life".

DespandeSavita P (2001) "Status of Educated Scheduled Caste in their Local Socio Cultural Life"

Jasmir .Sc (2005) "Empowerment of Socially and Economically Weaker Section of the Society through Education University".

Pande and Astone (2001) "Son Preference in Rural India : The Independent of Strucrural Vs Individual Factors".

Sobha and Venkateswaralu (2013) "Economic Empowerment of Dalits in Three Mandals in Chittor District".

Subha. I and Reddy MSN (2001) "Education for Quality and Empowerment of Women".

http://censusindia.gov.in/

Chapter - 8

Issues and Challenges of Tribal Women in India: A Socio Economic Perspective

Dr. Indira P M

Abstract

The Indian Constitution guaranteed Fundamental Rights like right to equality, right against exploitation etc,. to all the citizens of India irrespective of race, religion, caste, sex or place of birth as these rights were considered essential for the development of the personality of every individual and to preserve the human dignity. Article 15 of the Indian Constitution allows the State to extend special provisions for Scheduled Castes and Scheduled Tribes for their advancement. But India is experiencing an alarming surge in violence and crime rates particularly against women and children and hence now-a-days ensuring fundamental rights is a question of threat. The tribes in India are the most vulnerable sections of the society because of their socio-economic conditions. Though they are numerically small minority representing an enormous diversity of groups, the crimes against them increasing day-by-day. The present study attempted to scrutinize the problems and Challenges of violence against Indian tribal women on a socio economic perspective.

Key Words: *Tribes, Crime*

Introduction

The Constitution of Indian guaranteed Fundamental Rights like right to equality, right against exploitation etc,. to all the citizens of India irrespective of race, religion, caste, sex or place of birth as these rights were considered essential for the development of the personality of every individual and to preserve the human dignity. Article 15 of the Indian Constitution permitted the State to extend special provisions to women and children, special arrangements for SCs and STs and special provisions for the betterment of SCs and STs. But we can see a blatant violation of the Indian Constitution that the crimes against women and children increasing day-by-day in an alarming rate both inside the family and in the society. When we look into the down trodden people like tribes, the conditions are so pathetic.

The Constitution of India in Article 366 (25) prescribe that the Scheduled Tribes means such tribes or tribal communities as are deemed under Article 342 of the Constitution to be Scheduled Tribes'. These communities are suffering from extreme social, educational and economic backwardness on account of the primitive agricultural practices, lack of infrastructure facilities and geographical isolation. They are borne and brought up in such a type of miserable environment and they never try to come out from the shell created by them and the society.

Importance of the Study

The Indian State must aim to ensure that all sections of society share the overall prosperity of the country. It is widely recognized that a large section of the Indian population, especially the tribal communities, have not received the full benefits of development processes undertaken by the government. It is recognised that the tribal population is the most adversely affected among all sections of the society because of their socio economic background. In the growing consumer world, the present study is significant as tribes are one of the marginalised sections of the society, who found their livelihood by utilising natural resources (Pal. C. Gobinda, 2017).

Methodology of the Study

This is a theoretical research study where secondary data related to tribes published by different government departments are used like Annual report of Ministry of Tribal Affairs, The National Committee Reports of Tribals, National Crime Records Bureau reports etc. various articles, journals as well as websites have been used for obtaining necessary information.

Results and Discussions

Demographic Profile of Tribes

Tribes are more vulnerable to natural and human made disasters because of their marginal social standing and discrimination as well as their habitation in marginal spaces segregated from mainstream settlements. India has the second largest tribal population in the world, accounted 104.2 million i.e., 8.6 percent as per the 2011 census. There are 705 distinct tribes in India recognized by our Constitution. Other than this, in most Indian states,

Particularly vulnerable tribal group or Primitive tribal Group are also located. Such category shows the characteristics of pre-agricultural system of existence, that is practice of hunting and gathering, zero or negative population growth, extremely low level of literacy in comparison with other tribal groups. The regional demographic profile of tribes in India are shown below in Table: 8.1.

The total ST population in India as per the 2011 census was 1045.46 lakhs which constituted 8.6% of the total population of India. Of these, 5199.85 laks are females, i,e. 49.7%. The demographic profile of tribes in India shows that majority of STs belongs to States Madhya Pradesh, Maharashtra, Orissa, Andra Pradesh, Rajastan, Gujarat, Jharkand, Tamilnadu etc. Madhya Pradesh, Maharashtra, Orissa, Rajasthan, Gujarat, Jharkhand shows high percentage of female ST population. A majority of the Scheduled Tribe population is concentrated in the eastern, central and western belt. About 12% inhabit the Northeastern region, about 5% in the Southern region and about 3% in the Northern States. In Kerala it's only 246,636 in number. Bhil, Chenchu, Gond, Kondas, Lambadis, Sugalis, Adiyam, Kammrar, Kondkappus, Malais, Palliyar, Irular, Kammara, Kondakapus, Kota, Toda, Goud, Kuruba, Koya, etc are the major tribal groups located in Andhra Pradesh, Karnataka, Kerala and Tamilnadu. In these States, we can see around 25 Primitive Tribal groups also. In the case of Kerala , there are 43 distinct tribal groups names as Adiyam, Kammrar, Kondkappus, Malais, Palliyar etc. of which 5 are Primitive tribe groups (Cholanaikkan, Kadar, Kattunayakan, Koraga, Kurumba).

Table 8.1: Tribes in India: Regional Demographic Profile

North East States of India					
	No. of Tribes	***Population in State (In Lakh)***	***ST Population in State (In Lakh)***	***% STs in State to Total Population of State***	***% STs in State to Total ST Population in India***
Mizoram	15	10.97	10.36	94.4	01
Nagaland	05	19.79	17.11	86.5	1.6
Meghalaya	17	29.67	25.56	86.1	2.4
Sikkim	04	06.11	2.06	33.8	0.2
Tripura	19	36.74	11.67	31.8	1.1
Arunachal Pradesh	16	13.84	9.52	68.8	0.9
Assam	15	312.06	38.84	12.4	3.7
Manipur	33	28.56	11.67	40.9	1.1

(Contd...)

North States of India					
UP & Uttaranchal	15	1998.12	11.34	0.6	1.1
Himachal Pradesh	10	68.65	3.92	5.7	0.4
J&K	12	125.41	14.93	11.9	1.4
East States of India					
Orissa	62	419.74	95.91	22.8	9.2
West Bengal	40	912.76	52.97	5.8	5.1
Bihar	33	1040.99	13.37	1.3	1.3
Jharkhand	30	329.88	86.45	26.2	8.3
South States of India					
Andhra Pradesh	35	419.74	95.91	22.8	9.2
Karnataka	50	912.76	52.97	5.8	5.1
Kerala	43	1040.99	13.37	1.3	1.3
Tamilnadu	36	329.88	86.45	26.2	8.3
Central States of India					
Madhya Pradesh	21	726.27	153.17	21.1	14.7
Chhattisgarh	31	255.45	78.23	30.6	7.5
West States of India					
Gujarat	31	604.4	89.17	14.8	8.5
Rajasthan	12	685.48	92.39	13.5	8.8
Maharashtra	48	1123.74	105.1	9.4	10.1
Goa	08	14.59	1.49	10.2	0.1
Daman & Diu	05	2.43	0.15	6.3	0
Dadra & Nagar	07	3.44	1.79	52	0.2
Islands					
Andaman Nicobar	06	3.81	0.29	7.5	0
Lakshadweep	04	0.64	0.61	94.8	0.1

Source: Annual Report, 2012-13. Ministry of Tribal Affairs, Census 2011

Literacy and Schooling among Tribes

The fundamental move to develop a community is through education. Education is the only primary agent which can help individuals overcome income barriers, and expand the horizon of the community when it comes to making career choices, personal growth, build confidence, and a sustained development in well-being. It is the most supreme and vital parameter for a better tomorrow of the tribal population (Pujasree Chatterjee,2014). While analysing the education scenario, we can arrive at a conclusion that the literacy rate and Gross Enrolment Ratio among the tribal women of India are very low due to unawareness about the programmes and policies offered by the Central and State governments to them for their upliftment. Because of lack of education, they haven't enough confidence to deal with the privileged groups. When we analyse the literacy data of STs in India (Table:2), we found that females literacy level shows remarkable progress from 1961 to 2011, 41.97%. But still females lag behind males about 20%

as per the 2011 census. In Kerala, Cholanaickan tribe group shows a very low level of literacy rate (15.3%) as per the latest census.

Table2: Literacy Rates of STs by Sex

Year	*Scheduled Tribes - Persons*	*Scheduled Tribes - Males*	*Scheduled Tribes - Females*
1961	8.53	13.83	3.16
1971	11.3	17.63	4.85
1981	16.35	24.52	8.04
1991	29.6	40.65	18.19
2001	47.1	59.17	34.76
2011	58.95	68.50	49.40
% Increase in 2011 over 2001	25.18	15.82	41.97

Source: Census 2011, Office of the Registrar General, India

At all ages 49.4% is the ST female literacy rate as against 68.5% of male. In all age groups, female literacy rate of STs lag behind male literacy rate. The Literacy rate at all India level for different categories is given in Table 4.3. Details of Gross Enrolment Ratio for ST students at Primary, Upper Primary and Elementary levels for years 2014 to 2017 are given in Table:4. These data indicate that there has been decline of Gross Enrolment Ratio in 2015-16 and 2016-17. For ST Girls, It shows an increasing trend, in respect of higher education too. Gender Parity Index for Scheduled Tribe students has shown some improvement at senior secondary levels as well as at higher education level. However, it is constant at secondary level during 2015-16 to 2016-17.

Table 8.3: Literacy Rates of STs by Age wise

Age Groups	*Person*	*Male*	*Female*
All Ages	59.0	68.5	49.4
Oct-14	86.4	88.3	84.4
15-19	80.2	85.7	74.6
20-24	69.2	79.6	59.0
Adolescent (10-19)	83.6	87.1	79.9
Youth (15-24)	75.0	82.9	67.1

Source: Census 2011, Office of the Registrar General, India

Table 8.4: Gross Enrolment Ratio of ST Girls

Level / Year	*Primary (I-V) 6-10 Years*		*Upper Primary (VI-VIII) 11-13years*		*Secondary (IX-X) 14-15 Years*		*Senior Secondary (XI-XII) 16-17 Years*		*Higher Education (18-23) Years*	
	Girls	Total	Girls	Total	Girls	Total	Girls	Total	Girls	Total
2014-15	107.7	109.0	93.2	92.6	71.7	71.4	37.6	38.5	12.3	13.7
2015-16	105.2	106.3	96.1	95.2	74.4	73.7	42.2	42.8	12.9	14.2
2016-17	100.6	101.6	97.0	95.7	74.4	73.5	42.6	42.7	14.2	15.4

Source: Census 2011, Office of the Registrar General, India

Poverty among Tribes

Poverty and ignorance continue to keep the tribal poor and less dignified. Estimates based on Tendulkar Methodology of poverty ratios for the years for which large sample surveys on household consumer expenditure have been conducted by the NSSO. As per these estimates, ST people living below the poverty line in 2011-12 were 45.3% in the rural areas and 24.1% in the urban areas. In the case of both rural and urban people who belongs to below poverty line, the states like Chhattisgarh, Jharkhand, Madhya Pradesh, Maharashtra, Orissa shows the percentage above the national average. State-wise details for the year 2011-12 are given in Table: 8.5.

Table 8.5: Percentage of BPL ST Population (Tendulkar Methodology)

States	*Rural*	*Urban*	*States*	*Rural*	*Urban*
Andhra Pradesh	24.1	12.1	Kerala	41.0	13.6
Assam	33.4	15.6	Madhya Pradesh	55.3	32.3
Bihar	59.3	10.3	Maharashtra	61.6	23.3
Chhattisgarh	52.6	35.2	Orissa	63.5	39.7
Gujarat	36.5	30.1	Rajasthan	41.4	21.7
Himachal Pradesh	9.50	4.00	Tamil Nadu	36.8	2.80
Jammu & Kashmir	16.3	3.00	Uttar Pradesh	27.0	16.3
Jharkhand	51.6	28.7	Uttarakhand	11.9	25.7
Karnataka	30.8	33.7	West Bengal	50.1	44.5
All India	45.3	24.1			

Source: Planning Commission, 2011- 12

Drinking Water and Latrine Facility

According to Census 2011 data, while almost 47% of all households in the country have drinking water facilities, within the Scheduled Tribes premises, less than 20% of the ST households enjoy this convenience. More than one third of the ST households have to spend time and energy for fetching drinking water from far away sources as against only about 18%

of all households at all India level. Other sources of drinking water includes tank, pond, lakes etc. (Table: 8.6).

Table 6: Source of Drinking Water for ST Household

Location of source of drinking water	*Tap water from Treated Source*	*Hand Pump*	*Tube Well/ Borehole*	*Well*	*River / Canal*	*Spring*	*Other Sources*
Total	24.5	39.1	7.8	21.0	2.0	3.1	2.4
Within Premises	54.1	20.9	8.8	16.2	0.0	0.0	0.0
Near Premises	22.5	46.8	7.5	18.0	1.3	2.0	2.0
Away	9.8	39.1	7.7	28.2	4.2	6.5	4.5

Source: Census 2011, Office of the Registrar General of India.

According to Census 2011 data, only 22.6% ST households have latrine facility within the premises as compared to 46.9% households at all India level. While 49.8% of total households go for open defecation and 74.7% ST households still go for open defecation as per census 2011. At the State level, Lakshadweep scores highest percent (98.3%) of ST households with latrine facilities within the premises. In Kerala, the rate is 71.4%. Odisha is seen to be lowest with only 7.1% ST households against 22% of all households having latrine facilities within the premises.

Health and Hygiene

Health is an important source of human capital formation in any country. The tribes have very low level of awareness, consciousness, information and knowledge about the need to maintain life in healthy and hygiene condition that leads to low health-seeking behaviour among them. The diseases affecting tribal population vary from area to area, depending on the environmental and social conditions and cultural practices prevalent in each area. Especially vulnerable are the primitive tribes who have some unique health problems and challenges, needing special attention by the government. Many tribal people die of malnutrition, ignorance and superstitious beliefs. The essential characteristics of these communities are primitive traits, geographical isolation, distinct culture, shy of contact with community at large, economically backward etc. Accessibility to proper health facilities is very rare. Advanced checkups and treatments are not available and affordable to the majority of the tribal people. Health education and proper sanitary amenities are far from them. Regular medical clinics or camps, special assistance to diagnose and advance treatments in cities can make their life better.

While there is an increasing trend in the prevalence of chronic diseases such as diabetes, hypertension and cancer throughout India, associated with the use of tobacco, lack of physical activity and consumption of unhealthy diet, a similar increase is also being experienced by the tribal populations in India. The vector-borne diseases such as malaria have a huge and disproportionate adverse impact on the tribal population (Jai Prakash, 2019). The tribal districts contribute to 70% of the dangerous malaria strain and 47 % total malarial deaths in the countryas on 2016. Available evidence indicates that the prevalence of tuberculosis is significantly higher among tribal populations. That is 703 per 100,000 compared to the national average 256 per 100,000. The Saharias, a primitive tribe in Madhya Pradesh, is particularly vulnerable to TB, with alarmingly high prevalence of 1518 per 100 000 population. In the case of Kerala, there are many affected by cancer and most of them, abandoned by their dear ones. The Adiya and Paniya tribe in Wayanad are very poor and victims of these kinds of sicknesses. Though there are primary health centres, its services are very limited and not easily reachable. They depend on traditional system of medicine and do no access to modern system of medicine.

According to the National Family Health Survey 2016, the under-5 mortality among the tribal population was 57.2 per 1000 live births compared to 38.5 among others, and the infant mortality rate 44.4 per 1000 live births versus others of 32.1. A child born to a ST family in India has 19% higher risk of dying in the neonatal period and 45% greater risk of dying in the post-neonatal period compared with other social classes. Child malnutrition rates are also significantly higher and poverty more common for tribal populations as compared with others.

Economic Status

Scheduled tribes heavily depend on agriculture for both their subsistence and commercial purposes. In India, two third of the tribal population working in the agriculture sector. Schedules tribes are collectors of forest produce, hunter gatherers, shifting cultivators, nomadic herders and artisans. India's tribal population is over-dependent on agriculture and forest-related livelihood sources. While 43 % of non-tribals depend on agriculture, 66% of the tribal population survives on these primary sector livelihood sources. But in recent decades, the number of tribal farmers is coming down, and more are becoming agricultural labourers. In the past decade, 3.5 million tribals have quit farming and other related activities. Between 2001 and 2011 census reports, the number of tribal cultivators reduced by 10% while number of agricultural labourers increased by 9 %.

Crimes against Tribes

The crime against tribes in India is increasing in an enormous rate. Because of lack of education and literacy, the tribes are unaware about their life security and safety. Many cases are under reported to the authority as the tribes attitude and shrink in shell nature. They haven't get enough security from the government also. As per the National Crime Record Bureau statistics, crime against tribes occurred more in Madhya Pradesh, 2801 during the year 2018. It is 29.6% to all India total during the year 2018 and the second position is for the state Maharashtra. Among the southern states of India, Tamilnadu recorded the least number of crimes against Tribes. Crimes against STs during 2010-2018 are shown below (Table:7)

Even though the literacy and education level of India shows an increasing trend over the years, the different types of violent behaviour against tribal population increase day-by- day. Major crimes against the tribes categorised into murder, rape, kidnapping, abduction, dacoity, robbery, arson, hurt etc.

Incidence of crime committed against Scheduled Tribe women in India during 2001-2014 shown in below Table:8. Hurt and rape case reported to the police during these years shows a large digit. the total crimes reported in India during the year 2016 was 6568. The number of kidnapping case also shows an increasing digit over the years.

Table 7.8: Crime/Atrocities Against Scheduled Tribes, 2010-2018.

States	*2010*	*2011*	*2012*	*2013*	*2014*	*2015*	*2016*	*2017*	*2018*
Andhra Pradesh	803	802	666	672	390	362	405	341	544
Bihar	71	97	119	91	77	5	25	80	108
Chhattisgarh	507	336	344	331	475	373	402	399	612
Gujarat	155	153	221	224	223	248	281	319	770
Jharkhand	0	0	287	396	402	266	280	237	126
Karnataka	234	309	373	521	397	386	374	401	696
Kerala	294	281	124	135	120	165	182	144	244
Madhya Pradesh	88	231	1218	1296	1577	1358	1823	2289	2801
Maharashtra	1383	1284	307	407	443	482	403	464	1138
Odisha	0	0	688	790	533	691	681	700	303
Rajasthan	1319	1263	1351	1651	1681	1409	1195	984	1061
Telangana	33	23	0	0	333	386	375	435	618
West Bengal	110	41	91	122	107	84	83	122	66
Tamil Nadu	01	08	27	23	18	25	19	22	32
Total State	5877	5699	5912	6759	6815	6270	6556	7114	9457

Source: National Crime Records Bureau, Ministry of Home Affairs.

Table:8 Category Wise Crime/Atrocities Against Scheduled Tribes

Crimes	*2001*	*2005*	*2010*	*2011*	*2012*	*2013*	*2014*	*2015*	*2016*
Murder	167	164	124	143	156	122	225	132	232
Rape	573	640	640	772	729	847	949	967	974
Kidnapping	67	72	69	137	103	130	166	124	163
Dacoity	16	27	7	7	5	8	2	4	6
Robbery	73	49	5	9	15	7	12	9	10
Arson	108	38	33	24	26	33	28	25	13
Hurt	756	767	917	803	816	930	1150	963	979
Others	2732	2511	2927	2700	2759	3301	3045	2974	3156
Total	6217	5713	5764	5756	5922	6793	6827	6276	6568

Source: National Crime Records Bureau, Ministry of Home Affairs

According to the latest National Crime Records Bureau statistics, in 2016, rape accounted for 14.8 per cent of all crimes reported against STs, followed only by 12.7 per cent cases of assault on women, with intent to outrage their modesty. About 974 cases of rape were reported in 2016 against ST women, whereas 2,541 cases of rape were reported against SC women. Table:9 shows the murder of STs from 2001 to 2012. During these years, Madhya Pradesh recorded high number of murder of STs, 174 during 2012 followed by the south Indian state Andhra Pradesh, then Maharashtra, Rajasthan, Chhattisgarh. Dadra and Nagar Haveli and Andaman Nicobar Islands reported 7 murder case in the year 2003 and 2008. records shows that the state Tamilnadu exhibit a very least number in all types of crimes. A total of 122 cases of murder of persons belonging to Scheduled Tribes were reported in the year 2013 as compared to 156 cases in the year 2012, showing a decline of 21.8%. Madhya Pradesh has reported the highest number of cases (42 cases) accounting for 34.4% cases followed by Rajasthan (21 cases) accounting for 17.2% of the total such cases reported in the country during the year 2013.

Table: 8.9 Murder of Scheduled Tribes

States	*2001*	*2005*	*2010*	*2011*	*2012*
Andhra Pradesh	13	12	13	11	52
Bihar	3	0	1	2	3
Chhattisgarh	22	32	40	101	36
Gujarat	13	13	11	14	25
Jharkhand	18	30	21	6	6
Karnataka	1	9	16	3	26

(Contd...)

Kerala	3	1	1	0	1
Madhya Pradesh	71	126	102	139	174
Maharashtra	32	32	36	38	45
Odisha	9	20	14	13	4
Rajasthan	60	46	34	16	34
Tamil Nadu	0	0	9	0	1
Uttar Pradesh	3	0	0	6	0
West Bengal	0	0	0	0	4
Total State	266	358	301	352	412

Source: National Crime Records Bureau, Ministry of Home Affairs

Data regarding rape of STs during 2001 to 2012 shown in the table:10 below. Among the selected states, Madhya Pradesh recorded 401 number of rapes in the year 2012, followed by it Chhattisgarh recorded 154 numbers, and Maharashtra recorded 85 numbers. The total number of rapes in India during 2012 recorded as 946. A total of 847 cases were reported in the year 2013 as compared to 729 cases in the year 2012, thus showing an increase of 16.2%. Madhya Pradesh has reported 329 cases accounting for 38.8% of the total cases in the country during the year 2013. The total number of arson cases reported in India during 2012 was 82 numbers, of these 22 reported in Maharastra, followed by it Karnataka reported 14. Among the north Indian states, Tamilnadu and Kerala recorded zero number of cases in these category. West Bengal and Chhattisgarh also recorded zero arson cases during these years.

Table: 8.10 Rape of Scheduled Tribes

States	*2001*	*2005*	*2010*	*2011*	*2012*
Andhra Pradesh	23	36	57	66	45
Bihar	6	0	1	2	0
Chhattisgarh	71	110	136	123	154
Gujarat	27	40	35	31	38
Jharkhand	25	29	9	28	4
Karnataka	2	5	4	2	11
Kerala	30	26	21	50	65
Madhya Pradesh	294	411	414	460	401
Maharashtra	80	67	68	82	85

(Contd...)

Odisha	30	31	60	39	59
Rajasthan	53	27	46	51	48
Tamil Nadu	0	2	0	3	2
Uttar Pradesh	4	0	0	0	4
West Bengal	0	7	1	3	24
Total State	667	827	852	952	946

Source: National Crime Records Bureau, Ministry of Home Affairs

Table: 8.11 Hurt of STs

States	***2001***	***2005***	***2010***	***2011***	***2012***
Andhra Pradesh	269	117	126	177	245
Bihar	11	9	43	34	0
Chhattisgarh	101	74	18	205	108
Gujarat	118	118	82	93	135
Jharkhand	19	80	106	26	40
Karnataka	64	21	21	32	35
Kerala	17	21	47	22	33
Madhya Pradesh	401	423	722	490	553
Maharashtra	23	15	34	57	33
Odisha	214	119	180	48	100
Rajasthan	85	190	151	96	74
Tamil Nadu	8	0	0	41	34
Total State	1380	1300	1559	1341	1413

Source: National Crime Records Bureau, Ministry of Home Affairs

Table: 8.11 shows the hurt of STs. In this category Madhya Pradesh shows highest digit of 553 during 2012, followed by it Andhra Pradesh also recorded 245 number of hurt of STs. A total of 930 cases were reported during the year 2013 as compared to 816 cases in the year 2012, thus showing an increase of 14.0%. Madhya Pradesh has accounted for 21.9% of total 930 cases reported in the country followed by Odisha and Rajasthan. The highest crime rate of 6.4 was reported in Kerala as compared to the national average of 0.9.

Conclusion

Active involvement of women in the entire development process is essential for the overall socio-economic progress of any country. Therefore, raising the status of women in general and that of socially and economically backward women in particular is not just a moral necessity but a strategic one. In Indian Society, the weaker sections have been subjected to socio economic deprivation, exploitation, discrimination and injustice of all types even after the 60 years of independence. The condition of tribal people in India is so pathetic. This category of people not yet came to the main stream economic activities because of the socio economic environment and the cultural and traditional barriers created by themselves in their society. The crimes against tribal population in India is increasing at an alarming rate. With widespread displacement of tribals, women lose the secure conditions of life, making them vulnerable to sexual attacks. The changing Central and State governments are taking many steps for their upliftment and to promote the quality of life of these weaker sections of population but none of them get desired result because of their ignorant and illiterate character, lack of their reliability about the knowledge and information of government policies and programmes etc. For them, we have to take a better step for a better tomorrow, as the developmental goal never be achieved by compromising these groups.

Reference

Chatterjee Pujasree (2014),'Social and Economic status of tribal women in India : The challenges and the Road Ahead', International Journal of Interdisciplinary and Multidisciplinary Studies, Vol 2, No.2, ISSN: 2348 – 0343

Narain Jai Prakash(2019), 'Health of tribal populations in India: How long can we afford to neglect?', Indian Journal of Medical Research, Vol.149, issue:3

Pal C. Gobinda (2017), 'Tribal Resistance, Assertions of Identities and Atrocities: Suppressing the Voices of Truth', Journal of Economic & Social Development, Vol. - XIII, No. 1, ISSN 0973 - 886X

'Educational Statistics at a Glance', (2016) , Government of India Ministry of Human Resource Development, Department of School Education & Literacy, New Delhi

'Tribal Profile at a Glance', (May 2014) http://tribal.nic.in/WriteReadData/userfiles/file/Statistics/Tribal%20Profile.pdf

'Achieving Gender Equality, Women's Empowerment and Strengthening Development Cooperation', (2010), Economic and Social Affairs, Dialogues at the Economic and Social Council, United Nations, New York

'Report of the Working Group on Empowerment of Scheduled Tribes for the Eleventh Five Year Plan', (2011), Planning Commission, Government of India

'Report of the High Level Committee on Socio Economic, Health and Educational Status of Tribal Communities of India, Ministry of Tribal Welfare',(2014), Ministry of Tribal Affairs, Government of India

'Women and Men in India: A statistical compilation of Gender related Indicators in India', (2018), 20th Issue Social Statistics, Division Central Statistics Office, Ministry of Statistics and Programme Implementation, Government of India

Annual Reports (2017-18), Ministry of Tribal Affairs, Government of India

Census of India, 2011, Registrar General of Census, GOI, New Delhi

Reports of National Commission for Schedules Tribes, Government of India

Reports of National Crime Records Bureau, Government of India

https://ncst.nic.in/content/crime-against-scheduled-tribes/

http://www.focusonpeople.org/index.htm

http://ncrb.gov.in/StatPublications/CII/CII2018/pdfs/Table%203A.3.pdf

data.gov.in

http://ncrb.gov.in/StatPublications/CII/CII2013/Chapters/7-Crime %20against%20Scheduled%20Castes%20&%20Scheduled%20Tribes.pdf

https://shodhganga.inflibnet.ac.in/bitstream/10603/94474/11/11 chapter%202.pdf

Chapter - 9

Tribal Women's Health in India: Issues, Challenges and Strategies

Dr. Shilpa M. Sangam

Abstract

Indian Tribals groups are heterogeneous and usually living in remote and ecologically diverse climates and areas. They culturally firm and have developed strong magico-religious health care system. Health conditions in tribal areas have been described as deficient in sanitary conditions, personal hygiene and health education. Modern medicine has not been accepted in most tribal areas. The present paper attempts to address the health status, issues and challenges of the tribal women in India and also discuss some essential strategies for successful women entrepreneurship in the aspect of health.

Key words: *Health status, Health issues and tribal women*

Introduction

Tribal peoples are popularly known as Adivasis. Approximately, they constitute 8.6% of the nation's total populations, over 104 million people, out of which women are 51 million which amounts to almost half of the tribal population (Census 2011). They are concentrated mostly in the central belt of India and parts of the North-East. These tribal groups inhabit widely varying ecological and geo-climatic conditions such as hilly, forest, tarai, desert, coastal regions etc. in different concentrations throughout the country. Indian Tribals groups are heterogeneous and most of them remain at the lowest stratum of the society due to various factors such as geographical and cultural isolation, low levels of literacy, primitive occupations and extreme levels of poverty.

Health conditions in tribal areas have been described as deficient in sanitary conditions, personal hygiene and health education. Modern medicine has not been accepted in most tribal areas. They have developed strong magico-religious health care system and they wish to survive and live in their own style. This paper is an attempt to highlight the health status, issues and challenges of the tribal women in India and also discuss some essential strategies for successful women entrepreneurship in the aspect of health.

Objectives

1. To study the concept health and health status of tribal women in India.
2. To highlight health issues and challenges faced by Indian tribal women.
3. To suggest some essential strategies to improve health status of tribal women in India.

Concept of Health

Health is a very broad concept. It is an important aspect for the survival of human. It is a general condition of a person's mind and body usually meaning to be free from illness, injury or pains. WHO has defined health in 1946 as "a state of complete physical, mental and social well-being and not merely the absence of disease or infirmity".[1] Women's health has long been a concern for WHO but today it has become an urgent priority as it involves reproductive health which is a crucial component of a women's general health. The health is determined by the physical, emotional, social, spiritual, cultural, political and economic context of women's lives, as well as by biology. Health is considered as one of the most important factors contributing to the development of society.

Health Status of Tribal Women in India

Pandit Jawaharlal Nehru often repeated that "When women moves forward, the family moves, the village moves and the nation moves." And "You can tell the condition of a Nation by looking at the status of its women." In the words of Former President Dr. APJ Abdul Kalam, "Empowering women is a prerequisite for creating a good nation, when women are empowered, society with stability is assured. Empowerment of women is essential as their thoughts and their value systems lead to the development of a good family, good society and ultimately a good nation."

Health status is an important index of economic growth and development. The status of health of a given population has positively or negatively influenced nation's economic growth. Despite rapid strides in socio-economic development, health and education, the widening economic, regional and gender disparities are posing challenges for the health sector.[2] In any country the state of health is measured in terms of life expectancy, mortality rate, fertility rate, and many more. But it can't be ignored that all these indicators of health are dependent on other factors like per capita income, nutrition, sanitation, safe drinking water, social infrastructure, medical care facilities, employment status, poverty, etc., which affect the health of every individual. There is direct relationship between health and development.[3] Generally, at household level, cultural norms and practices and socio-economic factors determine the extent of health problems among women.

Tribal are characterized by a distinctive culture, primitive traits and socio-economic backwardness. Although scheduled tribes are accorded special status under the fifth/sixth schedules of the Indian Constitution, their status on the whole, especially their health still remains unsatisfactory.[4] Tribal communities in general and primitive tribal groups in particular are highly disease prone. Also they do not have required access to basic health facilities. They are most exploited, neglected and highly vulnerable to diseases with high degree of malnutrition, morbidity and mortality.[5] Their misery is compounded by poverty, illiteracy, ignorance of causes of diseases, hostile environment, poor sanitation, lack of safe drinking water and blind beliefs, etc. Some of the preventable diseases such as tuberculosis, malaria, gastroenteritis, filariasis, measles, tetanus, whooping cough, skin diseases (scabies), etc. are also high among the tribals. Some of the diseases of genetic origin reported to be occurring in the Indian tribal population are sickle cell anemia, alpha-and betathalassemia, glucose-6-phosphate dehydrogenase (G6PD) deficiency, etc.[6] Night blindness, sexually transmitted diseases are well known public health problems of tribals in India. Malnutrition is pervasive among tribals. Deficiencies have been detected in gross amounts of calcium, vitamin A, vitamin C, riboflavin, and animal protein. Southern tribes are known for their caloric and protein deficiencies. Maternal mortality is due to unhygienic conditions and inappropriate tribal practices. Studies on fertility and mortality trends among the tribal population of India have been found to be fragmentary and isolated. Limited studies are available on infant mortality and hardly any study is available on maternal mortality among the tribal population. However, a brief review of the available studies at zone wise showed that the total fertility rate were more or less similar to the Indian national population. Maternal mortality was reported to be high among various tribal groups but no exact data could be collected. The main causes of maternal mortality were found to be unhygienic conditions and primitive practices for parturition.[7] However, after a comparative analysis of the various indicators such as political organization, religion, ritual practices etc., among the different tribes of India, it has been observed that the status of tribal women is comparatively lower than that of tribal men. Moreover, the status of tribal women has gone from bad to worse as a result of the impact of social change which has affected the social structure of tribal society.[8]

Health Issues of Tribal Women in India

However the health issues are greatly influenced by thoughts, beliefs, notions, traditions and taboos of the tribal society. Apart from these socio-cultural barriers, the religion, education and economic factor do alter the health issues. These factors are the determinants of the health pattern of the individuals in a given society but bound to vary from a society to other, one area to other and so on.

Efforts have been made to collect available literature on the health studies among different tribal women in the light of several parameters i.e. sex ratio, female literacy, marriage practices, age at marriage, fertility, mortality, life expectancy at birth, nutritional status and health, child bearing and maternal mortality, maternal and child health care practices, family welfare programme, sexually transmitted diseases and genetic disorders. It may, however, be mentioned that health-related information is limited, most of the available populations are limited and most of the available studies are fragmentary in nature without an adequate sample size and standard methodology. The research findings of all the available studies are discussed in the context of the above said parameters. The following are the main problems or difficulties that are posed to tribal women's health.[9]

1. Malnutrition such as anemia, chronic energy deficiency (CED), vitamin deficiencies etc.
2. Communicable diseases like Malaria, Tuberculosis, Leprosy, HIV etc.
3. Non-communicable diseases such as Cancer, diabetes, Hypertension etc.
4. Reproductive health issues such as RTI's STIs.
5. Mental illness and subsequent addiction.
6. Genetic disorders namely sickle cell anemia etc.

Health Challenges of Tribal Women in India

1. Lack of awareness of health issues
2. Lack of health facilities in remote rural areas
3. Lack of emergency transportation
4. Discriminatory behavior by health care providers
5. Financial constraints

Strategies to Improve Heath Status of Tribal Women in India

First, the governments both at the Centre and States must recognize improvement in the health status of the tribal population as among the topmost priorities from policy point of view and ensure adequate budget allocations made including under the National Tribal Plan. The Government of India (GOI) constituted Expert Committee on Tribal Health has recommended that the government per capita expenditure on tribal health should be substantially enhanced and that 70 per cent of this should be spent on primary health care. Three World Bank supported the following innovative strategies to state health projects in Rajasthan, Karnataka and Tamil Nadu following innovative strategies to improve tribal population's access to health care and raise the quality of service provided.

1. Advocating and Awareness of Women's Health and Rights
2. Raising Awareness of Health Issues
3. Bringing Health Services to Remote Populations
4. Formulating of realistic development health plans
5. Providing Emergency Transportation for Expectant Mothers
6. Employing Health Workers from Tribal Communities
7. Changing the Behavior of Health Care Providers
8. Providing Financial Support

Conclusions

Health conditions in tribal areas have been described as deficient in sanitary conditions, personal hygiene and health education. However the health issues are greatly influenced by thoughts, beliefs, notions, traditions and taboos of the tribal society. Apart from these socio-cultural barriers, the religion, education and economic factor do alter the health issues. They have enjoyed lower health status resulting different kinds of diseases and ailments due to poor health care facilities and poor health seeking behaviours. In India, the National Health Services have often neglected the tribal people in general and tribal women in particular. In addition to the social and economic factors contributing to the low health status of this underprivileged group. Health Interventions must focus on tribal culture, medical training of tribal people and knowledgeable health care delivery system catering to the needs of the tribal women and more research.

References

1. K Park, Preventive & Social Medicine. 20th Edition. Jabalpur : M/s Banarsidas Bhanot Publishers. 2002. PP.14
2. Das k, Health as an economic indicator, kurukshetra, Volume 60 (10), August, 2012, P.6.
3. Sharma A. Pal, Rural Health Scenario in India, kurukshetra, Volume 60 (10), August, 2012, P.9.
4. Santhosam M Angeline, Samuel U., A Study on the Health Status of Elderly Irular Tribal Women in Kancheepuram District, IOSR Journal Of Humanities And Social Science (IOSR-JHSS) e-ISSN: 2279-0837, p-ISSN:2279-0845.Volume 7 (2), Jan.-Feb. 2013, P.1, www.Iosrjournals.Org
5. Balgir R.S., Dimensions of rural tribal health, nutritional status of Kondh tribe and tribal welfare in Orissa: a biotechnological approach, Proc. of the UGC Sponsored National Conference on Human Health and Nutrition: A Biotechnological Approach (Lead Lecture), Thane, 12-13th December 2004. PP. 47-57.
6. Balgir R.S., Health care strategies, genetic load, and prevention of hemoglobinopathies in tribal communities in India, South Asian Anthropologist. Vol. 4, 2004, PP 189-198.
7. Basu SK., A Health profile of tribal India, 1992. April:2(2):12-4; Pubmed PMID 12287763

   Basu, S. K.Tribal Health in India (Bdited). Manak Publishers, New Delhi (in press). 1993
8. Chauhan, Abha Tribal women and social change in India. A.C. Brothers, Etawah. 1990
9. NFHS-4 (2015-16), Tribal Health in India -Bridging the Gap and a Roadmap for the Future

Chapter - 10

Empowerment of Tribal Women and Education as a Tool

Dr. Naseema. PK

Abstract

The social order of every society revolves around several instincts and out of those, two are not only powerful, rather make a lot of influence on the society. They are the knowledge and the presence of educated women in the society. For achieving the second object, every society on the earth must endeavor on the first one, ie; process of imparting of education. But even now women are falling behind the necessary education about their basic rights in the basic unit of society, i.e., family. The hot debate over the subject of triple talaq till the recent judgment showed that it was not known to Muslim women that their right was violated, instead many silently suffered. Similarly the tribal women in India too lag behind as they are not given the necessary knowledge required in various fields. One of the solutions to their problems is creating an awareness of their legal rights through education. Of course empowerment regarding their rights should be inclusive of family system as well so that it will enrich them because real empowerment begins from one's own family. The purpose of this paper is to emphasize the women's education as a tool for empowerment of tribal women, focusing on its socio-legal aspects.

***Key words**: Women, Empowerment, Society*
Asst. Professor of Law, AMU, Centre, Malappuram

1. Introduction

It is true that no nation can ever be worthy of its existence that cannot take its women along with the men (Powell, 2007).The social order of every society revolves around several instincts and out of those, two are not only powerful rather, make a lot of influence on the society. They are the knowledge and the presence of educated women in the society. The former signals for the preservation of individual itself, whereas the later deals with the preservation of descent, especially the lineage of mankind. For achieving the second object, every society on the earth must endeavor on the first one, *ie*; process of imparting of education. This is equally applicable to all communities irrespective of their claim to divinity of their laws concerned. This is most relevant in the case of tribal women as they have been devoid of access to the realization of their rights whether constitutional or legal. Of course empowerment regarding their rights in family system is also to be addressed to them as it will enrich them and real empowerment begins from one's own family.Therefore, 'educating women' is the most powerful tool that can bring a change in the position of women in the society bringing reduction in inequalities and functions as a means of improving their status within the family (Sowjanya & Hans, 2018).

The status of women in a society is significant reflection of the level of social justice in that society. Elimination of all types of discrimination against the socially disadvantaged groups is a must for social justice to prevail. This is why there is a need to discuss about the issues of tribal women who lag behind the main stream andgovernment should focus empowerment of schedule tribe women and allocate separate funds. Education and nourishment of their confidence should be selected as key focus areas and they must be provided additional skills for value additions to their lives.

2. Empowerment

Empowerment is a multi-dimensional process, which enables the individuals to realize their full identity and powers in all the spheres of life. If we speak about empowerment of women, it is that process which brings equal status to women, opportunity and freedom, and thereby equipping her to be independent and confident. If they are empowered, they will become scientific, logical, open-minded, and self-respecting. They will become bold to shake away custom, belief and practices in the society that may tie them to the bottom level. Women empowerment is a process of enabling women to have access and make productive contributions to their economic independence, political participation and social development (Sowjanya & Hans, 2018). It helps to realize their identity and powers in all spheres of life. Women are mostly depicted as most respected and valued entities in Holy Books, but, found invisible in the development scenario. Denial of access even to the enjoyment of their recognized rights and rejection of opportunities to rightful place *etc*. prevails even today and it shows the true and pathetic position of women.

Through empowerment women acquire knowledge, skills and techniques which help them in their personal and social growth. They show sensitivity towards problems in the society rather than observing it. But they should be trained effectively for a meaningful involvement and here is the importance of their education in the correct perspective. Lack of education is the root cause for women's exploitation and negligence. The two gates that opens new world for them is literacy and education. Through these doors they can open the new skies by understanding constitutional and legislative provisions that are made to strengthen them. When women are educated, they will be able to contribute in nation building and thus the socio-political state of affairs of the whole world will definitely improve.

Gender equality is what women desire. It is not only the desire of women folk, but the need of the society as a whole. If half of the population remains deprived, ignorant and continue under this discrimination due to ignorance mainly, the country cannot move on to an era of prosperity, instead lag behind conflicts and confusions. Empowerment becomes the means of achieving the rights with dignity. And to achieve it, women should be taught in the needed perspectives and concerned disciplines. As Justice Krishna Iyer opined, "Women's exploitation is a reality and gender justice is a fragile myth, women emancipation lies in the education and in their awareness..." (Krishna Iyer.J, 1979). So empowerment calls for critical interventions by administrative and political wings to design approaches which suitably fit for the strategic developments of women. This is because women development and women empowerment are correlated conceptually and methodologically.

Empowerment means not only economic or status based improvements, but also liberation from man-made bondages. The whole concept of empowerment of tribal women need to be contextualized overcome all the obstacles like economic insecurity, absence of socio-political space etc. The tribal population is an integral part of India's social fabric. It is the second largest concentration after that of the African continent. Many studies related to the general enquiry of women exploitation and dependency shows that lack of education is responsible for women disempowerment.

Gender equality is a constitutional obligation for India. Our country has ratified various international conventions and human rights instruments like Convention on Elimination of All Forms of Discrimination against Women (CEDAW), The Mexico Plan of Action, the Nairobi Forward Looking Strategies, the Beijing Declaration as well as the Platform for Action *etc.*, In spite of the women's movement and all the above legal obligations, still exists a wide gap between the goals of the legal instruments, legislation, policies, plans and the situational reality of the women on the other hand.

3. Importance of Women Education

Women make almost half of the population and if they are empowered it will strengthen the national economy. Our country can become a developed nation only if women are uplifted. This great goal will be possible when she is educated and empowered. Education is considered as a powerful tool for women empowerment because it enables them to respond to the challenges, to confront their traditional role and change their lives. According to the Literacy Rate 2011 census, the female literacy levels as 65.46% where the male literacy rate is over 80%. But beyond and over literacy, there are more meaningful ways that education can do for women's rights and well-being. Education is the key to unlock the golden door of freedom for development. This paper discusses the impact of education, especially that in connection with tribal women and related rights to empower women to face the challenges and changes in life. Educating women is the key, not only to solve the conflicts of rights in legal arena, but also to enhance economic growth and sustainable development. Raising the education levels and literacy rates of women is one of the most effective investments for increasing female productivity as well as enhancing the well-being of family and children (OECD, 2008).

4. Education

Education is a *sine qua non* for the creation of society where the human being can realize their rights and development (Chauhan. J, 2013). Education is as important as heart is to human body. It is a fundamental right for the citizens of our nation. The Supreme Court of India held that right to education attaches to the individual as an inalienable human right (Avinash Malhotra v. Union of India). It has important role in eradicating inequality through inculcating rational thinking and independent outlook. In this perspective, it can be used as the most powerful weapon to fight an age old problem of our society, *i.e.,* backwardness of women. Nowadays we speak too much about women empowerment. But even now, major portion of women community is illiterate and backward. But how is true empowerment possible? From where should it start? It should be started from the family first. When one realizes the value, status, rights *etc.*, of oneself, the self-respect regenerates in one's own self which is the first step towards empowerment. Education will reduce inequalities inside and outside family. It is a means of improving their status within the family. If they are really empowered, it will be reflected in their improved livelihoods. Education of women is highly relevant because only the educated women can play a very dominant role whether in the economic or social scenario of the country.

Education will enable women to articulate their views and instill in them a sense of confidence to fight for their rights(Rajasekharan Nair.G, 2011). It is only through educating them; their mindset can be changed and tuned to the required frequency for a positive social change. But it is seen that poor and vulnerable women are usually more interested in skills training that meets their immediate „practical gender needs as opposed to longer term, "strategic gender needs" that directly tackle the basic underlying causes of female subordination (Moser, C. 1989).

Only when women are ready to remove the obscurantist mindset, they can transform themselves to be carriers of torchlight for a brighter future. As the former Prime Minister of India, Mrs. Indira Gandhi said when she was delivering a message to U N Women's Conference in Mexico on 26th June 1975, "So long as the woman has within her the archaic seed of dependence, no legislation or society can ensure her rightful position- status is the outcome of history, heritage and social and economic environment" (Amita Malik). In order to bring out this, women should realize her potential and be aware of her rights through proper education.

When tribal women are devoid of modern facilities like education its adverse impact is far severe than facilities like electricity or ample transportation because the lack of education act as the breeding ground for social vices and anti-social activities. Through education one's competence will be enhanced so that they can adapt physical and social environments and will enable the upward social mobility among people. It can provide opportunities for functional employment as well thereby opening economic growth which can change the rural landscape. In short, education act as tool changing human capital into a better socio-economic structure.

5. Educating of Rights- An Effective Way Out

India is a country of diverse culture where many are residing in underdeveloped areas or remote places like hills. The rural communities especially tribals are lagging behind modern facilities like education, electricity, health care facilities *etc.* If State could successfully educate them, it can not only transform the culture, but also make opportunities for functional employment and can lift the downtrodden rural map. One way of educating which could transform people is educating them of their rights. The skill development and realization of one's own rights will lead to a different picture of these women. India has the second largest tribal population in the world and its women find no space in formal business training programs thus limiting their employment options, economic returns and long term career development (Swaleha Sindhi, 2012).

Mostly it's a custom that after the marriage, bride's connections are practically severed and she will move to husband's place. From a carefree life to one of full of responsibilities through marriage, she has to plays a very decisive role in society and hence necessitates recognition of her status, rights and duties too. For this, she must be trained regarding the knowledge of domestic as well as family life. Though we have legislations covering the domestic relations they are not understood either, fully or partially, by the people especially women. Even though gender parity has been applied in formal forms, it is not enjoyable practically even on the knowledge level. This lacuna about the existing legislations regarding households can be solved by educating them. Thus the knowledge on this aspect will be useful for many desperate wives or at least provide them where to go and what are their rights which can be legally claimed in difficult situations. The correct knowledge regarding the rights of women in matters related to family will equip them not only to find remedies in challenging phases of life, it will also equip them to manage matters of family in a better way to avoid such situations and solve them even before complicating them.The family structure here is patriarchal where a culture of power relationship supports man's supremacy and here gender roles are socially constructed. As a consequence, a boy is looked upon as the perpetuator of the family line, and a girl 'a bird of passage' promoting a hierarchy of classification in which man centered issues take dominance (Veena Bhasin,2007)Hence, it's highly useful for them if they are enlightened upon their rights at least in their family. If they are made to form small groups like SHG program, it will be useful for women who are drop- outs of regular educational programs too. They can pay more attention to sanitationand health matters in households and can spread a health rights awareness. This will motivate women to take treatment from qualified doctors as they will be knowing the risks.

They don't even know the constitutional provisions that is envisaged for the upliftment of them through affirmative action. They should be familiarized with their constitutional rights. A module consisting of the following Articles shall be introduced to them after getting them translated to their own tribal language. They are Article 14 that confers equal rights and opportunities to all, Article 15 directing the State to prohibits discrimination against any citizen on the grounds of sex, religion, race, caste *etc,*Article 15 (4) that States to make special provisions for advancement of any socially educationally backward classes, Article 16 (4) for provisions for reservation in appointments or posts in favor of any backward class of citizens, which in the opinion of state, is not adequately represented, Article 46 to promote with special cares the educational and economic interests of the weaker section, especially the ST and protects the social injustice and all form of exploitation, Article 275 for grant–in aid for promoting the welfare of ST and raising the level of administration, Article 330 for reserving seats in the House of the People, Article 332 reserving of seats for Scheduled Castes and Scheduled Tribes in the Legislative Assemblies of the States and A. 335 that says that the claims of the members of the Scheduled Castes and the Scheduled Tribes shall be taken into consideration, consistently with the maintenance of efficiency of administration, in the making of appointments to services and posts in connection with the affairs of the Union or of a State. Also, as per A.244(1) tribal welfare communities to be setup for the welfare of the tribes and A. 22(2) provides that effective participation of tribal shall be ensured in the process of planning and decision making. When the tribal women themselves know about all these wonderful provisions they can contribute better as knowing one's rights, empower them from heart. It is with a noble goal for ensuring a better quality of life for the tribal population, the Tribal Sub Plan (TSP) Strategy has been adopted for all round development of tribal areas since Fifth Five-Year Plan. The TSP approach ensures allocation of fund for tribal areas from State Plan in proportion to the ST population in the State. The Tribal Sub-Plan (TSP) aims to bridge the gap between the Schedule Tribes (STs) and the general population with respect to all socio-economic development indicators in a time-bound manner. TSP is not applicable to states where tribals represent more than 60% of the population (Prsindia).

The government and civil society need to contribute immensely to add the quality of life of this vulnerable sections of our country. By empowering rural woman through education can thus enable them to live with dignity and self-reliance cutting across the barriers of customary biases and prejudices, social barrier of caste, class, gender, occupation and institutional barriers that prevent them from taking actions to improve their state both at the individual and collective level (Swaleha Sindhi, 2012).It must be remembered that right to vote is meaningless unless rural women are made aware, educated and imparted skills to understand the order of the day and this can bring change in their lives, in the family and lastly transform the holistic tribal landscape of India, through education, legal awareness, and socio economic independence (Swaleha Sindhi, 2012).Women empowerment is not an isolated task but depends upon many different variables like geographical location (urban/rural), educational status, social status, and age. Though we have sound plans, there are significant gaps between policy advancements and actualpractice at the community level. One prominent reason can be the patriarchal structure thatgoverns the households and less political participation in spite of the reservations for women.The role of women is substantial and crucial in tribal community because theywork harder and the family economy and managementdepends on them (Ramu Bhukya, 2015).

6. Conclusion

Empowerment is not a one day process and does not happen overnight. It may take time for women to realize their potential and make otherwomen aware about it and the government initiatives and policies. In this way, as a chain of events it continues and only this way the womenempowerment take place in the rural tribal area. Education can accelerate this process. Thus, promoting education especially to make them aware of their rights in the family as well as in the society is worthwhile in transforming society to a just society in which women can enjoy equality. This is of great importance in empowering them to accomplish their goals in different spheres of life. Thus educating in a way where socio-legal norms are given publicity and importance and adopting this approach to education wherein the need to correlate social norms and legal norms are of much value in bringing a transformation in the society. After all, the purpose of education itself is generating thoughts to create a progressive society. In many societies, women are under-represented in various areas, including business programs or other economic activities. This is more among tribal women who lags behind other women. In relation to tribal societies, this is having a high significance as India has the second largest tribal population in the world which is resulting in narrowing their employment options, economic returns and national growth.Empowerment includes higher literacy levels, education,better healthcare, equal ownership of productive resources, increased participation in economic and commercial sectors,awareness of rights and responsibilities, improved standards of living, self-reliance, self-esteem and self-confidence.

Upliftment of the status of tribal women is not just a moral imperative but also a strategic one if the aim is that of national upliftment. Not only economic empowerment, but also the political empowerment is also a need of the time because political participation is very vital in the development of the community as a whole. In this context, tribal women can secure their rights, as well as their identity by political decisions so that they may no longer be deprived from their basic human rights. At this juncture too, education making them aware about their voting rights, right to elect their representative *etc.* is to be given to them. This is necessary as the situation of ST female's participation to politics is very poor in rural area. Another area of concern is that tribal women engaged in agriculture, construction *etc.*, are un-organized and are exploited. The State should protect their labor rights and should make special steps to teach them labor laws and collective rights and implement labor laws for them.

Thus education leads to qualitative improvement in women's lives which in turn makes them feel dignified and enjoy the right to be themselves. They will no longer be passive victims, but actively create and shape their own future. When more and more tribal women would come forward for their own development, then only their progress would ensue. Without the educational development women can't make her status to society. The demand for literacy is to be generated within the family and community so that leadership qualities will be developed.

References

Amita Malik, *Quotable Quotes from Indira Gandhi* 34.

Avinash Malhotra v. Union of India, (2009) 6 SCC 398.

Chauhan.B.S. Judge, Supreme Court of India (2013) editorial, XIV NYAYA DEEP, 3 & 4.

Justice. Krishna Iyer. V. R., (1979) *Law and Life* Universal law Publishing.

Moser, C. (1989).Gender planning in the third world: Meeting practical and strategic gender needs, World Development 17 (11), Pages 1799-1825

OECD (2008), Gender and Sustainable Development: Maximizing the Economic, Social and Environmental Role of Women, Retrieved from http://dx.doi.org/10.1787/9789264049901-en,

Rajasekharan Nair.G, (2011) *Gender Justice under Indian Criminal Justice System* Eastern Law House Pvt. Ltd.

Ramu Bhukya (2015), Empowerment of tribal women in India, Indian Journal of Research 4.|

Russell Powell (2007). Catharine MacKinnon May Not Be Enough: Legal Change and Religion in Catholic and Sunni Jurisprudence, 8 GEO. J. GENDER & L 8, 1& 6.

Sowjanya Shetty and Hans, V. Basil (2018). Role of Education in Women Empowerment and Development: Issues and Impact, Retrieved from https://ssrn.com/abstract=2665898.

Swaleha Sindhi (2012), Prospects and Challenges in Empowerment of Tribal Women, IOSR Journal Of Humanities And Social Science 6, 46-54.

Veena Bhasin (2007), Status of Tribal Women in India, Journal Studies on Home and Community Science 1.

https://prsindia.org/report-summaries/tribal-sub-plan

Chapter - 11

Social Exclusion of Paliyar Tribal Women In Dindigul District of Tamil Nadu

Dr. T.S. Bala Gomala & V. Ariya Nathu

Abstract

Paliyar Tribal community in India has been most vulnerable community in the in equal, domination and exploitation ridden society. Tribal group's population of mainland South Asia. Tribal community population in India's 8.6% or 104 million people, According to the 2011 census, and a large percentage of the Nepalese population. They comprise a substantial indigenous minority of the population of India and Nepal. They are on the breadline of their socio-economic and political rights. Even after centuries, the unchanged condition of Tribal communities is leading in India. The violation of fundamental Human rights and the state brutality has been perpetrated on them, particularly on Paliyar Tribal communities have faced isolation and social discrimination like that of Dalits from the mainstream in the society. The Constitution of India has guaranteed equality of opportunity to all sections of society including the Tribal women. The Paliyar Tribal women are subjected to discrimination in many ways and Communication of media and also neglected the Paliyar Tribal women due to several reasons in the post-independence era in India. The media institutions have a corporate social responsibility of facilitating the empowerment of Paliyar Tribes who are the excluded sections of Indian society. The present paper explores within the large framework of Human rights in general life practices observed through field and social interaction highlights their food habit, marriage, health, worship and cultural festival practices. Besides the social significance of this study and statement of the problems and objectives of the study are presented in this chapter of Paliyar Tribal women in Dindigul District of Tamil Nadu.

Key words: *Paliyar Tribal Women, worship and cultural practices, Human Rights, Constitution of India, Discrimination, Indian Society, Social Justice and Empowerment of Paliyar Tribes.*

1. Introduction

Human rights are the birthrights of every human being and they form an integral part of the socio-cultural fabric of humanity all over the world. However, they are vulnerable to abuse of the violation and human rights can be understood as abstract norms and values protected in laws, constitutions and international conventions. Tribal peoples constitute 8.6 percent of India's total population, about 104 million people according to the 2011 census (68 million people according to the 1991 census). This is the largest population of the tribal people in the world. Tribalism implies the possession of a strong cultural or ethnic identity that separates one member of a group from the members of another group. Based on strong relations of proximity and kinship members of a tribe tend to possess a strong feeling of identity. The Tribal people in India have a long history even before the arrival of the colonial government. The Tribal societies that existed prior to the colonial intervention had their own rights and duties within their autonomous sovereign framework. The majority of the tribal population is found in the Eastern, Central and Western regions of India. They are mostly backward, deprived and oppressed sections of the Indian society.

Human rights have become prominent on the National and International agenda. Coinciding with the United Nation Declaration. The Indian Constitution also replicates that the State will not distinguish against any citizen on grounds of birth, place, ethnic, religion, caste and agreed that the promotion and protection of all human rights is a legitimate concern of the State. These include basic survival rights to health care, shelter, food and social security, the right to work, the right to education, and the right to participate in the cultural life of one's society. However, there is a huge gap between the ideal of the human rights laws and the reality of continuing gross human rights violations of Tribal communities in India.

2. Review of Literature

The review of literature is to guide the researcher in understanding the problem selected for research and then formulate the research design. With this view, the review of literature related to the themes of present investigation in terms of the previous findings, variables considered, methodology adopted and the gap in these is carried out by considering the available research reports.

Prakash (2003) conducted a study on the food habits of tribal households and tribal were forced to depend much upon the agriculture and mainly on produce like vegetables, rice and some coarse grains such as maize, millet etc.

Deogaonakar (2006) reported that Kolam Tribes attempts to depict an ethnographic profile of the tribe to discuss the socio-cultural and economic problems. Even the traditional methods follow the tribals. The tribal situation in south India and tribal development policies followed in general and programmes for Paliyans in particular are discussed. The socio-economic conditions of Paliyans life problems and developmental activities etc. The systematic analysed in this study.

3. Statement of the Problem

The Tribal population has a close traditional association with the territory or a tribal domain with the tribal community enjoying a collective command over the natural resources. In this way the Paliyar Tribals in Sirumalai and Kodaikanal are more associated with the territory and with their particular community. Tribal human rights provide fundamental insights into the causes, manifestations and consequences of human rights violations experienced by Tribal communities.The tribal economy can be termed as a subsistence economy or a primitive economy. A large number of tribes are still dependent on cultivation, food gathering and fruit collecting exercises for their survival. They are at the lowest stage of social and economic order in India.

Paliyar Tribal women have been discriminated against education, income, consumption, status and access to power they have a worse health record then men, they suffer from social, cultural and legal discriminated and often from violence, They are discriminated on ground of equity which refers to equality of opportunities and choice and efficiency. There is need for quantitative measurement for a complete set of cultural and rights indicators to assess women's rights. The rights of Paliyar tribal women as women and their right as indigenous peoples shall be understood as interlink and inter-related. Indigenous women are an integral part of indigenous people's collective identity, dignity, cultures and ways of life. Thus, the violation of the rights of indigenous peoples also directly affects indigenous women and the violations of their rights as women also affects them in different ways as indigenous peoples in relation to their welfare and wellbeing as indigenous peoples and as Paliyar Tribal women.

They are socially and economically weaker and also under object poverty and live in subsistence economy and general backwardness. This is because of their ill health which is a cause and consequence of poverty.

Paliyar tribal women mostly they suffer from the nutritional deficiency diseases like endemic goiter, anemia. Other manifestations were pot belied school children, small body sizes, underweight adolescents and short life spans. Another set of nutritional problems develop from unsanitary food supplies and water contamination, less calories of food intake, which have much reflection on the health status of paliyar tribes women. Low awareness among the paliyar tribal women in personal hygiene, poor sanitation, nutritional deficiency and poor mother and child health services, absence of health education, lack of national preventive programmes, and lack of available health services are responsibility for the poor health of the tribals. It is due to low income and other socio economic factors. Due to poor education system or lack of quality education, paliyar tribal women remain in a cycle of illiteracy. They are economically dis-empowered by not having land tenure inspite of their role and contributions as custodians of land and natural resources. Millions of tribal women depend on the land, forest and water for their livelihoods and for providing food security to their families and communities. The socio-economic and political status of paliyar tribal women, they continued to face severe violations of their human rights, both within their own community and in the wider society.

3. Objecetives of the Study

- To analyze the socio-economic background of the Paliyar tribal women.
- To assess the level of awareness about the health condition of Paliyar tribal women
- To identify the various problems faced by the Paliyar tribal women.
- To suggest suitable measures for the providing for the welfare of the Paliyar tribal women.

4. Hypotheses

The following hypotheses are proposed for testing in this study

- Awareness about the health condition and Constitutional provisions of human rights act does not vary across the different levels of Paliyar tribal women
- The Paliyar tribal women is more victimized for Untouchability practices in the study area

5. Methodology of the Study

5.1. Study Area

Descriptive as well as analytical method will be followed in the study. In order to achieve the objectives of the study 50 Paliyar Tribal women in the Dindigul Districts of Tamil Nadu will be choosen as the study area.

5.2. Universe and Sampling Design

Paliyar Tribal women problem is more as per the reports of the Govt and NGOs. According to the 2011 census the researcher fix the requirement of sample respondents. The study respondent belongs to the age group of 18-45 years old. Names of the Village in Sirumalai, Thenmalai in 50 Paliyar Tribal women is selected as respondents for this study.

5.3. Pilot Study

A pilot study is the primary work to gain clear cut and specific research perspective on the subject of investigation is undertaken. For simplifies the task of designing an interview schedule or questionnaire for this study.

5.4. Tool and Method of Data Collection

An interview schedule is developed to collect data. The interviewed schedule consists of both the fixed and open ended questions.

5.5. Sources of Data

There are two types of data used for study.

5.5.1. Primary data

Primary data was collected from the respondents by the researcher using personal interview schedule, focused group discussion, and other supplementary observational techniques.

5.5.2. Secondary data

Secondary data was also collected from the following sources: Books, Journals, Reports, National and International publications on tribal women from Govt. reports and NGOs.

6. Analysis and Discussion

11.1. Demographic Profile of the Paliyar Tribal Women

Variables	*Sub-Variables*	*Number*	*Percentage*
Age	20-30	16	16
	31-40	18	18
	41-50	16	16
	Total	50	50
Community/ Tribe	Paliyar Tribal Women	50	50
Religion	Hindus	50	50
Type of Family	Nuclear family	30	30
	Joint Family	20	20
	Total	50	50
Education	Illiterates	30	30
	Primary School Level	10	10
	Middle School Level	10	10
	Total	50	50

The above table shows that the demographic profile of the chosen Paliyar Tribal Women for this study. Among the 50 Paliyar Tribal Women, Majority 18(36%) of Respondents belonged to the age group of 31-40 (32%) of them belonged to 20-30 age category and the remaining 16 (32%) of them belonged to 41-50 age group. All the 50 respondents were only Paliyar Tribal Women and in fact, all the 50 (50%) respondents belonged to Hindu religion. The majority of the Paliyar Tribal Women live in Nuclear families. As per the observation, nearly 30% Paliyar Tribal Women live in Nuclear families and only 20% of the Paliyar Tribal Women live in Joint families. It is quite evident from the observations of the researcher that among the 50 Paliyar Tribal Women 10% Women had completed their Primary level of learning which means up to V standard and 30% Women are completely illiterates as they do not know even to read or write and 10% Paliyar Tribal Women have completed their Middle School Level of Education which means up to VII standard.

11.2. Facilities Available at the Households of the Paliyar Tribal Women

Electrical Facilities Available at the Households of the Paliyar Tribal Women	*No. of Respondents*	*Percentage*
Electrical lights Alone	25	25

(Contd...)

Electrical lights and Television	10	10
No Electrical Lights and Television	15	15
Total	50	50
Fuel used at the Households of the Paliyar Tribal Women		
Use Fire Wood	40	40
Use kerosene Stove	10	10
Total	50	50
Nativity Identity		
Ration Card	20	20
Voter ID	15	15
Do Not Have Ration Card and Voter ID	15	15
Total	50	50

Among the 50 Paliyar Tribal Women, 25(25%) Tribal Women's Houses have Electrical lights, 10 (10%) Houses have Television Sets, 15 (15%) Houses do not have the Electrical Facilities such as Electrical lights and Television Sets. Even the basic needs of the Paliyar Tribal Community are not met by the Government. Tribal Women 40 (40%) women use Fire wood as their fuel for cooking purposes and 10(10%) women use either Gas stoves or kerosene stoves for cooking. This reveals that the Paliyar Tribal Women still use the olden cooking methods like their ancestors, as they believe that cooking using fire woods would promote good health benefits. Among the 50 Paliyar Tribal women have only Ration cards, 20 (20%) women have only voter IDs and 15 (15%) women have both Ration cards as well as Voter IDs and 15 (15%) women do not have either Ration Cards or Voter IDs to exhibit their nativity.

11.3. Work and Leisure Time of the Paliyar Tribal Women

	Part time Work		***Season Time Work***		***Permanent Work***	
	N	%	N	%	N	%
Collecting Honey	28	28	15	15	35	35
Home Garden	12	12	10	10	8	8
Own Business	10	10	25	25	7	7
Total	50	50	50	50	50	50

Among the 50 Paliyar Tribal Women, there were 28 (28 %) women who collect Honey as their part time work , 15 (15 %) women collect Honey as their seasonal work, 35 (35%) women collect Honey as their permanent work as well as their leisure time work. There were 12 (12%) women who cultivate in their Home garden vegetables and fruits as their part time work , 10 (10%) women cultivate in their home garden as their seasonal time work, 8(8%) women cultivate in their Home garden as their permanent work as well as their leisure time work. There were 10 (10%) Paliyar Tribal women who do their own business as their part time work. 25 (25%) women do their own business as their seasonal time work and 7 (7%) women do their own business as their permanent work as well as their leisure time work.

7. Major Finding of the Study

- On the whole in Sirumalai Hills nearly 20(2.2%) women live in Mud houses with thatched roofs in Village like Thenmalai 10(10.0 %) women live in Cement house and asphalt roofs in village.
- In Sirumalai Hills some Tribal families are living in small caves which look like huts between two rocks. Some Paliyar women while roaming for collecting honey, medicine plant, herbal plant in the forest, they live in rocky caves in the interior forests as well as in open space in the forest.
- Paliyar Tribal Women who are living in Nuclear as well as in Joint families possess assets as Goats and Hens, 30 (3.4 %) women possess Cows and Hens as their assets.
- It is observed from the study that the Paliyar Tribal women have slowly started shifted from their traditional medicinal practices and have opted to take Allopathy medicines to get recovered from their illness. But, still many Paliyar Tribal women used to follow the traditional medicines for their illness and medicines used for specific illness has to be elicited from the Paliyar Tribal Women and it has to be documented so as to preserve the ancient medical practices that were followed by the Paliyar Tribal Women.
- The educational status of the Paliyar Tribal Women respondents was analysed it was found that there were more of illiterate (30%) and a few of the (10 per cent) respondents completed only primary level education. It is observed that most of the respondents were uneducated due to non-availability of school in the study area for the past few decades.
- Marital status revealed that majority of them (30.6 per cent) were married and living with their spouse. 14.9 per cent of the respondents come under the widow category. It is found from the study that majority of the respondents depend mainly on collecting honey and medicine plant (35 per cent) and also depend on agricultural coolie works for livelihood.

- The income of the respondents highlighted that high number (39.7 per cent) of the respondents were earning Rs. 1000 to 3500 per month. It is observed that 31.9 per cent of the respondents get to financial support from their daughters. 12.1 per cent of the respondents are getting financial support from their spouse and remaining 11.7 per cent of the respondents are receiving from their sons. The inference drawn from the analysis is that female children were taking care of their parents during illness in the lost stage of elderly Paliyar tribal women.
- When assessed the level of awareness of supportive systems and welfare of the elderly tribal people, the majority (35.2 per cent) of them responded that they did not know about the Government programmes. It is observed that the elderly people are not well aware of Government tribal welfare programmes due to ignorance and illiteracy.
- Based on the objective 'factors and extent of problems among the Paliyer tribal women's' the researcher finds factors and major problems of Paliyar tribal women in respect of their age, sex, dependency ratio, etc. and the conditions of the aged in respect of their economic dependency, number of dependants, living arrangements, persons supporting the aged, physical immobility, etc.
- Nearly 35 (35 %) women consume Vegetarian type of food, 15(15 %) women consume Non-Vegetarian type of food during the time of their Menstruation. Most of the Paliyar women prefer Vegetarian type of food during their menstruation time.
- The results obtained from the research are presented in this section. It is observed from the field that 40 per cent of the respondents have some kind of Physical problems like gastro intestinal disease, chronic constipation, chronic headache, joint pain, loss of vision, loss of hearing. These problems occurred due to food habits, climate condition and ageing factor. Malnutrition, as expected, is the most common health problem among the paliyar tribal women.
- In fact, 37 (37%) Paliyar Tribal Women consume Vegetarian type of food during their cultural function like marriage ceremony, 13 (13%) women consume Non-Vegetarian type of food during the marriage functions. The Paliyar Tribal women follow the best practice of simple, very economical marriage functions because they organise their marriage functions at their own homes or at the

temples. Besides, they provide mostly Vegetarian type of food and they adopt a community gathering ceremony.

- The Paliyar Tribes consider the age attainment of the girls or Puberty as an important ceremony and during this period they think that the girls have to be ritualistically treated and the girls are not allowed to do any household works. From the day of attaining puberty as well as the girls will be kept confined to one corner of the hut. Similarly the puberty the girls will be kept for seven days at home and on the seventh day a purification ceremony will be done at home inviting their tribal community friends and relatives.
- In addition, they from communicable diseases such as tuberculosis and malaria. Some tribal groups are also at high risk for sickle cell anemia. Generally tribal diets are seen to be deficient in protein, iron, iodine, and vitamins. And 10 per cent of the agricultural coolie workers have psychological problems. Because they were getting very low income, they cannot consume healthy food, nutrition and they do not get proper respect from the society.

8. Implications of the Study

It is the duty of the Government to empower the tribes especially the paliyar tribal women because it is the human right to educate them and they are excluded in the National development of our country in all aspects. The Central, State and Local- Self governments should take up the responsibility to formulate the suitable policies and development of the tribes and the paliyar tribal women. They Tribal community must be actively involved in policy making, planning, implementation and evaluation of tribal development programmes in India. The welfare and development of tribal Community should not be viewed in terms of material needs but equally in relation to non material needs and fundamental rights. The basic needs to be fulfilled in order to enhance their development respect of tribal areas which are deprived of basic needs, civic amenities and infrastructural facilities. It is a need to say that the occupational pattern in the life style practices of the Tribal Community need to be improved in order to develop their efficiency and coverage of self-employment and wage-employment. The Government and the NGO's should work for the achievement of the goal of gender equity and justice, goal of cultural promotion, goal of economic development in order to empower the Paliyar Tribal women.

9. Conclusion

The problems of Paliyar tribal women in the hill areas of Kodaikanal in Dindigul District, South Tamil Nadu it is found out from the in-depth analysis of the problems and its extent faced by the tribal women under study are more prone to be affected by physical, economical and psychological problems. Taking into account the nature of geographical location of the target and way of life, sources of livelihood have forced the poor elders to lead miserable life in the rest of their lives. To develop the appropriate measures policies and programmes to meet their needs and improve their living conditions and wellbeing in the context of respecting their rights as women and as indigenous peoples. Till today, there been no common legal framework at the national level to promote and protect the rights of the women domestic workers. As there is no alternative employment and their increasing age factors have become instrumental behind perpetuating their poor economic life. The constitutional guarantee, which governs and protects the rights and sovereignty of Tribal communities, need an immediate implementation. Otherwise, this would lead to a disappearance of the various Tribal communities from the human picture. The Tribal communities sovereignty is at stake by the intervention of non-tribes in their area. Therefore, there is an immediate need to constitute Tribal autonomy councils so that the Tribal communities themselves can look after the rules, implementation and development of the localities. The Government should provide awareness to the Paliyar Tribal Women to fight against the oppressive forces in the society and disseminate knowledge about to health condition of the Paliyar Tribal women to acquire benefits from the Government and NGO's so as to adopt the scientific innovations and technological advancements by developing their personality.

References

Chandran, D. (2012). A Paradox Within A Paradox: Emerging Signs Of Change In The Unappealing Tribal Scenario In Kerala, India,, Developing Country Studies, 2(6): Iiste

Chakarvarti, Sumi (2007) "Tribal Welfare And Development In India: Past, Present And Strategies With Special Reference To Agriculture And Forestry", New Delhi.

Dandekar (2004) "Aged In India" Anmol Publications Pvt Ltd, New Delhi.

Mitra A And Singh P (2008), "Trends In Literacy Rates And Schooling Among The Scheduled Tribe Women In India", International Journal Of Social Economics, 35

Nair, R. (2006) Human Rights In India: Historical, Social And Political Perspectives, New Delhi: Oxford University Press.

Poulter, S. (1998) Ethnicity, Law And Human Rights, The English Experience, Oxford Clarendon Press.

Revathi, E. (2013) Adivasis And Telangana The Hans India.

Virginius Xaxa, (1999) Tribes As Indigenous People Economic And Political Weekly, 34no.51 December 18.

Http://Www.tribal.com

Http://Paliyartribals.In

Http://Paliyartribals

Http:// Tribalwomen.in

Http:// Tribalpeople.in

Chapter - 12

Kudumbashree and Empowerment of Tribal Women: Evidence from Wayanad, Kerala

Fathima Fidha & Dr. Sukumaran M

Abstract

Now days Kudumbashree has been a phenomenon in the process of women empowerment. The initiatives taken by the Kudumbashree have been resulted miraculous result in this respect. The development strategies followed in the Kudumbashree activities has a holistic, economic and social welfare function. The eradication of poverty being the motto of Kudumbasheree has been achieved this for some extent. The women along with the men have been performing for the momentum growth of the economy and society. In short, the impact of Kudumbashree on the empowerment of women is very significant. It is needless to say that the benefit of the development activities should appropriate equally without any special consideration. But historically, sociologically and anthropologically, tribal women are far behind from the entire developmental programme. It is also anticipated that, even though Kudumbshree has been facilitating momentous growth in the socio-economic avenues it is least benefited to the tribal women. Due to several reasons they are not able to take advantage of this momentous growth. In this juncture, this paper is an attempt to examine the tribal women participation in Kudumbashree and the status of women empowerment among the tribes in Wayanad district. This study has been used primary data. Using simple statistics the data were analysed and made the inferences. The study found out that, the women empowerment status of tribal women participating in Kudumbashree has adequate level of empowerment than the non particiapants.

Key Words: *Kudumbashree, Empowerment, Tribal Women*

1. Introduction

Tribal community in general and tribal women in particular is the most marginalized and socially excluded segments in the society. The historical hangover of the tribal population from the oppression of mainstream population has its own deep roots in every aspect of life of tribal population. The different socio-economic, cultural and political conditioning has been deepening the psycho social environment of the tribal women. They are working hard even more than that of their counterparts. In every tribal society the role of tribal women in the process of income generation, decision making are relative higher in the tribal women. This high workforce participation of the tribal women results in myriads of related issues among the tribal women. Tribal women are seems to be illiterate, low educational status, poor health condition more over prone to violence and exploitation at large extent.

In Kerala, it is observed that, a large majority of unorganized lablour force directly or indirectly related to Self Help Groups. One of the most popularized SHGs in Kerala is Kudumbashree. Kudumbashree is a programme intended to eradicate poverty and driving force of women empowerment implemented by the State Poverty Eradication Mission (SPEM) of the Government of Kerala. Kudumbashree has been a buoyant initiative of the government towards women empowerment. Convergence with Panchayat Raj Institutions (PRIs) is seems to become the central themes of Kudumbashree idea. Convergence means seamless working together of the Kudumbashree and the Pnchayathi Raj Institutions. Presently Kudumbashree become a pivotal programme for women empowerment in Kerala. It is a fact that, the tribal women are entirely different from non tribal women in accessing many of the benefits of government programmes. Educational backwardness, poor social relations are some of the factors influencing in this respect. In this backdrop the present study is an attempt to examine the participation of tribal women in Self Help Groups and the status of their empowerment. This paper is discussing connecting the changes occurred or very emphatic among the tribal women those who are the members of SHGs and non members of any SHGs.

2. Significance of the Study

Kudumbashree (SHGs) plays a decisive role in empowering women empowerment in Kerala.Kudumbashree leads to sustainable social, economic development of women and a direct impact on their living status, educational, nutritional and health needs of their children, positively (Jomy Jose, 205) . It is observed that tribal women are reluctant to participate in the Kudumbashree programmes and activities and they have also low level of empowerment characteristics. They are often facing myriads of socio-economic and political issues compared to the main stream non-tribal women population and tribal women who are the members of any SHGs. In this context it is very significant to study the participation of tribal women in SHGs and to compare the major changes observable in the members of SHGs and non members. The report of the study will have a strong impulsion to the planners and policy makers to take initiatives to include all the tribal women in the purview of SHGs and ensure the sustainable empowerment and development of tribal women in Kerala.

3. Objectives of the Study

Following are the two objectives of the present study.

1. To examine the participation of tribal women in Kudmbashree.
2. To compare the socio-economic and political empowerment of Kudumbashree member tribal women and non member women.

4. Methodology of the study

The study has been used both primary and secondary data. The primary data were collected from 30 tribal women belongs to Kurichya, Kuruma and Paniya communities of Wayanad district. The secondary data were collected from some of the published sources like reports and journals. The data were collected using a research toll which comprises five questions and 15 statements.

5. Results and Discussions

This section presents the results of the study followed by discussions.

5.1. Membership of tribal women in Kudumbashree

Table. 12.1 Illustrates the percentage of tribal women having membership in Kudumbashree in the study area. From the data it is evident that, more than 56 percent of the tribal women have membership in Kudumbashree. It is also realized from the field experience that, this 56 percent tribal women, many are not active in the process and programmes of the Kudumbashree unit. It causes to lack many of the privilages enjoyed by the active members of Kudumbashree.

Table. 12.1 Number of tribal women having membership in Kudumbashree

Do you have Membership in Kudumbashree	*Number of Women*	*Number of Women in Percentage*
Have membership	17	56%
Not have membership	13	44%

Source: Field Survey, 2020.

5.2. Kudumbashree and Status of Women Empowerment Indicators

This part of the paper discusses about the relationship between participation in Kudumbashree and some of the women empowerment indicators of the tribal women in the study area. Here the indicators like training, skill development, confidence, general awareness, social status, decision making power, gender equality in the family, social relation, participation in the social activities, political participation, awareness on banking activities, participation in gramasabha, contacts with political leaders are discussed using cross tabulation of these indicators with the membership of the tribal women in Kudumbashree. The indicators of women empowerment were selected on the basis of field experience and personal discussion with scholars.

5.2.1. Kudumbashree and Training of the Tribal Women

The relationship between participation in Kudumbashree and access to training is presented in Table.2. From the data it is obvious that, majority of the tribal women who are the members in Kudumbahsree were got training in any of the specialization in production and socio-economic empowerment. It tells us that participation in Kudumbashree is a way to improve training and development of the individuals including tribal women. But still 50 percentage of the tribal women not get any type of training from any source.

Table. 12.2 Kudumbashree and Training of the Tribal Women

Are you member of any SHGs	*Have you got any training through SHGs?*		*Total*
	Yes	*No*	
Yes	15 (80)	2 (20)	17
No	0	13 (100)	13
Total	15 (80)	15(50)	30 (100)

Source: Field Survey, 2020

5.2.2. Kudumbashree and new skill of the Tribal Women

The relationship between participation in Kudumbashree and skill development is presented in Table. 12.3. From the data, it is evident that, the most of the tribal women participating in Kudumbashree were getting new skills. Here 58 percent of the tribal women participating in Kudumbashree are obtained new skill. It is very significant to note that, none of the tribal women who are not participating in Kudumbashree obtained new skills.

Table. 12.3. Kudumbashree and new skill of the Tribal Women

Are you member of any SHGs	*Have you learned any new skill through SHGs?*		*Total*
	Yes	*No*	
Yes	10 (58)	7 (42)	17 (56)
No	0	13 (100)	13 (44)
Total	10 (33.3)	20 (66.7)	30 (100)

Source: Field Survey, 2020

5.2.3. Kudumbashree and Self Confidence of Tribal Women

Self-confidence is one of the significant factors which influence the individual to life management. Greater social self confidence can also lead people to more effectively manage their social relations. This management of social relations does not imply that they are managed towards a specific objective, but more effective management would build trust and foster greater influence compared to those who mismanage their social relations (Greenacre etal. 2024). The study reveals that, more than 94 percent of the Kudumbashree participants acquired extra skills through Kudumbashree activities.

Table. 12.3. Participation in Kudumbashree and Self Confidence of Tribal Women

Are you member of any SHGs	*Whether your Self Confidence changed positively after joining in Kudumbashree?*		*Total*
	Yes	*No*	
Yes	16 (94.2)	1 (5.7)	17 (56)
No	0	13 (44)	13 (44)
Total	16 (53)	14 (46.7)	30 (100)

Source: Field Survey, 2020

5.4. Participation of Tribal Women in Kudumbashree and Social Relations

Social relation is another factor which stimulates the individual to become self-empowered. The existence of social relationship enhances the functioning of the individual by way of collective information. Such relationship leads to his personal growth and socio-psychological development. The individual but importantly also their social relationships matter in promoting what is generally considered the domain of the individual—personal growth (David etal, 2017). Table.4. describes the relationship between participation of tribal women in Kudumbashree and the change in their social relationships. The field data shows that, more than 94 percent of the tribal women those who joined in Kudumbashree have improve their social relations after joining Kudumbashree. It is very interesting and serious to note that, the tribal women who are not member in Kudumbashree have not improved their social relation.

Table. 12.4. Participation in Kudumbashree and Social Relation of the Tribal Women

Are you member of any SHGs	*Do you think that, your social relationship improved after joining in Kudumbashree?*		*Total*
	Yes	*No*	
Yes	16 (94.2)	2 (5.7)	17 (56)
No	0	12 (44)	13 (44)
Total	16 (53)	14 (46.7)	30 (100)

Source: Field Survey, 2020

5.5. Participation in Kudumbshree and Social Status of the Tribal Women

Development of women including tribal has been one of the objectives of planning in different political regime. Myriads of policies and programmes have been implemented to achieve this goal. All these steps were initiated to ensure the empowerment of women and thereby all round development of the economy and the society. Integration of women development and their empowerment becomesperceptible for the development of any country and this have contributed immensely to capacity building ofweaker sections in all emerging economies, including India (Amruth and Hemalath, 2018).

Table 12.5 Participation in Kudumbshree and Social Status of the Tribal

Are you member of any SHGs	*Whether your social status changed after joining in Kudumbashree?*		*Total*
	Yes	*No*	
Yes	15 (88.2)	2 (17.8)	17 (56)
No	0	13 (100)	13 (44)
Total	15 (50)	15 (50)	30 (100)

Source: Field Survey, 2020

Women

However, it is a fact that till now the empowerment of tribal women is not accomplished. It is noted that, there is a possibility to stimulate the question on tribal women empowerment through Kudumbashree. Table 12.5. exemplifies the relationship between improvement in social status and participation of tribal women in Kudumbashree. From the field study it is evident that, more than 88 percent of the tribal family has undergone commendable level of change in their social status at the same time the family in which women are not members in Kudumbashree does not have any change in their familial social status.

Table.12.6. Participation in Kudumbashree and Improvement in Decision making

The improvement in decision making power of the tribal women after joining in Kudumbashree has been presented in Table. 12.6 from the data it is pertinent that, about 83 percent of the tribal women who joined in Kudumbashree were improved their decision making power through Kudumbashree. At the same time no changes has been occurred to the non-participants in Kudumbashree. From the field experience it is also realized that, women who are participating in Kudumbashree having due importance in the decision-making of family matters or the are maintaining a sort of equilibrium with their counterpart.

Are you member In Kudumbashre?	*Does your decision making power improved after joining Kudumbashree?*		*Total*
	Yes	*No*	
Yes	14 (82.3)	3 (86.7)	17 (56)
No	0	13 (100)	13 (44)
Total	14 (46.7)	16 (53.3)	30 (100)

Source: Field Survey, 2020

Table. 6. Participation in Kudumbashree and Improvement in Decision making

Table 12.7. Kudumbashree and Participation in Social activities

It is very remarkable to note that, the social responsibility of the tribal women has been enriched with the influence of Kudumbashree. The field experience and the supporting field data reveals that, cent percent of the tribal women those who are the members of Kudumbashree are very enthusiastic in social activities. The result with respect to this element is presented in Table 12.7

Table.12.7 Kudumbashree and Participation in Social activities

Are you member In Kudumbashre?	*Do you're your interest towards social activities improved after joining Kudumbashree?*		*Total*
	Yes	*No*	
Yes	17 (100)	0	17 (56)
No	0	13 (100)	13 (44)
Total	17 (56)	13 (44)	30 (100)

Source: Field Survey, 2020

5.8. Participation in Kudumbashree and Awareness on Banking Services

The results of the study also enable to understand that, the percentage of tribal women having good awareness about the banking procedures and services. It reveals that the entire tribal women included in the Kudumbashree have good awareness regarding banking services and procedures whereas those who are not member of Kudumbashree not having awareness on banking procedures. It is presented in Table. 12.8.

Table. 12.8. Participation in Kudumbashree and Awareness on Banking Services

Are you member In Kudumbashre?	*Do you're your interest towards social activities improved after joining Kudumbashree?*		*Total*
	Yes	*No*	
Yes	17 (100)	0	17 (56)
No	0	13 (100)	13 (44)
Total	17 (56)	13 (44)	30 (100)

Source: Field Survey, 2020

5.9. Participation in Kudumbashree and Political Relation of Tribal Women

The study is giving the information about the link between participation of tribal women and their political relation. The data reveals that, the political relation of the tribal women is positive to those who are member of Kudumbashree. Whereas, tribal women not participating in Kudumbashree, not having relation with political parties or political leaders. The field data tells us that, 53 percent of Kudumbashree tribal women are maintaining good relation with political parties, whereas, 47 percent of the Kudumbashree tribal women not maintaining any relation with the political parties and political leaders. It is presented in Table. 12.9.

Table. 12.9. Participation in Kudumbashree and Political Relation of Tribal Women

Are you member In Kudumbashre?	*You have relation with political parties after joining in Kudumbashree?*		*Total*
	Yes	*No*	
Yes	9 (53)	8 (47)	17 (56)
No	0	13 (44)	13 (44)
Total	9 (30)	21 (70)	30 (100)

Source: Field Survey, 2020

10. Participation in Kudumbashree and Frequency of Attending Gramasabha

Gramasabha is a platform to understand the problem faced by the general public and to take remedial measures to solve the problems based on the urgency and deserving of the beneficiaries. When the actual beneficiary is indifferent to attend the gramasabha meetings often he/she will lose his/her benefits. But the engagement in Kudumbashree is acting as a source of information about the frequency of occurrences of Gramasabha and the benefits available to the tribal women. It will enable them to attend the gramasabha regularly to bag their benefits. The data reveals that, all the tribal women who have membership in Kudumbashree are regularly attending the gramasabha and raising their issues in the gramasabha and (Oorukootam).

Table.12.10. Participation in Kudumbashree and Frequency of Attending Gramasabha

Are you member In Kudumbashre?	*You have relation with political parties after joining in Kudumbashree?*		*Total*
	Yes	*No*	
Yes	17 (100)	0	17
No	0	13 (100)	13
Total	17 (56)	13 (44)	30

Source: Field Survey, 2020

6. Conclusions

From the discussion, it is emphatically revealed that, the participation in Kudumbashree developing sense of empowerment to the tribal women through its numerous socio-economic and political programmes. The involvement in Kudumbashree enables them to think rationally in different circumstances and act purposefully. It makes them to develop a sense of politics of socio-economic and political wellbeing. It is unhappy that many of the tribal women still keeping away from this endeavor. Bringing them also in the purview of Kudumbashree will definitely increase the magnitude of empowerment of tribal women. I demand the innovative policies and Programmes to accelerate the socio-economic changes of tribal women in Kerala.

References

Jomy Jos, (2015).Role of Kudumbashree And Women Empowerment: A Study of Thiruvananthapuram Municipal Corporation Areas in Kerala State, India" International Journal of Research – Granthaalayah, Vol. 3, No. 12(2015): 72-82.retrieved from: Http://www.granthaalayah.com, 23-02-2020, 06-27 AM.

Greenacre, Luke & Tung, N.M. & Chapman, T. (2014). Self confidence, and the ability to influence. Academy of Marketing Studies Journal. 18. 169-180.Vol.18, PP169-180.Retrieved form.https://www.researchgate.net.

David S. Lee1, Oscar Ybarra, Richard Gonzalez, and Phoebe Ellsworth. (2017). Through-We: How Supportive Social Relationships Facilitate Personal Growth. Personality and Social Psychology Bullettin.(SAGE). Issue published: January 1, 2018, pp 37-48, retrieved from. https://journals.sagepub.com/doi/full/10.1177/0146167217730371.

Amrutha R and A.V. Hemalatha.(2018). Women Groups and Changing Socio-economic Status.A Study of Kudumbashree in Kasaragod District, Kerala State. International Journal of Management StudiesVol.–V, Issue –3(6), pp 10-19. Retrieved from http://www.kudumbashree.org.

Chapter - 13

Economic Status of Scheduled Tribal Workers Working in Leather Tanneries in Vellore District, Tamil Nadu

Mr. S. John Sundar

Abstract

This study attempts to understand the economic conditions of scheduled tribal workers and working condition of leather tannery workers. The leather tanning industry and leather related industry give employment and business opportunities for many people. The rising cost of living compels the tannery workers to take up the job. The tannery workers are exposed to lot of chemicals for low wages. But this leads to health related problems at large. The state and central government can formulate suitable policies to increase the welfare of the tribal workers. This study helps to suggest increasing the economic conditions tribal of workers in leather tanning industry.

Keywords: *Tannery, Protective, Socio-economic, Health status, Tanning industry.*

Introduction

The leather and leather product industry is one of the oldest manufacturing industries that created an international market right from the middle of the nineteenth century. The leather industry employs about 2.5 million people. It is also an industry with strong links with the social structure through caste and community. Even today, a large number of people engaged in this industry are from traditional leather working castes, belonging to the lower castes or scheduled castes, popularly called Dalits, in the caste hierarchy. So it will be feasible to ascertain the status of the leather artisans in history before dealing into their present condition. The leather workers generally came from an agrarian background. Many of them were workers on the farms of others before joining work in tanneries.

Low wages, uncertainty of employment, rising prices drove them off from their native places. It is really difficult to accommodate increasing size of family on their meager source of income.

The industrial development in the post independence era has culminated in the definite improvement of the condition of labour in the organized sector. The corresponding benefits, however, did not filter down to the workers in the unorganized sector which accounts for more than 90% of total workforce in the country.Socioeconomic status (SES) is a combined measure of a person's work experience economically and sociologically and of a family's or individual's economic and social position in relation to others, based on education, occupation, and income. It is extensively used to assess the SES of an individual in the urban community and is based on three variables-occupation, education and income.

Scheduling Tribes

Arbitrarily critics adopted for scheduling tribes has created series anomalies with certain group, still claiming scheduled tribe status, while some communities which made considerable progress are still in the list. The area restriction for the purpose of according recognition to a particular tribe has also created confusion depriving the persons belonging to the same tribes but living in other districts, the benefits of concession and privileges.

Table - 13.1: District-wise Distribution of Tribal population of Tamil Nadu

District	*Total Population*	*Tribal Population*	*Total Population (%)*	*Total Tribal Population (%)*
Thiruvallur	3,728,104	47,243	1.1	5.94
Chennai	4,646,732	10,061	0.2	1.26
Kancheepuram	3,998,252	41,210	1.0	5.18
Vellore	3,936,331	72,955	1.9	9.18
Tiruvannamalai	2,464,875	90,954	3.7	11.44
Viluppuram	3,458,873	74,859	2.2	9.41
Salem	3,482,056	119,369	3.4	15.02
Namakkal	1,726,601	57,059	3.3	7.17
Erode	2,251,744	21,880	1.0	2.75
The Nilgiris	735,394	32,813	4.5	4.13
Dindigul	2,159,775	8,064	0.4	1.01
Karur	1,064,493	575	0.1	0.07
Tiruchirappalli	2,722,290	18,198	0.7	2.29
Perambalur	565,223	2,584	0.5	0.33
Ariyalur	754,894	10,722	1.4	1.35
Cuddalore	2,605,914	15,702	0.6	1.98
Nagapattinam	1,616,450	3,756	0.2	0.47

(Contd...)

Thiruvarur	1,264,277	3,034	0.2	0.38
Thanjavur	2,405,890	3,561	0.1	0.45
Pudukottai	1,618,345	1,283	0.1	0.16
Sivaganga	1,339,101	790	0.1	0.09
Madurai	3,038,252	11,096	0.4	1.40
Theni	1,245,899	1,835	0.1	0.23
Virudhunagar	1,942,288	2,294	0.1	0.29
Ramanathapuram	1,353,445	1,105	0.1	0.13
Thoothukkudi	1,750,176	4,911	0.3	0.61
Tirunelveli	3,077,233	10,270	0.3	1.29
Kanniyakumari	1,870,374	7,282	0.4	0.91
Dharmapuri	1,506,843	63,044	4.2	7.93
Krishnagiri	1,879,809	22,388	1.2	2.81
Coimbatore	3,458,045	28,342	0.8	3.56
Tiruppur	2,479,052	5,458	0.2	0.68
Total	72,147,030	794,697	1.1	100

Source: Census of India 2011

The distribution of scheduled Tribal population among the different district in the state is presented in table no - 13.1 Based on this, the tribal topography may be broadly divided into three categories, viz., (1) Tribal concentration areas (2) dispersed tribal area and primitive tribal area.

Table - 13.2:Tribe wise Population in Tamil Nadu (2011 census)

S. No	*Tribe*	*Male*	*Female*	*Population*	*Total Tribal Population (%)*
1	Adiyan	2247	2179	4426	0.56
2	Aranadan	72	66	138	0.02
3	Ervalan	1438	1433	2871	0.36
4	Irular	94521	95140	189661	23.86
5	Kadar	325	325	650	0.08
6	Kammara	537	515	1052	0.13
7	Kanikaran,Kanikkar	1879	1958	3837	0.48
8	Kaniyan, Kanyan	1042	1095	2137	0.27
9	Kattunayakan	23360	23312	46672	5.87
10	Kochuvelan	4	3	7	0.0009
11	KondaKapus	265	256	521	0.07
12	Kondareddis	5028	4819	9847	1.23
13	Koraga	61	40	101	0.01
14	Kota	155	153	308	0.04
15	Kudiya, Melakudi	36	30	66	0.008
16	Kurichchan	3181	2919	6100	0.77
17	Kurumbas	3380	3443	6823	0.86
18	Kurumans	15949	15016	30965	3.90
19	MahaMalasar	43	34	77	0.01
20	MalaiArayan	75	97	172	0.02
21	MalaiPandaram	710	729	1439	0.18
22	MalaiVedan	3701	3514	7215	0.90

(Contd...)

23	Malakkuravan	10013	9632	19645	2.47
24	Malasar	3259	3172	6431	0.81
25	Malayali	181704	176276	357980	45.05
26	Malayekandi	107	103	210	0.03
27	Mannan	99	112	211	0.03
28	Mudugar&Muduvan	661	589	1250	0.16
29	Muthuvan	200	190	390	0.05
30	Palleyan	114	117	231	0.03
31	Palliyan	1146	1106	2252	0.28
32	Palliyar	2643	2645	5288	0.66
33	Paniyan	4898	5236	10134	1.27
34	Sholaga	3066	2899	5965	0.75
35	Toda	957	1045	2002	0.25
36	Uraly	6491	6495	12986	1.63
37	Generic Tribes*	27701	26936	54637	6.87
	Total	4,01,068	3,93,629	7,94,697	100

Source: Census of India 2011.

As the table no - 13.2 shows most of tribal communities of Tamil Nadu are small, with population below 5000. Only 16 communities have a population above 5000. However, we cannot identify any district having the representation of all the tribes.

Among the tribal population of Tamil Nadu state, Malayali inhabiting in Dharmapuri, Tiruvannamalai, Vellore, Pudukottai, Salem and Tiruchirapalli districts form the largest tribal community. Malayali numbering 3,57,980 (as per 2011 census) form 45.05 percent of the tribal population of the state. Irulas numbering 1,89,661 form 23.86 percent of the tribal population come next to Malayalis. Kattunaicken form the third largest tribal community in Tamil Nadu. They represent 5.87 percent (46,672) of the tribal population in the state as per 2011 census.

Occupation

The occupational status of schedule tribe population as per 2011 census provided in table 13.3 reveals that only 44.60 percent of tribals were employed or engaged in the main occupation. On the other hand, 45.48 percent of the tribals were unemployed or non-workers and 9.92 percent among them were marginal workers.

Table - 13.3 : The Occupational Status of ST Population 2011.

S. No	*Occupation*	*No. of workers*	*Percent of Workers*	*No. of Workers*	*Percent of Workers*
		Main workers		*Marginal workers*	
1	Cultivators	106099	29.93	6765	8.58

(Contd...)

2	Agricultural labourers	145721	41.11	47551	60.30
3	Household Industry	5279	1.49	2921	3.70
4	Other works	97342	27.40	21621	27.42
5	Total	354441	100	78858	100.00

Source: Census of India 2011.

It can be observed that among the tribal main workers 41.11 percent were agricultural labourers and 29.93 percent were cultivators. In marginal workers, agricultural workers consists of 60.30 percent and 27.42 percent were other workers. Table no - 13.3 gives the details of the distribution of tribal workers in Tamil Nadu as per 2011 census.

Objectives of the study

The objectives of the study are as follows,

1. To analyze the socio-economic characteristics of tribal respondents.
2. To examine the working conditions of the respondents.
3. To suggest suitable corrective and remedial measures.

Methodology of the Study

This study is based on the primary as well as the secondary which is collected from the Vellore district of Tamil Nadu. The convenient sampling has been adopted for the study. The primary data was collected through well-structured questionnaire, which comprises of general information, for socioeconomic condition in tribal people. The secondary data was collected through various books, journals, articles, periodicals, newspapers, websites, and theses.

Profile of the Study Area

Vellore district is one of the 37 districts in the Tamil Nadu State of India. Vellore City is the headquarters of this district. After the Independence in 1947, Vellore became a part of the erstwhile Madras state. According to 2011 census, Vellore district had a population of 3,936,331 with a sex-ratio of 1,007 females for every 1,000 males, much above the national average of 929. A total of 432,550 were under the age of six, constituting 222,460 males and 210,090 females. Scheduled Castes and Scheduled Tribes accounted for 21.85% and 1.85% of the population respectively.

Table - 13.4: Gender wise classification

S. No	*Gender*	*Frequency*	*Percent (%)*
1	Male	95	64.0
2	Female	55	36.0
3	Total	150	100.0

Source: Filed Survey and Analysis

The above table no - 13.4 shows the gender of the respondents, 64% of the male respondents. 36% of the respondents opined that female responds.

Table - 5: Educational Qualification Wise Classification

S. No	*Educational Qualification*	*Frequency*	*Percent (%)*
1	Uneducated	63	42.0
2	Primary	45	30.0
3	SSLC	28	19.0
4	HSC	10	7.0
5	DEGREE	4	2.0
6	Total	150	100.0

Source: Filed Survey and Analysis

The respondents are classified into four categories according to the qualification as SSLC, HSC, Under Graduate and Uneducated Table no - 13. 5 portrays 42% of the respondents are at illiterate level, 30% of the respondents have complete their Primary school level (SSLC), 19% of the respondents have complete their SSLC, 7% of the respondents have complete their HSC Level and only 2% of the responded Degree level.

Table - 13.6: Occupation Wise classification Occupation

S. No	*Occupation*	*Frequency*	*Percent (%)*
1	Agriculture	125	83.0
2	Private Employee	7	5.0
3	Daily Wager	15	10.0
4	Other	3	2
5	Total	150.0	100.0

Source: Filed Survey and Analysis

Form the above Table no - 13.6 state that 83% of the respondents are come Agriculture Occupations, 10% of the respondents are come Daily

Wage category, 5% of the respondents are Private Employee, 2% of the respondents are other category.

Table - 13.7: Income Wise Classification

S. NO	*Income*	*Frequency*	*Percent (%)*
1	BelowRs.5,000	45	30
2	Rs.5,001-Rs.10,000	35	23.00
3	Rs.10,001-Rs15,000	32	21.0
4	AboveRs.15,001	23	16.00
5	AboveRs.15,001	15	10.00
6	Total	150	100.0

Source: Filed Survey and Analysis

The above table no - 13.7 clearly shows that 30% of the respondents monthly income range from below 5,000 23% of the respondents monthly income is between Rs.5001 - 10000, 16% of the respondents monthly income is 10001- 15000, and only 10% of the respondents earns a monthly income range above Rs.15001.

Table - 13.8: Land Holding Size

S. No	Land Holding Size	Frequency	Percent
1	Below 1 Acre	45	30.0
2	2 to 3 Acre	80	53.0
3	3 to 4 Acre	15	10.0
4	Above 4 Acre	10	7.0
5	Total	150.0	100.0

Source: Filed Survey and Analysis

It is evident from the above table no - 13.8 that 53.0 percent of the respondents are have 2 to 3 Acre land in their own, 30.0 percent of the respondents are have Below 1 Acre land in their own and 10.0 percent of the respondents are have 3 to 4 Acre and only 7.0 percent of the respondents are have Above 4 Acre.

Conclusion

The results of the study reveal that there is a need to improve the economic condition and health needs of the leather tannery workers. Protective measures should also be provided to reduce the various morbidities. Economic status of the workers is more important for economic production of the industry and also in developing good socio economic status for the worker's family. It is necessary for the health care provider, various stakeholders to identify such factors, thus the monitoring and care provided can be improved. Their socio-economic status will be improved only if adequate measures are taken to overcome their problems.

References

1. Annual Tribal Sub-Plans, 20012-2013 and 20013-20014, Director of Tribal Welfare, Chennai
2. Development of Indian Tribes, Prakash Chandra Mehta, Discovery publishing house, New Delhi, 2006
3. Janaki, D. "Socio-Economic Conditions of Tribal Women in South India", Chennai, Dhana Publications, 2000.
4. Nang Helina Mantaw, "Tribal Development", New Delhi,classical Publishing Company, 2003.11.
5. Policy Note, Adi Dravidar and Tribal Welfare Department, Demand No.4, Government of Tamil Nadu, 2014.
6. Singh, K.S. "People of India, Tamil Nadu", Volume XL, Madras, Affiliated East-West Press Pvt, Ltd, 2001. pp. 906-907.

Chapter - 14

Social Exclusion and Tribal Women

Kavi Mozhi. M Dr. P. S. Sreedevi Nandini. P

Abstract

Not depending on others tend to women empowerment but standing on their own. But most often women were stigmatized and excluded from the societal norms which are prevailing for more than centuries. Social exclusion is meant to be the denial of control over participation in societal, Economical, political and cultural life, denial of human rights and the denial of ghetto mentality. Social exclusion and stigmatization doesn't have vast difference where both imply the denial of rights. Most often women were excluded and stigmatized. It is only through Education women has the opportunity to acknowledge themselves and creates a way to overcome the hurdles of being excluded. Tribal women are being excluded in the arenas of domestically, societal, economic, political and legal perspectives. Social exclusion provides a base for being superior or inferior in the same society or culture. Thus Social exclusion and stigmatization has to be degraded from the society to empower women especially tribal women. This can be achieved by providing proper education and creating awareness among people.

Key words: *exclusion, stigmatization, education, tribal women*

Introduction

Social exclusion is a form of discrimination. The term social exclusion was coined in France in 1974, defined as a rupture of social bonds. It has been interpreted differently in different contexts at different times. So, it is very difficult to define it rigorously. It was used to mention various categories of people, characterized as mentally and physically ill or handicapped, suicidal people, aged invalids, abused children, substance abusers, delinquents, single parents, marginal asocial persons and other social misfits (Silver, 1994). When people are being neglected from participating in the social, political and economic parts of their community it is termed as "Social Exclusion". Social Exclusion happens in major parts of the world in different perspectives based on their color, class, gender, religion, ethnicity etc., In India most often it occurs on the basis of Caste, ethnicity and gender, community, and disability. Gender discrimination plays a major role in India for more than centuries. Women tend to be slaves in ancient days. Kings consider it as a pride to enslave women of the opposing team. It is obvious that during the period of Mughals women were accustomed to a new practice named "Burkha system". During the reign of Kings and thrones women of certain community were named "Devadasis" considered to be the wives of God which jurisdicates the rights of Women? From the past days women were being excluded and suppressed but now the footing of the story changes and women attained greater heights and still to be the greatest. These are being achieved mainly by the women residing in urban areas and not in rural areas which question the empowerment of women. Apart from empowerment tribal women are being excluded in receiving their basic rights and awareness. Social exclusion leads to social stigmatization and marginalization.

Characteristics of Stigmatization

- Comprises defined social categories
- It is enrooted with social relations.
- It neglects people's rights which they desire to attain and fulfill their life

Functions of Social Exclusion

Christine Bradley (1994) pointed out five mechanisms of social exclusion namely Geographical Segregation, Intimidation, Physical Violence, Corruption and Barriers to entry.

Geographical Segregation

This happens when people are being stigmatized based on the geographical boundaries. In India most often certain community of people isbeing obligated to live outside the villages and is branded as being proletariat. They are made to live and construct their residential places and dwellings outside the villages or at the periphery of village or town. Most of the tribes live in hills and forests and are excluded from the mainstream population. This creates major hygiene issues among tribal women.

Intimidation

Intimidation is the voluminous arm used for social exclusion. A threat to harm, verbal abuse are may be used as a term of intimidation. It can be observed at every level in a society. Intimidation is a major form of control used by men over other men and women. Most probably it was supposed to use over women domestically, in working areas and politically. Tribes are being subjected to intimidation till now.

Physical Violence

Physical violence is another form used for social exclusion. When threat of harm does not work, physical violence is used. It can be committed by the state, community, group or individuals. Violence against women in the household and against poor people and ethnic and religious minorities reported is to be practiced all over the world. Domestic violence is rooted in the norms of gender inequality and patriarchy. Domestically it plays major role rather than socially. Most often women are being subjected to Physical violence by men. Tribal women in this sense are tended to more affective since they were being harmed by all in the society.

Barriers to entry

At many places and in many spheres, people excluded are neglected from entry.. Entry restriction is still prevalent in major villages of the country. Tribes are being greatly subjected to this type of social exclusion where most of them were not allowed to enter in the preserved places. Other than documents, transition costs are another way to place hurdle in the entry of the excluded. Transition costs are the costs that are involved in acquiring a good service above and beyond its actual price.

Corruption

Corruption is the main cause of many social evils in India. It is prevalent all over the world. The people who are excluded from obtaining goods and services do not have the required necessary amount to pay for securing jobs, health care and other public services. It causes insecurity among the excluded. Corruption neglects access to resources, opportunities and information.

The Poorest Areas Civil Society Aproach to social exclusion

The Poorest Area Civil Society programme focuses on five specific socially excluded groups in India namely women, Scheduled Tribes, Scheduled Castes, Muslims and people with disabilities . Its projects aim to reduce the gap between socially excluded groups and the society by helping them to learn their own rights to empower themselves.

Effects of Social Exclusion

Social exclusion results in the following main consequences:

- It leads to various kinds of bereavement.
- It leads to the impoverishment of human life and develops a poorer sense of well-being.
- It paves way for inequality, poverty, unemployment and involuntary migration.
- It leads to social stigmatization and marginalization.
- It intuits fear complex within the community.
- It puts various restrictions on the excluded about their free and full participation in the economic, cultural and political activities.
- It gives negative impact on the quality of life.

Tribal Women and Social Exclusion

It is obvious that women have been excluded in many areas even now a day, especially tribal women, since they were underestimated by their own community and society and lacks Education. Social exclusion is also the major reason which prevents them to get educated. Most often tribal women hesitate to get in to the group mainly because of the fear of discrimination. Tribal women face inequality at higher rate than urban women. Tribal women have many implications to hinder their empowerment. Mostly tribal women work in unorganized areas and informal sectors which have the probability of being vulnerable, being abused and insecurity which fence them to be empowered. All those factors lead to the mechanism of social exclusion.

Stigmatization and Women Empowerment

Not depending on others doesn't denote women empowerment but standing on their own. Women comprises of more than fifty percent of the population. But the literacy rate is low in comparison with that of men. Women in a nation like India are having ample opportunities to empower themselves. But only the small amount of urban and educated women are being benefitted and aware of it. And those people tend to overcome the hurdles and barriers and break the effect of stigmatization imparted to them. Women in rural areas especially tribal women are not aware of it which prevents them to empower their own self. It is only through Education and proper training such women could be empowered.

Ghetto Mentality and tribal women

The word "ghetto" symbolizes a part of city where minority people usually live often due to the oppression from society. Tribal people majorly fall in to this category. They were accustomed to the ghetto mentality for which they don't have any desires to conflate with the society. Tribal women are not intended to fuse with others exclusively in this manner. They neglect works, food, customs and marriage interrelated with other community. In this case both tribes and society are not stepping forward to fuse with one other.

Suggestions

- Impart more awareness among rural people.
- Meet the needs of women to achieve greater success.
- An authentic rule has to be made.
- Propagating laws to everyone.
- Higher Education to be mandatory for all women.

Conclusion

The stigmatization among women was found to be maximum among tribal and uneducated families and tribal women are being largely excluded by society. The discrimination is also found in Educated and tribal areas but in smaller scale in comparison with urban areas. Thus more awareness about the real state and Education has to be imparted among women to empower themselves without which it would not be achieved in a greater scale.

References

Shetty S. Sowjanya, (2019), "Education for Skill Development and Women Empowerment" EPRA International Journal of Economic and Business Review – Peer Reviewed Journal, vol.7, Issue-2, e-ISSN: 2347-9671/p- ISSN: 2349-0187

Roy Rajarshi, (2009), "Women Education and Development: Perspectives, Issues and Concerns" , ISBN: 978-81-7541-460-0

National Perspective Plan for Women 1988-2000, (1988), Department of Women and Child Development, GoI, Ministry of HRD.

www.pacsindia.org

www.youarticlelibrary.com› social exclusion

Gupta K Shailendra (Nov-Dec, 2016) "Study of Women Empowerment through Skill Development and Vocational Education in India" International Journal of Applied Sciences Research, Vol.3, Issue 07, EISSN: 2349-2899, ISSN: 2349-4808, Retrieved from https:// arseam.com.

Chapter - 15

Importance of personal hygiene among adolescent women's in rural India

Lukkumanul Hakkim S

Abstract

Indian rural women suffer many problems and problems in their daily lives when it comes to equality, education, work as a source of income for the family, etc. But they also face the fight during the days they have menstruation. They face many inhuman and follow unhygienic treatments only because of the lack of awareness towards knowledge, security and dignity without social taboos, which is their social right. This document attempts to highlight the problems related to what women face, especially in rural India, in the name of menstruation and achieve the objectives set in the light of the relevant literature available in the field. The researcher tried to focus on how to avoid negative results that affect self-esteem and confidence along with their general well-being. Suggestions are given in relation to issues mentioned in the document, such as attention and promotion of menstrual hygiene.

Keywords: *Rural India, Menstrual Practices, awareness & promotion to menstrual hygiene.*

Introduction

Menstruation is a physiological process in women that serves as the beginning of their reproductive life. But this process is considered impure in Indian society. Because of this, women do not get the right information about good practices to follow during menstruation. This can lead to the development of reproductive tract infections (RTI). Due to the lack of knowledge of normal physiology, several restrictions are imposed on women during their menstruation in the form of a restriction to attend functions, touch food, etc. Good hygiene practices such as proper use of sanitary napkins and proper washing of the genital area. they are essential during menstruation Women should have access to clean sanitary products that can protect their health throughout their reproductive life.

Menstrual hygiene depends on several factors, such as educational level, socioeconomic status, cultural habits and their beliefs and values. Women, particularly in rural areas, often wear disposable or reusable clothing as absorbents during menstruation. The use of clothing as absorbents during menstruation increases the susceptibility of women to develop infections of the reproductive tract (ITR). Women of reproductive age should maintain proper hygiene through regular use of sanitary pads during menstruation. There have been many studies among teenagers. But very few reports have been published on the menstrual practices of women living in rural areas. Therefore, we conducted this study to investigate menstruation-related practices among women in a rural community.

Importance of Menstrual Hygiene in Women in India

The guidelines point to interventions at the state, district, block and school levels and describe the steps for all the ministries involved: Health, Rural Development, Human Resources, Women and Children and Tribal Development. These recommendations are part of the Swachh Bharat Mission; therefore, they recognize that women and girls have special hygiene and sanitation needs due to menstruation. It also establishes indicators of success, not primarily those related to the provision of infrastructure, such as toilets, sanitary napkins and incinerators, but considers that the development of life skills for girls and women to access this infrastructure is an important v indicator: Having adequate knowledge and feeling supported, and developing skills to experience a period of guilt and shame is an important component of the guidelines.

However, menstrual health cannot be achieved only through government efforts without addressing it as a social problem, which requires interventions at the social, community and family level. Since menstruation is a natural biological process, an average woman bleeds for approximately seven years of her life throughout her reproductive life. Despite this, even in this so-called era and scientific age, society pretends that menstruation does not exist.

This culture of silence worsens for women due to myths, taboos and different stigmas around menstruation and its current association with impurity. It is quite unfortunate that we are now less enlightened than in ancient times, when it seems that we gave more reverence to the female body and offered prayers to even the bleeding goddesses as seen in the Kamakhya temple in Assam and elsewhere. Many communities restrict the entry of women to kitchens and temples during their period. Some tribal communities confine their women to live separately in homes or menstrual huts, which may be welcomed by these women as a respite from daily tasks and hard work; However, some may find it stigmatizing. More studies and research are needed to understand the attitudes of women who menstruate towards such isolation.

According to a UNICEF study conducted in 2011, on which government guidelines are based, only 13% of girls in our country know menstruation before menarche. The same study indicates how impoverishing and debilitating the lack of menstrual hygiene for these adolescents: 60 percent missed school due to menstruation, 79 percent felt poor confidence, 44 percent felt ashamed and humiliated by restrictions, so that menstrual mismanagement adds to gender discrimination by reducing the subjective and objective conditions of young women. It negatively affects women's education, equality, maternal and child health, important goals for the country!

A study by AC Nielsen showed that 23 percent of teenagers drop out of school after starting menstruation. Another study by the Institute for Development Studies (IDS) revealed that many adolescents face great difficulties due to the lack of adequate infrastructure and sanitary facilities in their respective schools. The research also found that, despite being part of the curriculum, issues related to menstruation were not discussed in schools.

The magnitude of the problem has caused the government to pay attention to the issue in recent years; In 2004, the Tamil Nadu government became the first state to recognize the need for MHM and included it in its sanitation program. The Ministry of Health and Family Welfare has also recently introduced a scheme that aims to spread awareness of menstrual hygiene among adolescent girls (10-19 years old) in rural areas. The objective of this scheme is; increase awareness of menstrual hygiene, increase access and promote the use of high quality sanitary pads, and ensure that the elimination of compresses is done in an environmentally friendly manner. Under this scheme, accredited social health activists (ASHA) sell teenagers at very low and affordable prices (6 for a package of 6 napkins).

The United Nations Children's Fund (UNICEF), Wash United and the Collaborative Water Supply and Sanitation Council (WSSCC) are some of the entities currently working in space with the government, but the scale to be achieved is enormous : for 112 million adolescents and future Mothers should be contacted with information on menstrual hygiene and myths, and they should be provided with appropriate sanitary facilities in schools and at home.

MHM therefore needs a strong championship inside and outside the government. It may need to be highlighted as an important component of Swachh Bharat, or it may be reduced to individual efforts and initiatives of interested officers at the district level to carry out MHM guidelines. In addition, the lack of effective coordination between various ministries can be a challenge and will need strong supervision and messages.

Measures

Now, the awareness of one day has increased at the basic level about many things, be it education, rights, etc. Similarly, rural women have also faced many things about menstruation practices and hygiene, but even more efforts must be made. Government's point of view for the development of the country and also as an individual, we need to fulfil some obligation by changing our attitude towards menstruation. Many initiatives have been taken to improve the field of hygiene and menstruation practices. The awareness program should be carried out on a regular basis, especially in rural areas where women and girls can freely attend and understand the importance of hygiene and menstrual practices.

1. Disposal of used sanitary napkin should be done through the installation of incinerators in schools where girls can easily dispose of solid waste.
2. The local production of sanitary napkins by self-help groups should be promoted.
3. The attention of the medical and paramedical health professional is necessary to promote menstrual hygiene.
4. The availability of adequate washing facilities in schools and the workplace for menstrual management should be maintained.
5. The mother, family and community should receive advice on physiology and menstrual hygiene on a regular basis.
6. The promotion of menstrual hygiene should be included in the school curriculum. School teachers should be trained regularly so they can have a clear idea about how to deliver reproductive health education in class.
7. The availability of services, including subsidized sanitary napkins, is a step forward to initiate acceptance of the practice.
8. Kishori Shakti Yojana (adolescent empowerment scheme) under the Integrated Child Development Scheme (ICDS) in 1991 and this scheme could be used to meet the reproductive health demands of adolescents.

9. Mahila Mandal and Stri-Sabha), traditional midwives, shopkeepers, etc., should participate to store and distribute sanitary napkins, since girls would feel more comfortable if they bought sanitary napkins.

Conclusion

Women and girls face many problems, as we can see in their experiences about menstruation management, hygiene practices related to that, the availability of sanitary pads, clean water facilities; napkin removal, use of old clothes during the menstrual cycle And so many like that. But, the point is that these problems could not be solved simply by discussing about it or by executing any scheme for it. The mentality regarding the menstruation of people who belong to rural areas should be channeled in such a way that girls feel safe and secure when sharing their physiological changes in front of their family members. This required a lot of work from the stakeholders of our societies, where they must take initiatives to advise people about the creation of a productive and health environment for girls or women.

The government of India is also taking several initiatives, but they really need to work on the reality of the land, which remains negative when it comes to executing its scheme. An effective review by the government of India is required. Similarly, academic institutions should also take initiatives to teach how menstruation practices could affect the health of girls or women. Therefore, teachers should also take responsibility for promoting the correct information to others so that social myths or taboos can be eradicated.

References

1. Arumugam, B., Nagalingam, S., Varman, P. M., Ravi, P., & Ganesan, R. (2014). Menstrual hygiene practices: Is it practically impractical?. International Journal of Medicine and Public Health, 4(4)
2. Garg, R., Goyal, S., & Gupta, S. (2012). India moves towards menstrual hygiene: subsidized sanitary napkins for rural adolescent girls—issues and challenges. Maternal and child health journal, 16(4), 767-774.
3. Pandit, D., Bhattacharyya, P. K., & Bhattacharya, R. (2014). menstrual hygiene: knowledge and practice among adolescent school girls in rural areas of West bengal. IOSR Journal of Dental and Medical Sciences (IOSR- JDMS), 13(6), 19-24.
4. Pathak, N., & Pradhan, J. (2016). Menstrual management and low-cost sanitary napkins. Economic & Political Weekly, 51(12), 27.

5. Priya, S. S., Alliretnam, A. S., & Shankar, R. (2016). Menstrual problems and hygiene among rural adolescent girls of Tamil Nadu-a cross sectional study. Indian J Obstetr Gynaecol Res, 3(2), 126-31.
6. Shah, S. P., Nair, R., Shah, P. P., Modi, D. K., Desai, S. A., & Desai, L. (2013). Improving quality of life with new menstrual hygiene practices among adolescent tribal girls in rural Gujarat, India. Reproductive Health Matters, 21(41), 205-213.
7. Shanbhag, D., Shilpa, R., D'souza, N., Josephine, P., Singh, J., & Goud, B. R. (2012). Perceptions regarding menstruation and practices during menstrual cycles among high school going adolescent girls in resource limited settings around Bangalore city, Karnataka, India. International Journal of Collaborative Research on Internal Medicine & Public Health, 4(7), 1353-1362.
8. Tiwari, M. (2017). Green Orientation & Green Management Practices as CSR in Academic Institutions.
9. Tiwari, M. (2017). Work Life Balance of Female Employees in Private Institutions, Gwalior: An Investigation. [10]. Tiwari, M., & Pant, P. (2017). Changing Roles of Teaching Professionals: Issues & Challenges.

Chapter - 16

Status of Tribal Women in Karnataka: Reference to Policies and programmes

Dr. M. H. Hullur

Abstract

India is a largest concentration of tribal people. The tribal's are children of nature and their lifestyle is conditioned by the eco system. India with a variety of eco-systems presents a varied tribal population throughout its length and breadth. For the developing and upliftment of tribal communities, government is making many developmental strategies and efforts by launching the various tribal development schemes/programme. The tribal women, constitutes, half of the total population like other social group. The tribal women are more illiterate than men. In related to health issues, the tribal women face more problems related to reproductive health. When primary and secondary subsistence activities are counted, women work more than men. The paper throws light on tribal women's development and progress, literacy and also support with some of valuable recommendations which are support from the government for the development of tribal in India. It Develop a comprehensive policy on tribal development, which derives inputs from people at the grass root level to ensure sustainable development that is ecologically sound, people oriented, decentralised and culturally accepted.

Keywords: *Status of women; Development policies and Programmes, Tribal, India, Eco-system.*

Introduction

India as a whole is characterised by sharp gender disparities, although women's status varies considerably by region. On virtually all frontiers of human societal pursuits-economic, educational, scientific, legal, political, official, political and religious sphere Indian women suffer profoundly. For all time there are socio-cultural factors, which validate for the status of women in particular society. It is always culture, determines the position of women in a society, gender roles are socially constructed. The family structure in India is patriarchal, patrilocal and patrilineal. Patriarchy denotes a culture of power relationship that promotes man's supremacy and women subjugation. It encompasses institutional endorsement of man's ascendancy within the family and other social structures. It justifies the normative process pertaining to the recognition and sustainability of his dominance in society.

In India women are discriminated due to several historical, religious and other reasons. A girl child is suppressed from the movement she is born in terms of personal development. She is made to undergo the feelings of being inferior and feeble. She is denied the prospects for personal expression.

There are various hypotheses about why women have relatively high or low status. The common premise is that women status is high when they contribute substantially to primary subsistence activities. Women position is low in the societies where food getting is entirely men's job like hunting, herding or intensive agriculture. In the historical times when warfare was essential, men were more esteemed than women. Likewise in the centralised political systems men had high status. Men in most societies contribute more to primary subsistence activities, as women have infant and child care responsibilities. However, women contribute substantially to primary subsistence activities that depend heavily on gathering and horticulture and in which men are away on labour or pastoral duties while sub-sistence work has to be done. When primary and secondary subsistence activities are counted, women work more than men.

Karnataka Population 2011

As per details from Census 2011, Karnataka has population of 6.11 Crores, an increase from figure of 5.29 Crore in 2001 census. Total population of Karnataka as per 2011 census is 61,095,297 of which male and female are 30,966,657 and 30,128,640 respectively. In 2001, total population was 52,850,562 in which males were 26,898,918 while females were 25,951,644. The total population growth in this decade was 15.60 percent while in previous decade it was 17.25 percent. The population of Karnataka forms 5.05 percent of India in 2011. In 2001, the figure was 5.14 percent. Recently as per Karnataka census data, 74.25% houses are owned while 23.02% were rented. In all, 70.06% couples in Karnataka lived in single family. In 2011, 61.11% of Uttar Pradesh population had access to Banking and Non-Banking Finance Corporation. Only 4.84% of Uttar Pradesh population had internet facility which is likely to improve in 2021 due to Jio. 6.32% of family in Uttar Pradesh owned car while 25.60%

owned two wheller. In few months we will also get details of election data for Karnataka.

Karnataka state has achieved commendable progress in all walks of life in the post- independence era. The Government of Karnataka has launched series of development programmes for the empowerment of women and weaker sections. Tribal development is a multi-directional process which demands active mobilization of tribes and participation of various stakeholders of tribal development in the process of development. Public-Private Partnership is essential to achieve the goal of tribal development in the new millennium. Karnataka state has witnessed several tribal development initiatives over a period of time. For the developing and upliftment of tribal communities the tribal development planners and administrators have made efforts by launching the various tribal development schemes/ programme. The problems of communication, government assistance and the communities cooperation have, to a more in number, has been overcome and there is no reason why the all-out efforts could not succeed to upgrade the tribal mass in endeavor towards ensuring faster, sustainable and more inclusive growth, the Government of Karnataka has committed itself to improving capabilities and productive endowments among the economically disadvantaged and socially marginalized sections of the State.

Review of Literature

There are a good number of studies, explaining the causes and consequences of backwardness and the low socio economic status of tribal women. Such studies are related to a general enquiry on women exploitation and dependency. These studies have identified lack of education, absence of skills and training, lack of property rights, social isolation and segregation and male control over resources and reproductive rights as responsible for women disempowerment.

Ashok Kumar (2015) highlighted the socioeconomic condition of Jenukuruba tribal community in Mysore district. This study revealed that, the Jenukurubas are social and economically very backward compare to other communities, even tribal communities. These people are suffering from illness, illiteracy, poverty, lack of food and other problems.

Ajay Saraogi (2013), highlighted the status of women in tribal society in India, and he explained anthropologists have been recently divided on the status of women in Indian tribal societies. The actual treatment, legal status, opportunity for social participation and the character and extent of work, all determine each in a specific sense and manner, the status of women in a society. All these four determinants are independent from each other and not casually related. The correlation between them is empirical and not conceptual.

Das (2012) in an attempt to find out the level of autonomy and decision making power of tribal women and the impact of socio-economic status on decision making roles concluded that the tribal women enjoy autonomy at their household level, especially in social aspects and at some point enjoy equal rights along with their husbands in economic matters. But due to low literacy rate and unemployment the community participation of the women is inactive and autonomy levels are very low.

According to Franzmen (2000) and Scott (1988) the religious sphere, which is most dominating among tribes, constitutes a major field for male domination. In fact, women are deprived of public authority, while religion legitimizes gender hierarchy. The subordination of women in religious activities and their denial of access to positions of religious leadership has been a powerful tool in most world's religions in supporting the patriarchal order and the exclusion of women from the public forum. The religious sphere is a major field for male dominance, and a strategy to deprive women of public authority.

Justification of the Study

Achievement of tribal mainly depends upon tribal are more participation in the development programme. Mostly it has been keen observed that due to hazard of participation, the programme, and enactment by the tribal area become only government schemes/programme without tribal people participation. Therefore, it is necessary to understand the progress and success of scheme or programme. Hence, the present research paper has been undertaken.

The socio-economic status of women is the position which they attain as a reason of the various norms, beneficial and obligations in the society. It is often found that women are the most vulnerable section of the society relative to their male counterparts, and they often happen to be last receivers of the opportunities offered by the development of the country. Tribal women are more isolated in term of education, employment and health facilities than the mainstream women. So, they might be are more deprived when compared with their male counterpart as well as women from other communities. So, in this regard, this study is an attempt to highlight the socio-economic status of Bettakuruba women in a district called

Chamarajanagara. The Bettakuruba are the tribal group who are the original inhabitant of the hilly region: consequently they are bound to be isolated from the mainland as well as its development. Hence, in such a case, it is of the upmost importance to find out the socio and economical condition in which they are living in order to help them to come closer to the stream of development.

Objectives of the Study

- To study the status of the Tribal women in Karnataka state.
- To analyses the welfare polices and Programme to tribal communities in Karnataka
- To understand the health condition of Tribal Women

Status of Tribal women

The tribal in India constitute about eight percent of the total Indian population, the material states in which poor tribal women live are-low wages, poor nutrition, and lack of access to health care, education and training. The need of the hour is to 'empower' the tribal women so that they live the life of equality and dignity which are being denied by our society. 'Power' is key word of the term 'empowerment' which means 'control over resource (physical human, intellectual, financial) and ideology (belief, values and attitudes)." The material assets may be of any type-physical, human, financial, such as land, water, forests, people's bodies and agencies, labour, money and access to money, and knowledge information. Ideas can be included in intellectual resources. Control over ideology signifies the ability to generate, capacity to propagate, capacity to sustain and institutionalize specific sets of beliefs, principles, values, attitudes, actions and behaviour, 'virtually' determining how people perceive think, and function in a given socio-economic and political environment.

But the women especially the tribal women have not been able in making control over material assets, intellectual resource and ideology as yet in spite of constitutional provisions in regard to raising their status enhancing their quality of life, bringing about gender equality and gender justice. Empowerment of tribal women not only refers to economic liberalization but also to access to opportunity, right to decision making and access to education, health services and information. When we talk to empowerment of tribal women, it requires to deal with some of the complex issues that are central to women's empowerment and gender equality and to adopt a holistic approach. Empowerment of tribal women can be achieved through supporting tribal women's human rights by strengthening initiative for a broader ratification and a more effective implementation of normative instruments pertaining to tribal women. Integration of legal literacy for tribal girls and women at all level of the educational system can serve a lot in this direction. Promotion of the attainment of gender parity, tribal women's full citizenship and equal participation in policy making is a prerequisite for true democracy at the local, national and international levels by assisting them is the elimination of stereo typed roles and expectation. Besides, it is of immense importance that tribal women should also have access to economic and labour opportunity through work, and carrier choices so that they will become self-dependent and economically secure.

Women from weaker sections of society have suffered long due to repression. They are considered as a weaker sex and are given a subordinate status in the society. She is protected by the father in her childhood, by the husband in her adulthood and by the son in her old age. The factors of sufferings of women particularly tribal women are deeply rooted in the socio-cultural beliefs in India.

The tribes in India constitute about eight percent of the total India population. This means that about four percent of the total Indian population is tribal women. The material state in which poor tribal women live are-low wages, poor nutrition and lack of access to health care, education and training. The normal tribal women are active part of our workforce. They bear the burden of 'paid' work as a part of the workforce and unpaid work in the house. It is said to see that besides constitutional protection, development has not benefitted tribal women. They are still at the lowest rung of development. Empowerment (in legal terms) of tribal women can be ensured through supporting tribal women's human rights by strengthening initiatives for a broader ratification and effective implementation of normative instruments pertaining to tribal women. Integration of 'legal literacy' for girls and women at all levels is a pre required for preservation and as safe-guard to their human rights.

Promotion of the attainment of gender parity tribal women's full citizenship and equal participation in policy making is also a per-requisite for true democracy at the local, national and international levels. It is required to assist chem. in the elimination of stereotyped roles and expectations with a view to promote more equitable sharing of responsibilities and rights in the family and in society at large. Besides, it is of immense importance that tribal women should also have access to economic and labour opportunities through work and carrier choices so that they will become self dependent and economically secured. Education, employment and empowerment are the three 'E's for the advancement and progress of the tribal women.

Girl Child

Tribes too have son preference but do not discriminate against girls by female infanticide or sex determination tests. Boys and girls do not have similar inheritance laws. Tribal girls do not inherit land, except in matrilineal societies or under special circumstances.

Her Work as a Child

Among tribes under study girls are not considered as burden because of their economic value. In all the four societies girls participate in all types of work at home and agricultural activities along with their mothers.

Education

The education is a fundamental right that provides opportunities for socio-economic uplift. The girl child is deliberately denied and the future opportunity of the total development. The reasons associated with not educating girl child are financial constraints, early marriages, submissiveness, motherhood, and parental perception of education on women's worldview.

Beneficiary of the Father's Property

The concept of patriarchy prevails in all the four societies, yet views regarding inheritance were different among the four groups. The inheritance of household property is determined by customary laws.

Married Women

Tribal women in India contribute positively to the local economy and participate along with men in subsistence activities. In reality, women do more work than men. They participate in all agricultural activities (except ploughing) and other sectors of indigenous cottage industries. They share major responsibilities in the production process. In addition, they have to manage household chores, which is a stupendous task. Child rearing is also the responsibility of the women.

Woman's Work

Married women in the study area carry out all types of work at home as well as outside that are demand of mixed agro-pastoral economy. Apart from looking after the house, children and cattle major portion of the agriculture is done by women who do weeding, hoeing, harvesting and threshing.

Women's Role in Economic Sphere

It is Concerned with life in the village, such as crafts, house building, watermills and work on boundary walls, there is division between men's work and women's work. Among Gaddis and Bhutias the men are shepherds and women grow crops for food. It is equally valid for Bhils and Bodhs, there too men are out on different duties and women grow crops for food. However the boundaries are not so clearly marked, as there is overlapping and deviations from the rule. There are as well cases where the rule is inflexible and times when change is possible.

Major portion of agriculture is done by women who do weeding, hoeing, planting, harvesting and thrashing except ploughing (which are done by men) in the fields adjacent to houses or far off fields. The other activities of women include looking after the house, children and cattle. Food processing and cooking is women's job. It is the women who with the assistance of children are largely responsible for the cattle, water fuel and fodder. This permits them considerable time away from home and the village. When they are away from home, they are free to talk to whom so ever they please, male or female, of any caste or creed. As a consequence, communication among women and between men and women is as high as it is among men.

Tribal women are very strong and courageous in the handling of environmental imperatives as can be demonstrated in the trekking and work pattern under the severe limitations of the harsh environment. Several studies dealing with pastoral societies indicate that the position of women in such societies is not very high because the actual care of the livestock and handling of economic affairs is entirely a male domain. However among Gaddis and Bhutias, though women do not directly help in handling of livestock, they do look after their husbands during migrations and they cook for them and carry loads.

In the traditional societies which lack market system, the business of everyday living is usually carried on gender division of labour (Illich, 1982). In the study area, the division of labour is mainly between herding and agriculture. In all other tasks

Women's Role in Social Sphere

Role of tribal women in the Social Sphere is not only important in the economic activities, but her role in non-economic activities is equally important. Formation and continuity of family health and home is the domain of the women. Women's role as wives, mothers, and organisers and as basic foundation of other dimensions of social life is of extreme importance. Among Gaddis, as men are out for pastoral duties, the socialisation of children automatically becomes mother's business, in the early years of life at least. The Gaddi family assumes mother centeredness with the children and some important decisions falling to the sphere of women's intervention. The role of women in childbirth, funerals and fairs and festivals is an important part of village life. In the tribal areas, women are carriers of traditional information in absence of written records. They are crucial actors in the preservation and dissemination of such knowledge. They are not only competent food producers and house makers but are also the transmitters of rich local oral traditions.

Women's Role in Political Sphere

The role of women's empowerment for a just society was highlighted in the Beijing Conference (1995). In all the four societies under study, women power does not extend to societal or political spheres. The economic power of the women in the household is not translated in to corresponding community authority. They are not ignored at household level but are not given due credit and importance at official level. Women supremacy is restricted within the family domain and does not extend to social or political spheres. It is interesting to note that although by convention every village Panchayat has a female member, the lady never bothers to attend the meeting or to take any active interest in the proceedings of Panchayat. Sikkim has a tradition of collective decision making by communities through the institution of *Dzumsha.* However traditional institutions do not witness a significant role for women and *Dzumsha* is constituted of males only. In the absence of a male member, a female can represent her family unit. If a male head is absent from *Dzumsha* meeting, he is fined, however if represented by female head, she is liable to pay half the amount for her absence. This shows that women have a secondary importance in public affairs and community decision-making. Women are generally bypassed and marginalised either they lack the requisite skills, or because women's heavy and unending domestic responsibilities makes attending meetings and participating in decision making difficult. It always happens that men take over the more profitable activities.

Voting Rights

Tribal women take pleasure in their voting rights and about 85 per cent of women in the study area exercised their right. Most of them follow the advice of their husbands or some of them are under pressure to accept the wishes of their husbands. All the tribal societies in the study area are patriarchal in which men dominate in public sector. However, in their own world women have a freedom, and a self-expression. They can only be understood on their own terms. With the onset of development programmes economic changes are taking place but tribal women remain traditional in their dress, language, tools and resources, because they grow food crops rather than cash crops. Significant changes have taken place in the two decades separating the United Nations Conferences on women in Mexico City (1975) and the meeting in Beijing (1995). Modernization is bringing changes, which affect men and women differently. Modernization brought by outside agencies is set in a male-biased ideology, women are seen as inherently 'incapable'; the new techniques are aimed at men by men. Male values are also reflected in the view that development is solely dependent on technological and economic advances. Such values exploit both the environment and vulnerable groups such as women (Hewitt, 1989: 351). The thought that women are being treated shabbily, women centered programmes for developments were evolved which tended to overlook the importance of man-woman relations. Inadequate planning and implementation as well as culture resistance gave rise to more gender disparities. The association between cultures, economic organisations and different patterns of women's labour force participation ought to be implicit. Though efforts have been made in almost all countries to improve the status of women but it is still an unequal world.

Role of Government

The Department of Tribal Welfare was formed specifically to address the needs of STs in Karnataka. The concept of the Tribal Sub-Plan (TSP) and its counterpart the Special Component Plan (SCP) emerged in the National Fifth Five-Year Plan. The objectives of the TSP are poverty alleviation, protection of tribal culture, education, health care and providing basic minimum infrastructure. Poverty alleviation includes programmes in agriculture, animal husbandry, sericulture, horticulture, village and small industries as well as all employment-generating schemes such as *Swarna Jayanthi Swarozgar Yojana* (SJSY). Tribal education is given importance by the State Government. Social Welfare Department of the State is looking after the educational needs of these communities. Various programmes are implemented to provide educational facilities to students belonging to the scheduled tribes. The State Government is opening nursery and women welfare centres, *Asharm* schools (free residential schools) pre-metric hostels, for boys and girls, *etc*. From 1995-1996 onwards Karnataka Government has started scholarship scheme for the ST children. The students from 1st to 10th standard can avail this privilege. Financial assistance is provided by the Social Welfare Department. Apart from the efforts made by the State Government some of the non-governmental agencies and associations, trusts and individuals have taken interest in tribal educational welfare programmes in Karnataka. Institutions such as Vivekananda Girijana Kalyan Kendra (VGKK) in Mysore district is a well-known centre working for the upliftment of the *Soliga* tribes. The centre has residential tribal school, vocational training and market facilities for tribal products.

Role of Non-Government Organisations (NGOs)

The role of NGO's in tribal welfare activities, though small, has been significant for introducing qualitative changes in the lives of the people. Vivekananda Girijana Kalyana Kendra, Swami Vivekananda Youth Movement, Development Through Education (DEED), Foundation for Educational Innovations in Asia (FEDINA), Coorg Organisation of Rural Development (CORD), Samagra Grameena Ashrama, Janashikshana Trust, Chintana Foundation, Samvriddi/Krupa, Vanavasi Kalyana Ashrama are some of the well-known NGOs involved in the tribal development in Karnataka. It is possible to make development work more effective and sustainable through engagement with the local community, which has a better understanding of its own socio-economic needs, traditions and culture than non-tribals. Their participation in programmes, funded by the Government and voluntary organizations helped build confidence in the people to utilize the services thus offered and has provided feedback for modification and re-orientation of programmes. Under the India Population Project (IPP-9) project, the Health Department and NGOs trained tribal girls as ANMs and they were posted to sub-centres in remote tribal areas. These ANMs are now providing good healthcare services to tribal women and children[11]. Government-owned PHCs at Gumballi and Thithimathi were handed over to Karuna Trust and Vivekananda Foundation respectively and are being run as model PHCs.

In B.R. Hills, Mysore, Vivekanada Girijana Kalyan Kendra (VGKK), an NGO, is promoting the traditional knowledge systems of tribals and has integrated traditional healthcare system with modern medicine. Tribal knowledge of herbal medicines is also being promoted by them[11]. However, the degree of effectiveness of various schemes in terms of programme implementation in these sectors is not evident in the three critical areas of health, education and poverty reduction. The magnitude of the problem is so great that a large percentage of tribal families are poor and lack access to resources that would improve their education and health status. The human development status of the tribes of Karnataka is more than a decade behind the rest of the population of the State and thus they remain poorest and most deprived of all sub-populations in the State.

The present review attempts to highlight the limited research carried out on the health of the ethnic tribes of Karnataka. It identifies the gaps that need to be filled up to understand the health issues for better health care management of these tribes. It also underscores the potential of integration of the rich traditional practices of the ethnic tribes with present day knowledge and healthcare. Concerted inter-sectorial efforts are needed from policy makers, researchers, care providers, non-profit and social organization to improve the health status of the tribes of Karnataka.

Conclusion

Role of women is not only of important in economic activities, but her role in non-economic activities is equally important. Women's role as wives, mothers, organizers and as the basic foundation of other dimensions of social life is of utmost importance. The tribal women in these areas occupy an economically significant place that is reflected in the generally high position and the importance that they have. The socio- economic equality of sexes can be observed in the attitudes and practices concerning marriage, divorce and household harmony. The tribal women work very hard, in some cases even more than the men. However these women are not backward. They have power in their own sphere, no men tell them what to do. They are responsible for their own share of work and share the benefits of their own work as long as the unit of production and consumption remains the home. Their own perception and that of their men, is that women share major share of socio-economic activities and consequently they are respected, well thought of and think well of themselves. The concept of patriarchy, which prevails in subsistence societies, conveys respect rather than envy between the genders (Illich, 1982). Despite the fact that tribal women live their lives as dependents throughout their life cycle: as daughters, sisters, and wives; or as mothers of sons, they have far more power and independence than modern sub-urban housewives. A woman always has it in her power to leave her husband if she is angry, dissatisfied or unhappy. She has great freedom of movement as children, if any, remain with the husband Her labour is sufficiently in demand so that she can move not only back to her natal family but also to a sister's husband's house or a more distant kinsmen's house She can stay there till such times as she returns to her husband's house or finds a new one. There is no great need for her to return to the natal village although this is the usual practice. Whenever a man in these regions acts on an assumption that his authority will be accepted simply because he is a man and fails to take into account the wishes or feelings of his wife, sister or daughter, he often gets himself into trouble. There is no way for a man to force women' compliance with his wishes. Her economic ability and consequent social position has resulted in special institutional privileges that are bestowed on the women. In spite of having freedom they seldom have a voice in the political sphere. They are not ignored at household level, but are not given due credit and importance in political and religious subjects. They are like invisible hands shaping and maintaining the structure of society.

All the tribal societies in the study area are patriarchal in which men dominate in public sector. However, in their own world women have a freedom, and a self-expression. They can only be understood on their own terms. With the onset of development programmes economic changes are taking place but tribal women remain traditional in their dress, language, tools and resources, because they grow food crops rather than cash crops. Significant changes have taken place in the two decades separating the United Nations Conferences on women in Mexico City (1975) and the meeting in Beijing (1995). Modernization is bringing changes, which affect men and women differently. Modernization brought by outside agencies is set in a male- biased ideology, women are seen as inherently 'incapable'; the new techniques are aimed at men by men. Male values are also reflected in the view that development is solely dependent on technological and economic advances. Such values exploit both the environment and vulnerable groups such as women (Hewitt, 1989: 351). The concept that women are being treated shabbily, women centered programmes for developments were evolved which tended to over-look the importance of man-woman relations. Inadequate planning and implementation as well as culture resistance gave rise to more gender disparities. The association between cultures, economic organizations and different patterns of women's labour force participation ought to be implicit. Though efforts have been made in almost all countries to improve the status of women but it is still an unequal world.

Reference

Bhasin, V. 1989. *Ecology, Culture and Change: Tribals of Sikkim*. Delhi: Inter-India Publications.

Bhasin, V. 2005. *Medical Anthropology: Tribals of Rajasthan*. Delhi: Kamla-Raj Enterprises.

Scott, John Wallach. 1988. *Gender and the Politics of the History.* New York: Columbia University Press. Sered, Susan S. 1994. *Priestess, Mother, and Sacred Sister*. Oxford: Oxford University Press, Oxford.

Pattanaik, B.K., Gender Justice, Women Empowerment and Maternal Health, Yojana, Vol. 40 No. 11, 1996.

Ghosh, D.K. : Scheduled Castes and Scheduled Tribes: Some Reflections on Poverty characteristics and Poverty Alleviation Programmes, Indian Economic Association, New Delhi, 86th Conference Volume, 2003

Government of India, Census. 2011. [accessed on May 7, 2014]. Available from: http://www.censusindia.gov.in/2011census/populationenumeration.aspx .

Malnutrition high among Koraga children. The Hindu. 2012 Feb 11; [Google Scholar]

Demographic Status of Scheduled Tribe Population of India. 2013. [accessed on May 7, 2014]. Available from: http://www.tribal.gov.in/WriteReadData/CMS/Documents 201306110208002203443 Demographic Status of Scheduled Tribe Population of India. pdf .

Dr. B.R. Manjunatha1, Prof. M.R.Gangadhar, Socio-Economic Status of the Bettakuruba Tribal Women: a Case Study from the Chamarajanagara District, Karnataka: *Online Journal of Anthropology, vol. 14, n. 1 (2018) 129-137*

Bistee AR, Sreeramulu G. Status of scheduled tribes in Karnataka. Indian Streams Res J. 2014;3:1–5. [Google Scholar]

Economic survey of Karnataka, 2012-13. [accessed on May 7, 2014]. Available from: http://planning.kar.nic.in/node/128.html .

Government of Karnataka. Status of Scheduled Tribes of Karnataka. In: Karnataka Human Development Report. 2005. [accessed on May 7, 2014]. Available from: http://planning.kar.nic.in/sites/planning.kar.nic.in/files/khdr2005/English/Main%20Report/10-chapter.pdf .

Hathur B, Basavegowda M, Ashok NC. Hypertension: An emerging threat among tribal population of Mysore; Jenu Kuruba tribe diabetes and hypertension study. Int J Health Allied Sci. 2013;2:270–4. [Google Scholar]

Nanjunda DC. Functioning of primary health centers in the selected tribal districts of Karnataka-India: some preliminary observations. Online J Health Allied Scs. 2011;10:1–4. [Google Scholar]

Mavalankar D. Primary Health Care under *Panchayati Raj*: Perceptions of officials from Gujarat. Asian J Dev Matters. 2009;4:23–8. [Google Scholar]

Ajay Saraog.,(2013).*StatusofTribalWomeninIndia*,http://www.importantindia.com/9429/status-of-tribal-women-in-india/

Awias, M., A. Tosib and A. Mohd., (2009)."Socio-economic empowerment of tribal women, an Indian perspective". *International journal of rural studies* (IJRS), 16(1): 1-11

Kumari, R., (1998). *Gender, work and power relations: a case study of Haryana*. New Delhi: Har-Anand Publications.

Mishra, B. K., (2009). "Status of tribal women in Orissa". In: M. Das and P. Daspattanayak, (Ed.) *Empowering women issues, challenges and strategies.* New Delhi Dominant Publishers and Distributors Pvt. Ltd, pp: 203-209

Nagaraja. S and Pallavi. S. K., (2013). "Socio-Economic Status of Tribal Women: A Case Study in Karnataka", *Global research Analysis*, 2 (10).

Panda, S., (2008). "Socio-economic status and domestic violence against tribal women". *Man & Development*, XXX(3):55-68

Puttaraja, Heggade, O. D., (2012). "Economic Empowerment of Tribal Women in Karnataka : A case study in Mysore and Chamarajanagara Districts", *Stud tribes and Tribals*, 10(2), 173-181.

Scott, J. W., (1988). *Gender and the Politics of the History*. Columbia University Press, New York

Shrabanti M., Haobijam, V., Alok Sen., (2014). "Socioeconomic Status of Kuki Tribal Women: A Case Study

Veena Bhasin (2007) Status of Tribal Women in India, Studies on Home and Community Science, 1:1, 1-16ISSN: 0973-7189 (Print) (Online) Journal homepage:

http://www.tandfonline.com/loi/rshc20

Chapter - 17

Contemporary Stigmatisation of Devadasi Women of South India

Popy Devi Nath
Ms. Bastobee Borsaikia

Introduction

Devadasi system is a practice of dedicating girls, as young as early teenagers, to deities as "temple girls" or "dancing girls". The Devadasi was the proverbial dancing girl of India. She served God (Deva) and men who assumed godly status (Kings), as a servant (Dasi). The Devadasis of South India were part of a tight knit community, which included dancers and musicians. In modern era they came to be known as the IsauVellalars, a group of hereditary performing artists belonging to the farming community. There were two groups, PeriaMelam and ChinnaMelam. PeriaMelam included the soloists and Melakkarars, while ChinnaMelam included dancers and their accompanists. The ritual of dedicating a girl to temples is as old as the temples themselves. In Chola times, it was believed that dedicating girls to temples would ensure long lives for the king, queen and their sons. The belief that the gods had to be pacified with various gifts ensured the dedication of girls. The dedication was further enhanced by the dasi's ability to sing and dance for the god. The people of the time believed that if gods were pleased, there would be rain and prosperity. This also ensured the admiration and respect for Devadasis in society. The girl dedicated to temple had to be born in Devadasi community. The dedication took place between the age of 6-9. Usually a senior Devadasi had to formally recommend the name of the girl to the temple authorities. The head priest usually officiated in the ceremony, directing the girl to sit near the sanctum Santorum of temple. There The Archaka tied Tali (a sacred thread) around girl's neck, representing the Deva. Before tying the tali to girl's neck it was placed at the feet of the Deva. The girl was then led to the Mandapam (outer precinct of temple), where nattuvanar formally began teaching her. Once the girl was dedicated, she became the vassal of the temple. That means, although she enjoyed benefits endowed by temple, she had to adhere to the rule of temple. The ritual cycle of initiation (typing pottu), incorporation (sadanku) and consummation (prayojanam) was a parallel to a brahmin wedding. At the same time, rituals related to Devadasi - Sadhakapuja (dancing initiation), Gajje puja (dancing debut and tying the ankle bells). Kutcheri (formal professional engagement), were important signifiers of her role outside the temple. So, her marriage marked both her biological, sociological life cycle and her progress in acquiring professional skills. During the pottu (a gold pendant) tying ceremony, the girl had to fast and remain in a ritually purified house. Senior Devadasis would go to temple on day of ceremony to fetch bride's pottu, sari & puja items. In evening, the girl was dressed like a Brahmin bride in sari gifted by temple and then taken to temple. After going around in circumambulation, the wedding party assembled in front of main sanctum where prayers were offered to the deity by Gurukkal. The Deity was offered a gift. At the commencement ritual with flowers, coconuts, nuts and the pottu were placed at the feet of the deity. After Archana, either priest or a senior Devadasi tied the pottu around girl's neck. In ancient times, the pottu ceremony was far more elaborate, the tying of pottu was accompanied by full-scale marriage rituals with priest acting as groom. The groom did mantraupadesa and the Devadasi was taught 5 or 8 syllables according to the tradition of temple. After the pottu ceremony the girl was sent home where the family arranged a feast. The pottu was then removed and kept safe during her first mensuration. During 20th century, the pottu was hidden in a rose garland to escape the eyes of law and later given back to girl for wearing. Then During the Sadhaka Puja, the first step of dance (Adavus) were taken by striking the feet on the ground covered with paddy heralding prosperity, wealth & fertility. She then went around the spot 3 times. She then offered a coconut, betel leaves, nuts, fruits to her Guru. Gajje puja was performed 2 yrs after SadhakaPuja,Vidwans were invited to asses girl's talent. The ankle bells and new clothes on a tray were taken around to be blessed by visitors. Then Guru tied the bell around her ankles and girl would start performing. A ceremony called Muttirai was also done in few temples where Devadasis belonging to Shiva temple were branded with trishul and the ones belonging to Vishnu temple were branded with Sankh or chakra. The branding seal was made of silver.

In the past Hindu society, Devadasis had a number of religious duties and services to perform. Epigraphical and literary sources confirm that this practice of keeping "wives of Gods" dates back to 8th century AD of the Sangam Age, when Karikala, an illustrious Chola king appointed girls in temples to wash the temple floors with cow dung, light the lamp and spread flowers on all corners of the temple every evening. Most well-to-do families invited Devadasis to dance and sing devotional songs in numerous Hindu festivals, the presence of whom was considered auspicious, divine and a blessing. At a point in ancient India, Devadasis were a much respected community in Hindu society. They were revered for their religious duties.

From Handmaidens to Prostitutes

The gradual malignancy of Devadasis began with the arrival of the Europeans to the Indian subcontinent. For an average European of the 15th century, the idea of a form of art, such as dance, offered to God was seen as petty and unbelievable. A dancing female with such grace and utter disregard to the Western medieval mind-set soon invited criticisms and harsh downplaying of their role of in Hindu society. They began to be termed as "nautch-girls", meaning "dancing girls", a seemingly derogatory term for the Devadasis. Soon, the practice started attracting appeals and petitions to the Viceroy of Indian states for its termination. "Anti-nautch movement" were started by several organisations against this practice, most of which were backed by Christian missionaries. The constant slander of Devadasis which frequently was directed to the religion of Hinduism as a whole, led to the dishonour of the community. Devadasis were no longer considered auspicious and were seen as mere pieces of meat who mostly existed to feed the sexual pleasures of upper caste men. Whilst facing the societal power of the upper caste organisations, Devadasis lost their only source of livelihood and were compelled to resort to prostitution. Men began to keep Devadasis for their own personal lustful benefits, thus exposing this vulnerable community to the malicious treatment which later began to be continued for the years to come. With the advent of such character assassination of Devadasis, soon enough, these women began to lose their respectable position in society.

Thus, a term that once meant handmaiden of God, later came to be equated to prostitution.

Legal Measures

India is obliged to end institutions similar to slavery, the exploitation of children, human trafficking and forced marriages under Articles 10(1) and 10(3) of the International Covenant on Economic, Social and Cultural Rights; Articles 8(1), 23(3) and 24(1) of the International Covenant on

Civil and Political Rights; Articles 6 and 16(1) of the Convention on the Elimination of All Forms of Discrimination Against Women; Articles 19, 24(3), 32(1), 34 and 36 of the Convention on the Rights of the Child; and Article 1 of the Supplementary Convention on the Abolition of Slavery, the Slave Trade, and Institutions and Practices Similar to Slavery.

Legal Framework work various laws have been enacted in the past to stop the menace of Devadasi system.The following are the Devadasi protection act in India:

The Bombay Devadasis Protection Act, 1934

The Madras Devadasis (Prevention of Dedication) Act, 1947

The Karnataka Devadasis (Prohibition of Dedication) Act 1982,

The Andhra Pradesh Devadasis (Prohibition of Dedication) Act, 1988,

The Andhra Pradesh Devadasis (Prohibition of Dedication) Act, 1947

The Maharashtra Devadasi Protection and Rehabilitation Act 2005

The tradition is still very much prevalent in states like Andhra Pradesh, Tamil Nadu, Karnataka and Orissa and Maharashtra etc.

The National Commission for Women has also taken initiatives to end the "Devadasi System" predominantly present in Southern States of India. The National Human Rights Commission has taken cognizance of a complaint drawing its attention towards the inhuman treatment being meted out to the girls and women, who are forcibly taken to the temple of Goddess Mathamma for offering in Thiruvallur District of Tamil Nadu and adjoining places. As the ritual goes, a girl is dressed like a bride and after the ceremony; she is unrobed by five boys, virtually leaving her naked. Thereafter, she is forced to live at Mathamma temple, deemed to be like a public property, and face sexual exploitation. She can neither live with her family nor get educated. Allegedly, this practice is another form of Devadasi system, which is still practiced in some parts of Tamil Nadu and Andhra Pradesh.

The Commission has observed that the allegations made in the complaint as well as in the media report, if true, amount to violation of human rights including Rights to Life, Education and Dignity of the victims. Accordingly, it has issued notices to the Government of Tamil Nadu and Andhra Pradesh calling for reports in the matter.

The National Human Rights Commission has found that on the 3rd October, 2016 in Tamil Nadu, the cheeks of about 20 children were pierced with two meter steel rods as part of a ritual for speedy recovery of the then ailing Chief Minister of Tamil Nadu, Ms. J. Jayalalilthaa. It has asked the

Additional Commissioner of Police, Law and Order, North Chennai, Tamil Nadu to register a case under sections 326/341/34/120B, IPC against those who forced them face this torture. The officer has also been asked to inform about the disciplinary action taken against the erring police officials, who were, admittedly, present at the site and did nothing to stop the criminal act. Further, the Commission has issued a notice to the Principal Secretary (Home), Government of Tamil Nadu to submit a report on the steps taken to stop such rituals (National Human Rights Commission, India).

"Prevented young girl from being from dedicated as Devadasi in Savadanti...although for today we have prevented no criminal case has been booked as the entire family and people around vehemently parroted that the girl was possessed and the rituals performed were to tackle the possession...the success of prevention is diluted by reality that they will find some other way to destroy the girl's life"- said Dr. Sunitha Krishnan of Prajwala, a Hyderabad-based charity which rescues and rehabilitates victims of sex trafficking.

Current Scenario

Although laws exist which strictly ban the above practices, evidence indicates that such rules are often violated, there's no doubt that women of this community continue to their misery, which remains untold and unheard of. Most women have now resorted to back-breaking meagre means of income like agriculture, wage labourers, construction workers, etc., if not prostitution. But a large number of women continue to be chained to the ground by forced prostitution. The lifestyle of these women continue to remain unhealthy and beyond any moderation due to societal pressure and constant degradation. Health index of the Devadasis today, remain alarmingly low. Most of the women are diagnosed with AIDS, and other sexually transmitted diseases due to having forced to have sexual intercourse with numerous men a day. Their children remain incredibly malnourished.

Itavva Jodatti, a devadasi and an executive officer at Mahila Abhivrudhi Mattu Samrakshana Samsthe (MASS), a charity that works with more than 3,600 devadasis in Karnataka, says banning the practice doesn't mean all of the devadasis' problems will disappear. "The path of transformation hasn't been easy, as many women have HIV and other health problems but don't have access to good medical facilities and employment," Jodatti says. "The scars of this age-old practice will take time to heal, and things can improve if our children have better access to mainstream education so they can lead a life of dignity"(Sahariah, 2017).

Conclusion

Devadasi tradition of religious devotion has been exploited for commercial gain. Devadasi families and communities has been destroyed generation after generation. Superstitious beliefs such as that having sexual relationships with young children offers protection from certain diseases are an added cause child trafficking. Now most of the devadasi are having price tag of AIDS, HIV andother health issues at a young age.

Eventually, they also give birth to children, which makes it impossible for them to get out of the system even if they want to. Unwillingly or unknowingly their body, dignity and respect are deteriorated.Life without education is a human rights violation. Devadasis need education in other to achieve their goal and transform their life.

Government should take initiatives to educate people against superstitious belief in this matter because this system is harming individuals and society as well, rather than bringing blessings to the family from the deity.

References

V. Sriram (2007)TheDevadasi and the Saint: The Life and Times of Bangalore Nagarathnamma

https://nhrc.nic.in/press-release/important-interventions-6

https://www.facebook.com/prajwala.in/photos/a.213618581985030/965194186827462/ ?type=3

https://yourstory.com/2017/04/devadasis-india?utm_pageloadtype=scroll

https://escholarship.org/uc/item/37z853br

Shingal, Ankur (2015)" The Devadasi System: Temple Prostitution In India", UCLA Women's Law Journal

Chapter - 18

An Anthropological analysis of Patelia Tribal women in Karnataka state

Dr. Prabudha S. Kamble

Abstract

The Patelia women are tribal in nature and are located in Bidar district of Karnataka State. The Patelia women work very hard, in some cases even more than the men as they attend the domestic house work and also the work outside the home. The women speak Hindi and Kannada language in their daily lifeand are in practice of clan exogamy form of marriage.The Patelia women celebrates a number of festivals throughout the year. Some of them are Holi, Dhuleti, Rakhi, Navratri, Dussehra, Diwali, Janmashtami, and Shivratri. This study has made an attempt to present the social cultural profile of patelia women in Karnataka state.

Keywords: *Tribe, Patelia, women, Anthropology, Karnataka, analysis*

The term 'Patelia' is derived from the term Patel which locally means a local 'headman' in the village settlement.The Patelia women, as women in all social groups, are more illiterate than men and assume themselves superior to the other Tribal women.The Patelia play different roles in their day to day life like parental, conjugal, domestic, kin roles, occupational, community and as an individual member.(wikipedia.org/wiki/Pateliya).

The Patelia women work very hard, in some cases even more than the men as they attend the domestic house work and also the work outside the home. The women are under the pressure of patriarchal in which men dominate in all sectors of life. However, in their own world women have a freedom, and a self-expression. With the impact of modernization and socio economic changes the women have remained traditional in their dress, language, tools and resources, as they grow food crops rather than cash crops.

The Patelias are distributed in to twelve states across the Indian Territory and are in majority found in Central India and sparsely populated in different states like Gujarat, Maharashtra, Rajasthan, Madhya Pradesh,Tamil Nadu, Dadar and Nagar Haveli,Delhi, Telangana,Jharkhand, WestBengal and Karnataka. Among the western Indian Patelia tribe, only 57 inhabit Karnataka, most of them in Bidar district alone. (Lal RB, Padmanabham SV, Mohideen A 2003).

The women speak Hindi and Kannada language in their daily life few also speak Marwari and Mewari language. Children go for Kannada, Marathi and English medium schools.

The community women traditionally are in practices of settled agriculture and are landless or the land owned is medium and small, and insufficient to sustain their daily needs. The poor go to work in the stone quarries and to cities to work in different Industries. They profess Hinduism, and worship local deities such as Devkarji, Mataji, and Kalka Devi.

The Patelia women are non-vegetarian in nature. They take mutton, chicken, eggs and fish along with vegetables. Maize and wheat and Jowar constitute staple diet. Rice is taken occasionally. They eat pulses of tur, urad, gram, chawala and moong. Ground nut and sunflower oil is used for cooking purposes. Vegetables like tomato, potato, ladies finger, fenugreek leaves and coriander are used in daily cooking. Locally available fruits they take from fields and trees. They make use of roots and tubers also which they gather from the forest. Consumption of alcoholic drinks is common among both men and women. They distill liquor from mahua molasses. They smoke bidi and use tobacco.

The Patelia women are in practice of clan exogamy form of marriage therefore we find exogamous clans among them. Though the clans are grouped into different categories they see equality among themselves. The people are classified in to different clans like Jadhav, Rathod, Chauhan and Pamar. The Jadhav clan is composed of Damor and Khaped. Chauhan includes katara, mori, and Dundawa.

As the other tribal women and nontribal women are in practice of getting married here Patelia women also get married but they are monogamous in character. The women prefer community endogamy with clan exogamy. The age at marriage is from fifteen to twenty years among girls and for boys eighteen years to twenty five years.Marriage by elopement is also prevalent in the community but in many cases Negotiated marriage which ends in arranged marriage is found in most popularity. The symbols of a marital status of a women are black beed necklace tied by her husband *mangalsutra,* nose ring or nose pin *natani*, rings in one or two toes of both the feet of women who has got married. The pateliasare patrilineal in descent and patrilocal in residence, hence the daughter in law goes to reside with husband after marriage. Bride price depends upon the financial status and as per negotiations done before marriage by the kins of the bridegroom. The bride price is paid in the form of cash, gold and house equipments. Divorce is permitted in case of conflicts between families and widow remarriage is also acceptable by the community people. In case the divorced family had children than it's the responsibility of the father to take care of the children as it is the descent line of the community.

The family in which the woman live is called a nuclear family, very rarely are found the joint families and many as extended families. The most preferred type of family is the extended family. The women have contributed a lot in building inter family linkages within the community and outside the community. They participate in various agricultural activities and domestic works like collecting fuel and fodder, few are also employed in salaried jobs. They have and are contributing very much in developing the family. They also participate in religious and socio economic activities like running a self-help group and helping other community women financially. The decision making in general is done by the eldest male in the family. In absence of male head in the family the family is lead by female head and all decisions are made by her.

The marriage ceremony of the women is carried out after the age of 14 to 16 years for a girl. As the boy's party comes in search of a bride they are invited and welcomed by the parents and relatives of the bride. After acceptance by both the families for a marital relation after several negotiations, the bridegroom's party visits once again to solemnizing the marriage. The marriage is officiated by a priest preferably a Brahmin priest. The pooja is performed for the family deity and the marriage pendal is erected on the next day.Marriage rituals are performed in the bride's house. The groom with the procession comes to the bride's house. Four rounds of the sacred fire are made by the bride and the bridegroom. A feast is arranged by both family. After the rituals the bride leaves with her husband to the groom's/house. Consummation of marriage takes place at the bridegroom's house.

After marriage the married couple get their official status after begetting a child. In most of the case the first preferred child is the male child. It also an auspicious occasion to hear about the pregnancy or carrying a child. The pre-delivery ritual *Udiitubudu / godibharana* is carried out in the seventh month of her pregnancy. The wife remains at her parent's house during her confinement. As part of ritual performances a coconut and wheat are put in her lap and the wife needs to embrace her husband's elderly female kin. During the child birth and before the child birth the services of institution or the midwife is obtained.*Chhatti* is celebrated on the sixth day. The house is cleaned and clothes are washed in order to maintain the purity. The mother takes a purificatory bath in lukewarm water added with neem leaves. The pollution period for the mother happens to be extended up to forty days to the day of worshipping the well. After that she starts doing normal work.

The Brahman priest is consulted during naming ceremony of the child, death rites and marriage. The Gosai works as a temple-priest. The barber serves on the occasion marriage and death rites of the Patelias. They have commensally norms with all the groups except the Harijans take girls from the Bhils. But these cases are very few and are of rare occurrences. The Patelia are receiving educational 'facilities in the schools and colleges. They send their children to schools and put them in the hostels too, whenever it becomes necessary. They educate the girls also.

The Patelia women celebrates a number of festivals throughout the year. Some of them are Holi, Dhuleti, Rakhi, Navratri, Dussehra, Diwali, Janmashtami, Shivratri, Dashera and Ramnavmi. They have a rich oral tradition. They do garbadance by dandiaduring Navratri festival. The women sing folk songs. Traditional inter-community linkages are found with a number of communities in the area. (Gujarat State Gazetteer 1972 -P 200)

In the community the dead are cremated. In case of death of children below three years of age they are buried. The funeral rites in such cases are completed within three days. Otherwise pollution period is observed for twelve days in case of adults. Bones are collected on the second day in a small earthen pot and later on disposed off in the nearby River. Dash karma is held on the tenth day and *pagadi*, succession rites on the eleventh day after death. The funeral feast is held on the twelfth day. Eldest son acts, as the chief mourner. The widow makes four reverse *phera*rounds of her husband's corpse before taking the corpse for cremation. On the eleventh day, she wears new dress and after this she can be remarried if she desires so.

Conclusion

An attempt has been made in this article to give a brief account of Patelia tribal woman with anthropological perspective. To present an ethnographic profile of the Patelia tribe has been made here in this study. The present study is based on the secondary data those were available in various departments, Gazetteer and Reports and census.The focus is on the few patelia community people distributed in Bidar District of Karnataka State.

References

Gazetter of India, Gujarat State Gazetteer, Panchmahal District, Government Press, Ahemedabad 1972, P 200

Government of India, Census. 2011. [accessed on May 7, 2014]. Available from: http:/ /www.censusindia.gov.in/2011census/population enumeration.aspx .

Government of Gujarat. Tribal Development Department. Tribal Research and Training Institute https://trti.gujarat.gov.in/pateli

Government of Karnataka. Status of Scheduled Tribes of Karnataka. In: Karnataka Human Development Report. 2005. [accessed on May 7, 2014].

Availablefrom: http://planning.kar.nic.in/sites/planning.kar.nic.in/files/khdr2005/ English/Main%20Report/10-chapter.pdf .

Lal RB, Padmanabham SV, Mohideen A, editors. Part I. Vol. 22. Mumbai: popular prakashan; 2003. People of India Gujarat; pp. 108–10. [Google Scholar]

Wikipedia, the free encyclopediahttps://en.wikipedia.org/wiki/Pateliya

Chapter - 19

Tribal Women in their Traditional Social Settings: An Anthropological Appraisal

Dr. K. S Pradeep Kumar

Abstract

Scheduled Tribe communities in India have a distinct way of while, which is quite different from the so called 'main stream' population. They are the most disadvantaged and weaker section of the population even though contributing a lot in preserving, promoting and maintaining the cultural and linguistic diversities in the country. Usually, some kind of differentiation can be seen in almost all the tribal communities and it is often exists in the form of clan and gender. Gender is the most prominent identity in the society even though it is not visible as such and it has a defining role in work distribution, selection of traditional decision making authorities, accessibility to public spaces, etc., Tribal women has been playing a crucial role in the overall life of the society by managing family affairs, engaging in agricultural operations, collecting tubers, decorating house, etc., but they are not getting their due share in various facets of socio-cultural life. Tribal women in many communities are -not consulted in taking important decisions, not permitted to become religious specialists, not selected as traditional hereditary Chiefs, and not able to participate in ritual dances and public performances. However, the status and public space provide to tribal women may vary in accordance with the particular socio-cultural features of the community. The paper is an attempt to appraise the status of tribal women in their traditional social settings with reference to a few tribal communities in various States of Indian union. An effort has also been made to identify the different factor that influences the status of women in tribal societies.

Key Words: *Matrilineal, Patrilineal, 'purity', 'impurity', matrilocal, matriarchy, etc.,*

1. Introduction

The tribal communities are the real indigenous people of India. They might have started their life in the large river basins of central and western

India and later fled to the present day hilly forest terrains of the various parts of the country due to the influx of 'aggressive, militant and greedy populations' to their age-old habitats. Before that they were self-sufficient and self-reliant people in all aspects and were in fact rulers of the area, governed and ruled by their own customary norms and practices. Shifting cultivation, food gathering and hunting were the major sources of livelihood.The Scheduled Tribes (ST's) are the most disadvantaged and weaker section of the population of the Indian union. However, they contribute a lot in preserving, promoting and maintaining the cultural and linguistic diversities of the country.

Women in Tribal Societies

Tribal communities contribute a lot in protecting and promoting the richness and diversity of human culture. One of the most significant identities within a tribal community is that of gender. Traditionally members of a particular community share more or less common livelihood resources, material conditions, beliefs, rituals and practices, etc., but gender has a defining role in deciding the nature/degree of participation of an individual in many aspects of life. The role of women in tribal societies is very crucial as they play a major part in managing day to day family affairs and livelihood activities. Tribal women are imperative in the persistence of many aspects of local culture. Their ornaments, dress code, bodily decorations, hair style etc, add a lot in enriching culture and tradition of the country.

Tribal women accounts for 5.20 crores of Indian population. They are spread over in 705 ethnic groups and together with their men folk forms 8.6 percentage of the total population of the country. Generally, the tribal societies recognizes more or less equal role to women and men. Absence of bride burning and domestic violence, favourable sex-ratio, high participation of women in economic activities, and low infant mortality rate are some of the indicators for the same. It is because of the specialty of tribal ethos that the women of tribal societies can maintain a comfortable position in the society. However, in spite of the better status enjoyed by tribal women in compared to women in other societies by and large the status of tribal women is very low in compared to the men folk of the community since they have little access to knowledge, to economic resources, to power, and lowest degree of personal autonomy.

Matrilineal Societies

Garo and Khasi Tribal communities in North East India are following matrilineal system and transferred the property through female members.

They practice matrilocal residence and enjoy relatively higher position in the society, (Mitra & Singh, 2007; Burman Roy, 2012[1]). In Adiyan, a matrilineal community of Wayanad district in Kerala, women has a deciding role in selecting the *Chenmakkaran*[2], who plays an important role in the society. However, women have no role in the selection of *Kuntumoopan*[3] and *Nattumoopan*[4]. Male members of the community select the *Nattumoopan,* (Sini, 2019:18-20). Women are also not participating in the ritual dance associated with the Gadhika ceremony. Thus, in matrilineal societies, where the properties and clan legacy are inherited through mother, the actual management of the property and decision making authority rests mainly on male representatives.

Patrilineal Societies

Kurumbar is one among the Particularly Vulnerable Tribal Groups (PVTGs) in Kerala and they occupy second in population amongst the five PVTG communities of the State. They follow patrilieny. '*Panjakad Vellama*', a mode of shifting cultivation, is the major economic activity of the Kurumbar. *Manookaran* is the soil and agricultural expert of the community and he supervises the agricultural operations in a hamlet. Besides, *Manookaran*, a Moopan for looking after the entire affairs of a hamlet, and *Kuruthala* and *Bhandari* for assisting them in discharging their roles are the major functionaries of a hamlet. All of them are from the male population. The households of a hamlet are erected around a plane open space, where all the members of a hamlet sit together by evening, after the days agricultural work, and spent the evening by singing and dancing. Both men and women are actively participated in the evening get-together.

Traditionally, marriage through elopement and service are practiced. The boy has to be stayed at the house of the girl, to whom he desires to get married even if a consensus has been reached between the families and elders, over a considerable period of time to prove his expertise in doing *panjakad* cultivation and other works. He would get the girl as bride only if he can impress the girl's family. There are cases where the proposal for marriage in the nature mentioned above had been rejected by the girl's family even after one year's service of the kind mentioned above from boy's side. Thus, the girl and her family has a say in finalizing a marriage proposal even though she is treated as 'some one to be looked after' to a certain extend. The above mentioned aspects clearly state that Kurumbar women are active participants at social gatherings, agricultural activities and rituals of the community eventhough the society is patrilineal and men as power holders of the socio-cultural life.

Munda, a tribal community which is distributed in Jharkhand, West Bengal, Chhattisgarh, Orissa and Bihar practices shifting cultivation and follows patrilineal, patriarchal and patrilocal family. But the woman in the community enjoys full liberty to choose her life partner and she can break the marriage bond at any time and marry another person with/without intimation to her husband. The practice of Bride price is also prevalent amongst them, (Selvi, 41:2019). All these reveal that the status of women in patrilineal societies is not much different from those of matrilineal one.

Kinnauri Women

Even though the women of Kinnauri[5] tribal group in Himachal Pradesh inherit no property due to the practice of patrilineal inheritance, they enjoy greater freedom than other tribal women due to the prevalence of matriarchal system. Kinnauri women can marry at any age or to lead a life with out opting for marriage by becoming a *jomo*[6]. Her consent prevails over family's decision in marital affairs including the choice to the practice of polyandry or to stay with monogamy. Widow remarriage is permitted. Women can divorce her husband as per her choice. After marriage women takes all the responsibilities and important decisions in family. They also do all the activities in the agricultural field except plugging. Eventhough Kinnauri women do not hold any official position in society they equally participate in socio-religious functions, (Negi, 2019:72-74). Thus, it is clear that women in Kinnauri tribal group enjoy better position and status than women in many tribal communities of the country.

Status of Women in Tribal Societies

Status is a relative concept and it changes over time and population. A single instance is not enough to determine the status of women; but a 'multi-dimensional cluster of variables' is required to assess the status. For tribal societies, the participation in subsistence activities forms one of the major determinants of status, (Sini, 2019:15). Some kind of a categorization can be seen on the nature and type of works available to the members of a tribal community. Such an arrangement is based on rough estimation about the risk factor, physical strength required, and prestige attached with the work. Those that require a high degree of the factors mentioned above such as honey collection, and hunting[7] are usually managed by the male gender both in patrilineal and matrilineal communities. Such works can be termed as volatile works and those works that needs less physical strength, low risk and prestige, for instance shifting cultivation, and settled cultivation, can be termed as non-volatile works. Non-volatile works may again fall in two categories, viz., one that is detached from the household and the one that is carried out in a household. The first category has the active participation of both males and females while on the second usually females are the active participants. In many tribal societies, such as Kurumbar of Attapady area in Palakkad district, non-volatile works have prominence and in such societies women play greater role in the day to day affairs of the hamlet and enjoy better status. But in some societies such as Cholanaikan volatile works have prominence and the chance for women to participate equally with men in day to day affairs is less and it in turn reduces their status.

Traditionally almost all the tribal communities have one or the other form of art forms that provides momentum and liveliness to social gatherings, and the performance of them are often associated with life cycle rituals and ceremonies. Participation and role ofwomen in traditional art forms is an indicator of their status. Many tribal communities such as Kattunayakan and Kurumbar of Wayanad and Palakkad districts, respectively, in Kerala have varying art forms where both females and males can participate, or only male or female can participate. In some other communities for instance Mannan of Idukki district in Kerala, only males can participate in ritual dances. Elder women of Mannan community may make guest appearances at special instances during the performance of the ritualistic art form, where only males can participate actively during the presentation. All these reveal that women have better social status in Kattunayakan and Kurumbar communities of Kerala. Thus, participation in social gatherings and public performances is a direct indicator on the status of women in tribal societies.

Another area that has a direct role in determining the status of women is the concept of 'purity' and 'impurity' prevalent in the society. Women are generally considered as 'unclean' during menstruation and child birth and are treated as 'impure' during the period. By taking into account of this attributed 'impurity' women are debarred from holding priestly positions and to act as community leaders by holding hereditary social positions. The 'state of impurity' attributed to women due to menstruation and child is a major reason for their oppression and discrimination (Aneesh and Jilly, 2019:50). Traditional leaders of the political system and specialist in religious matters, known by various titles in different communities are all occupied by male representatives. Many occupations in Munda tribal group are barred to women for ritual reasons (Selvi, 41:2019). One of the reasons for the lesser role and participation of women in the political and religious decision making is their 'state of impurity'.

Sini (2019:16) points out that 'a closer and discrete analysis of prevailing social institutions, economic pursuits and norms, religious and political affairs would help to assess the status of women in a society'. According to Lowie[8] 'actual treatment, legal status, opportunity for social participation and the character and extent of work', all of which may not co-exist in any society, determine the status of women in a society. In view of the above mentioned aspects it is clear that the status of tribal women can be measured as per the nature and type of works available, personal autonomy, participation in social gatherings and public performances, notions of 'purity' and 'impurity' and accessibility to authority.

Another important aspect regarding the gender status in tribal communities is its non-visibility. The gender division is not usually explicit in a tribal community since the community sentiments, and division of people in to various clans and lineages are much stronger than it. Community identity, clan ties and sentiments in tribal communities are felt to be 'primordial' and even 'natural'. Scholars are of the opinion that the members of the tribal communities by being an ethnic community feel that 'their community has existed 'from time immemorial', and that its symbols and traditions posses a 'deep antiquity', which gives them a unique power' (Smith, 1998: 707). More over being a small group and living in the company of other communities tribal community members feel their beliefs, practices, way of life, etc. are different from the 'desirables[9]' (Deshen, 1974; Mines, 1975; Epstein, 1978)'[10]. So, they give more emphasis to their community's distinct identity in order to retain their cultural distinctiveness and feel their 'space' in the social system. This in turn masks the gender identity within a tribal community and the women members of a particular tribal community are not in a position to identify them as belonging to a particular group in contrast to their male counterparts. Thus, even though all of them are suffering from a common pattern of discrimination in various facets of socio-cultural life many often they never consider that as a partially against the women gender of the community.

Conclusion

The above mentioned descriptions proves that women have command and supremacy in some tribal societies, equal or nearly equal to their men folk in some others, but generally they remain subservient to men. The status of women is not much different in partilineal and matrilineal societies, but the peculiar socio-cultural features of a community can raise the women's status as in the case of Kinnauri society. The concept of 'purity' and 'impurity', which has a biological relation, is an important factor for discrimination against women in tribal societies. Gender identity and consciousness are not visible in many tribal communities and it in turn leads to the absence of recognition of many partialities in socio-cultural life a part of discrimination against women.

References

Aneesh, M.S and Jilly John. 2019. 'Transition from Tradition to Modern: The Changing Scenario and the Role of Women in Tribal Community'. In K.S Pradeep Kumar (Ed.). *Contemporary Socio-Cultural Scenario of Tribal Women in India: Challenges and Prospects*. Kozhikode. KIRTADS.

Benson, E. Janet. 1998. 'Politics and Muslim Ethnicity in South India'. In M.S Chana (Ed.). *Ethnicity and Identity: An Anthropological View Point*. New Delhi. Cosmo Publication: 140-63.

Negi, Pooja. 2019. 'Tribal Women and Traditional Life: A Study of the Role of Women in the Culture of Kinnaur in Himachal Pradesh'. In K.S Pradeep Kumar (Ed.). *Contemporary Socio-Cultural Scenario of Tribal Women in India: Challenges and Prospects*. Kozhikode. KIRTADS.

Selvi,G.Shenthamil. 2019. 'Tribal Women and Tradition Life of Munda'. In K.S Pradeep Kumar (Ed.). *Contemporary Socio-Cultural Scenario of Tribal Women in India: Challenges and Prospects*. Kozhikode. KIRTADS.

Sini, M. 2019. 'Status of the Adiyan Women: An Overview'. In K.S Pradeep Kumar (Ed.). *Contemporary Socio-Cultural Scenario of Tribal Women in India: Challenges and Prospects*. Kozhikode. KIRTADS.

Smith, D. Anthony. 1998. 'The Politics of Culture: Ethnicity and Nationalism'. In Tim Ingold (Ed.). *Companion Encyclopedia of Anthropology*. London: Routledge: 706-34.

Notes

1. For more see Aneesh and Jilly John, 2019:47-48
2. Clan head of the community
3. Settlement head
4. Territorial chief of the community
5. Kinnaur in Himachal Pradesh, situated in Western Himalayas, has a unique culture. Simultaneous existence of Hinduism and Buddhism can be seen in the region.
6. Nun in Buddhism
7. Hunting is banned now but in certain regions hunting, which forms a necessary part of some particular ritual is permitted on certain grounds.
8. See Sini 2019:16
9. Desirables are the accepted behavior patterns of a society, which are often determined by the notions of the majority group.
10. See Benson (1998: 142)

Chapter - 20

Problems and Challenges of Kalvarayan Malai Tribal People

Dr. K. Pushpam, and K. Manivasakam,

Abstract

In India, Tribes are distributed geographically all over the country, Many Anthropologists have tried to classify the Indian tribes according to their geographic distribution is terms of zones, territories and regions some of the important aspects taken into consideration to classify tribes are geography, historical background language, racial features, demography, economic conditions and social life. The country has the tribal population is 10.43 crore, constituting 8.61% of the total population. The largest number of ST's contributing 14.69% to the total percentage of ST population of India particularly in Madhya Pradesh. The present paper explains the problems and challenges of the tribal people in Kalvarayan Malai.

Introduction

The tribal populations of the country, as per 2011, census is 10.43 crore, constituting 8.6% of the total population 89.97% of them live in rural areas and 10.03% in urban areas. In 1961 30.1 million, ST population has increased to 104.3 million in 2011. According to the 1991 census, the country has the population of the scheduled tribes 67.8 million, which is 8.1 per cent of the total population of the country. The scheduled tribe's population has been increased after 1951. Before India attained independence, the tribes were identified and enumerated as aboriginals, after independence, the Government of India listed the tribes and placed them in a schedule, hence the tribes came to be known as scheduled tribes. They were not practiced by system of dowry, caste division even divorce and widow remarriage are socially accepted among them. They are an exemplary society when it comes to social practices yet. They live a life of poverty and discrimination. The paper tries to understand the tribal community of Kalvarayan Malai people major problems and challenges like social, religious, and educational, health related problems and many more. The researcher also recommended some suggestions regarding the issues or challenges of tribes.

Need for the study

The tribal culture and lifestyle desired that development policies are evolved to suit is Autonomy. Many studies have their own strength to understand the problem in a particular time and space. However, very few anthropological studies move out of the behavioral and cultural contexts. The larger issues of tribal people do not receive any socio-economic, political, and ecological factors with the accessibility, affordability and availability of health service. The tribal therefore, needs to be protected against leading isolated life, away from towns and cities, through a network of new roads and technologies. The present paper tries to understand the tribal community of Kalvarayan Malai people major problems and challenges like social, religious, and educational, health related problems and many more. This study also recommended some suggestions regarding the issues or challenges of tribes.

Review of the study

In 2011, while 40.6 per cent tribes were below the poverty line, the proportion among the rest was 20.5 per cent. The key indicators among tribes remain very poor related to the health care. For example, according to the National Family Health Survey 4 (NFHS-4) (2015-2016), the under-5 mortality among the tribal population was 57.2 per 1000 live births compared to 38.5 among others, and the infant mortality rate (IMR) 44.4 per 1000 live births versus others of 32.1. ST family in India has a child born 19 per cent higher risk of dying in the neonatal period. Compared with other social classes 45 per cent greater risk of dying in the post-neonatal period.

According to a UNICEF-assisted study reveals that Disparity for tribals relative to rest of the population comes from Kerala State where in 2013 the lowest IMR of 7 per 1000 live births was reported. The rate in tribal community of Wayanad, the district having the largest tribal population in Kerala, was 41.47.

Compared with other populations Child malnutrition rates are also significantly higher and poverty more common for tribal populations. In a cross-sectional study conducted in 2015, three-fourths (76.6%) of the 2926 under-5 children surveyed among tribal district of Melghat in Maharashtra,

India, were found to be severely or moderately undernourished. The situation of under nutrition is extremcly worrisome in most tribal areas.

Objectives of the study

- To study the problems and challenges of tribes in the study area
- To suggest the suitable recommendations for the tribes

Area of the study

The present study selected the study area as Kalvarayan Malai in the Kallakurichi district. 54 respondents are selected in the study area.

Tribes

A group of people who live and work together is called tribe. A tribal society is a group of tribes organized around kinships.

Research design

The present study follows the need to understand problems and challenges of tribals, through focus on development strategy used to improve status and quality of life of tribals. The study has been adopted descriptive in nature.

Methodology

The literature used to write and analyse the socio-economic challenges of tribes in this paper is collected from various secondary sources like internet, research articles, government reports and websites.

Tools of data collection

The researcher framed that the interview schedule is the most suitable tools for data collection. Hence the researcher used self prepared interview schedule to elucidate the data required for the study.

Data Interpretation

Table - 20.1: Health Problems of faced by Tribes

S.No	*Particulars*	*No.of Respondents*	*Percentages*
1.	General problems	21	39.0
2.	Reproductive health problem	18	33.3
3.	Malnutrition.	15	27.7
	Total	54	100

Source: Primary Data

Of the total respondents selected for the study, tribes are facing the problems necessitating health seeking among the tribal's can be broadly classified in to three groups namely General problems (39.0 percent) followed by Reproductive health problem (33.3 percent) and Malnutrition (27.7 percent).

General, they are facing many issues related with the health of the community utilization of Government facilities, Community needs, Community participation, Role of Ngo's, Financial constraint, Land alienation, Poverty and indebtedness, Education cultural problems concept of private property and separatism.

Reproductive health related they are facing many challenges like , accessing health services, Lack of awareness of health issues, Lack of health facilities in remote rural areas, Discriminatory behaviour by health care providers and Health and nutrition.

Malnutrition related to People suffers a lot and find difficulties even for tea snacks and food. People face many health problems such as cholera, vomiting, diarrhea fever and other diseases such as sexually transmitted diseases.

Table - 20.2: Socio-Cultural challenges

S.No	*Particulars*	*No. of Respondents*	*Percentages*
1.	Social structure	14	26.0
2.	Economy	19	35.1
3.	Religious life	11	20.4
4.	Women in the political sphere	10	18.5
	Total	54	100

Source: Primary Data

Of the total respondents interviewed for the study, tribes' people are facing challenges related to economy- role of women in tribal economy, economic problems due to deforestation and land alienation, unequal wage structure, and exploitation at work place, (35.1 per cent) followed by social structure, descent, inheritance and succession and marriage and divorce (26per cent) , Religious life –taboos and the place of women in the traditional tribal religion and place and status of women as religious functionaries (20.4 per cent) and women in the political sphere- tribal women in the traditional political structure and tribal women in the present day political structure of the state and nation (18.5 percent). Till now no significant changes taken place in Kalvarayan Malai. Tribe's people do not have any transport facilities only one bus is hired to these areas, which take the people down the hills and shall return in the evening.

NGO/ SHG's Contribution

NGO and SHG's are helps them for cultivation by providing seeds for tomato, potato, carrot, beetroot, ladies finger, brinjal, banana etc. It helps peoples for their own use and to generate their income through selling it. NGO's helps them to express their opinion and mingle with the social culture. It provides the encouragement and refreshment for their exposures. NGo's provides elder caring program education program, women empowerment, community program and adolescent and youth programmes.

Findings

- The present study find out the tribes are facing the problems and challenges in general.
- The present study represents the people met the economic challenges in day to day their life.

Recommendations for rectifying the tribe's challenges and problems

The following recommendation and suggestions are reducing the tribes problems and challenges. There are

1. Raising awareness of health issues
2. Bringing health services to remote populations
3. Providing emergency transportation for expectant mothers
4. Employing health worker from tribal communities
5. Changing the behaviour of health care providers
6. Providing financial support
7. Other innovations ensuring sustainability and spreading the innovations.

Conclusion

Social and economic justice, equality of status and opportunities, assurance of the individual's dignity are ensured by the Constitution of India for all the citizens among other things. The constitution of India is enriched with several provisions for schedule castes and schedule tribes to safeguard and promote their cultural, social, educational, and economic interests to bring them in the mainstream of the nation.

References

1. Community Seva centre
2. Cscngo.org

3. People Democracy, June 21, 2015.
4. Shodhganga.inflibnet.ac.in
5. World bank.org/en/news
6. Vineeta Chawla, Tribals in India: current status and treatment given by public, by youth Ki Awaaz in society, 7th January 2011.
7. youth Ki Awaaz .com
8. sociology Guide-A students guide to sociology
9. https://www.academia.edu.
10. The Indian Journal of Medical Research
11. Pujankumar sen, *Indian society continuity and change,* ICFAI University.

Chapter - 21

A Critical Appraisal on the Issues and Challenges of Tribal Education in Kerala

Dr. Remmiya Rajan P & Ms. Anjana

Abstract

The backwardness of the scheduled tribes is mainly due to the high incidence of illiteracy and very low level of education among the tribal people. Hence, the educational status of the scheduled tribes and the role of governance in this direction are highly essential. It is well known that the educational background of tribes is very discouraging as compared to the rest of the population. So, education is an important avenue for upgrading the economic and social conditions of the Scheduled Tribes. The dropout rate of tribal students in School education is very high in recent days. Nobody conducted a research study in this area to bring an awareness on financial and educational schemes for School education among tribal students and their parents. So the researcher decided to study in this area because the upliftment of tribal community is the urgent need in this era, School education is the foundation stone of the development of any society.

Keywords: *Tribal Education, Critical Appraisal*

Introduction

The importance of education in the process of economic, political and social change has been widely recognised and well documented all over the world. The changes in the educational system should also reduce the social gaps by enabling proper recognition to whatever extent one is able to pursue or acquire a skill. The tribal community all over India has been subjected to various forms of deprivation such as alienation from land and other resources. Although certain constitutional safeguards are provided, there has been no economic, social and political mobility across this community. The Scheduled Tribes remain abysmally backward and socially excluded, still living in harsh environs.

Education is an important parameter for any inclusive growth in an economy and it is an important avenue for upgrading the economic and social conditions of the Scheduled Tribes. Literacy and educational attainment are powerful indicators of social and economic development among the backward groups. The male female gap in literacy and educational attainment among the scheduled tribes is significant. Scheduled Tribes are geographically, socially isolated and economically marginalized communities. In the post-Independence period, sincere and concerted efforts were made for the economic and educational development of tribal's. Despite of these efforts the performance of the tribes in education is still much lower than the Scheduled Castes. This has led to drop outs and directly impacted their overall educational status.

Rationale of the study

Despite the sincere and concerted efforts by the government for the overall development of the scheduled tribes, they are still far behind in almost all the standard parameters of development. They are not able to participate in the process of development, as they are not aware of most of the progrmmes and policies made for their upliftment. This is mainly due to the high incidence of illiteracy and very low level of education among the tribal people. Hence, the educational status of the scheduled tribes and the role of governance in this direction are highly essential. It is well known that the educational background of tribes is very discouraging as compared to the rest of the population. So, education is an important avenue for upgrading the economic and social conditions of the Scheduled Tribes.

Statement of the problem

The back wardness of the scheduled tribes is mainly due to the high incidence of illiteracy and very low level of education among the tribal people. Hence, the educational status of the scheduled tribes and the role of governance in this direction are highly essential. It is well known that the educational background of tribes is very discouraging as compared to the rest of the population.

Objectives of the study

(1) To study the educational status of tribal community in Kerala

(2) To study the critical issues and problems in the field of tribal education.

(3) To develop awareness of various schemes of government in promoting tribal education

1. Analysis and interpretation of the study

A. Scheduled tribes literacy Rate

Year	*Total*	*Male*	*Female*
2001	64.40	70.80	58.10
2011	75.81	80.76	71.08

Source: Census of India 2011

B. To study on the dropout of total tribal students of Waynad district

Academic Year	*Total number of students*	*Tribal students*	*Total Dropout*
2010-11	126132	26017	2718
2011-12	126213	27427	3365
2012-13	125767	28738	713
2013-14	124452	29566	1 264
2014-15	122816	30179	1463

Source: General Education Department, GoK

The drop-out rate of ST students is 5.81%. A survey conducted by the Kerala Institute of Local Tribal Education in Kerala: A Critical Appraisal Administration in association with local bodies and the Scheduled Tribes Welfare Department reveal pathetic living conditions of the Scheduled Tribes communities in the State. Most of them drop-out from schools at the primary level itself. Data on school education describes the low enrolment and high drop-out among tribal students in Kerala at each sections of school. This inequality in education is predominantly damaging the all tribal society.

C. To study on the critical issues and problems in the field of tribal education.

If we analyse the real issues of tribal population for taking education then we must find that there is higher concentration of poverty among the tribal population in both the rural as well as urban areas. Their weak resource base, their low position in socio economic and political hierarchy, illiteracy, their relative lack of access to facilities provided by developmental measures; and their inadequate participation in institutions are mainly responsible for their backwardness as well as access to education. It is indeed a matter of deep concern that why the fruits of development fail to reach the weaker sections of our society despite our planned efforts.

They are as follows:

1.	Medium of language	Language is one of the important constraints of tribal children which prevents them access to education.
2.	The Location of the Village	The physical barriers create a hindrance for the children of a tribal village to attend the school in a neighboring village.
3.	Economic Condition	The economic condition of tribal people is so poor that they do not desire to spare their children or their labour power and allow them to attend schools
4.	Attitude of the parents	As education does not yield any immediate economic return, the tribal parents prefer to engage their children in remunerative employment which supplements the family income.
5.	Teacher Related Problems	In the remote tribal areas the teacher absenteeism is a regular phenomenon and this affects largely the quality of education.
6	Lack of Proper monitoring	Proper monitoring is hindered by poor coordination between the Tribal Welfare Department and School Education Department. Government Policies and Programmes for Tribal Education

D. To develop awareness about various schemes of government for promoting tribal education

Schemes Of Governments	Facility awareness
Post Matric Scholarships To St Students (Class Xi And Above)	Scholarship Amount Of Rs.230 To Rs.1200 Per Month
Pre-Matric Scholarships To St Students (Class Ix And X)	Rs.150/- Per Month For Day Scholars And @Rs.350/- Per Month For Hostellers, For A Period Of 10 Months In A Year.
National Overseas Scholarships (Nos) For St Students For Studying Abroad	Annual Maintenance Allowance Of £9900/-, Annual Contingency & Allowance Of £1116/-, Tuition Fees As Per Actuals And Other Admissible Fees Are Provided For Candidates In United Kingdom.
Scheme Of Strengthening Education Among St Girls In Low Literacy Districts	Educational Complexes Impart Not Only Formal Education To Tribal Girls But Also Train The Students In Agriculture, Animal Husbandry, Other Vocations And Crafts To Make Them Economically Strong.

(Contd...)

Peripatetic Education to the Primitive Tribes	To impart Lower Primary education to Particularly Vulnerable Tribal Groups and other similar Scheduled Tribes, Peripatetic centres & single teacher schools have been set up in tribal dominated inaccessible areas of the State
Tutorial Scheme for Students	The scheme is intended to provide special coaching to students of High School and Plus I & II classes to increase pass percentage. The monthly tuition fee would be directly given to parents for providing tuition through nearby tutorials.
Gothra Sarathi	The scheme is for arranging transportation facilities to students living in the interior forests and inaccessible areas, in association with the Education Department, Local Governments and the Parent Teachers Association.
Samuhya Patanamuri (Community Study centre in tribal hamlets)(New Initiative)	To solve the linguistic and dropout issues and to create ambience for education in hamlets, department has started 100 Community Study Centres in tribal hamlets throughout the state during 2017-18. One educated tribal youth from same community has been selected and who works as a facilitator and social worker. The Centre is equipped with computers with internet, LED TV, furniture, reading materials etc. About 30 students are accommodated in each centre.
Special Incentive to Brilliant Students	*The scheme is for providing incentives to the brilliant students from ST communities who perform well in academics and come out with meritorious performance.*
Pre – matric &Post-matric Hostels for Tribal Students	*With a view to provide residential education to tribal students in remote areas, the department is operating 106 Pre-matric hostels and 5 Post matric hostels for providing boarding, lodging and tuition facilities to ST students. It is proposed to start 4 Post matric hostels during 2018-19.*
Ayyankali Memorial Talent Search and Development Scheme	Under the scheme, talented tribal students (day scholars) studying from 5th standard to 10th standard are the target group and continuous assistance is being provided to them to excel in academics and extracurricular activities. Every year, 200 students studying in 5th standards will be selected under this scheme through an intelligence test.
Assistance for Study tour to School & College going Students	Under this scheme, Post matric students are given financial assistance for participating in excursions and study tours. Also, the scheme intends to conduct Bharat Darshan/All India Tour for selected tribal students with the approval of the SLWG.
Assistance to Orphans	This scheme is intended to provide special assistance to the scheduled tribe children who have no parents to look after. Assistance is given to care takers of such children. Each beneficiary is given Rs.1000/- per month.
Supply of Laptop to Students	The scheme is envisaged to provide Laptop to ST students of professional courses in approved University/institutes. The courses covered are MBA, M.Sc Computer Science, MCA, MBBS, BDS, BAMS, BHMS, BVSc.& AH, B.Tech and M.Tech and other Post Graduation Degrees

(*Contd...*)

Gothrabandhu- Engaging Tribal teachers in primary schools(New Initiative)	To ensure proper education to tribal children, one educated tribal youth (men or women) with TTC/B.Ed qualification from the same locality with knowledge in tribal dialect and Malayalam is selected and trained to function as mentor teacher in Primary Schools
Vocational Training Institute & Training Centres for Scheduled Tribe students	There are two Vocational Training Institutes for Scheduled Tribe students functioning at Thiruvananthapuram(Kuttamala) and Idukki(Nadukani) for imparting training in 3 trades approved by National Council For Vocational Training. More over 11 vocational training centres are functioning under this department.
Incentive to Parents of ST Students	An amount of Rs. 50/- per month is given to parents of ST students studying in LP classes, who have 75% attendance in an academic year.

Kerala State Backward Classes Development Corporation (2014)

Thus many schemes for promoting tribal education has been brought by the government but the tribal community is unaware about it.

E. Government Policies and Programmes for Tribal Education

- Starting from the First Five Year Plan Period1 (1951 1956) the government is steadily allocating financial resources for the purpose of tribal development.
- Towards, the end of the plan (1954), 43 Special Multipurpose Tribal Development Projects (MTDPs) was created.
- During the Third Five Year Plan Period (19611966), the government of India adopted the strategy of converting areas with more than 66 per cent tribal concentration into Tribal Development Blocks (TBDs). By the end of Fourth Five Year Plan (19691974), the number of TBDs in the country rose to 504.
- Additionally, in 1972 the Tribal Sub Plan Strategy (TSP) was implemented by the Ministry of Education and Social Welfare. TSP was based on twin objectives of socioeconomic development and protection against exploitation. It was generally implemented in the areas where the Scheduled Tribe population was more than 50 per cent of the total population.
- The PESA (The Panchayats Extension to Scheduled Areas) Act, 1996 in fact, has made it mandatory for the States having scheduled areas to make specific provisions for giving wide-ranging powers to the tribes on the matters relating to decision-making and development of their community.

- A centrally-sponsored government scheme of ashram schools exclusively for ST children from elementary to higher secondary levels was initiated in the 1970s. But the poor quality of education in ashram schools, however, has undermined confidence in education as a vehicle for social mobility. The Janshala Programmeis a collaborative effort of the Government of India (GOI) and five UN Agencies–UNDP, UNICEF, UNESCO, ILO and UNFPA –a community based primary education programme, aims to make primary education more accessible and effective, especially for girls and children in deprived communities, marginalised groups, Scheduled Caste/Scheduled Tribes/minorities, children with specific needs.

Conclusion

Tribal students are backward in School education due to poor Socio-economic status of the family. One of the main factors of the lack of School education among tribal community is unawareness. Not only the parents but also the children are unaware about the financial and educational schemes for School education. The dropout rate of tribal students in School education is very high in recent days. Nobody conducted a research study in this area to find out the awareness on financial and educational schemes for School education among tribal students and their parents. So the researcher decided to study in this area because the upliftment of tribal community is the urgent need in this era, School education is the foundation stone of the development of any society.

From the study we have to identify the constraints in revamping of tribal community to School education, especially the unawareness on financial and educational schemes for higher education. We can diagnose the level of unawareness and provide suitable measures to inculcate awareness among tribal community about the importance of School education and the way they achieve it.

References

Aerthayil, Mathew. (2008). Impact of Globalisation on Tribals. New Delhi: Rawat Publication

Shashi. (1991). Tribal, Culture, Economy and Health. Jaipur: Rawat PublicationBasu,

Dr.Durga Das. (2007). Introduction to the Constitution of India. Nagpur: Wadhwa Publication

Kabitakumari, Dr. Sahu; 2014; 'Challenging Issues of Tribal Education in India' International Journal of Economic and Finance; Vol No: 3, Pp. 48-5

Kakkoth, Seetha; 2005; 'the Primitives Groups of Kerala: A Situational Appraisal'; Journal of Social Science

Mathur, P.G.R. (1977). Tribal Situation in Kerala. Trivandrum: Kerala Historical Society

Pratiksha. (2014). Tribal Situation in India. New Delhi: Centrum Press Report of Ministry of Tribal Affairs on Tribal Education. Government

Sah, D.C., Sisodia., & Singh Yathindra. (2004). Tribal Issues in India. New Delhi: Rawat Publication

Shirsath, Shivadas; 2014; 'Adivasi Tribes: Nature and Concept'; Online International Interdisciplinary Research Journal; Vol No: IV

Srihari, M., & Joy, Jobin; 2014; 'A case study on the school dropouts scheduled tribal students of Wayanad district, Kerala'; Research Journal of Education Science; Vol: 2 (3).

Chapter - 22

Status of Malapandaram Women in Kerala

Salini. R & Dr. PK. Muthukumar

Abstract

The Malai Pandaram or otherwise termed as Hill Pandaram is a scheduled tribe. They are mainly distributed in the high range areas of Kollam and Pathanamthitta Districts. The 2011 Census recorded their population as 2,422. In the Travancore region they have a patios referred by others as Pandaram Basha. With others they converse in Malayalam and educated use the Malayalam script for writing. The Malai Pandaram's economic life is overwhelmingly forest based. They are landless as well as seminomadics in nature. Presently, the government has allotted plots to groups in which they have erected their huts. The mean sof life of these people is gathering of forest products. Some of them have traditional knowledge in herbal medicines. Satha or Ayyappan is their principal deity and their settlements are located near the Sastha temples like Aryankavu, Achankovil and Sabarimala The present article unfurls the problems encountered by the malapandaram tribe of Kerala. Malapandaram is one of the semi- nomadic tribes located mainly in the premises of Periyar Tiger Reserve, to the south of it and in the vicinity of the Kollam district. The study highlights the problems encountered by this tribal community. The particular problems extracted from the study were, problems in finding employment for a minimum standard of living, lack of education, lack of stable income, threat of displacement, distance to educational, medical institutions, rules and regulations of the government, exploitation by the agents and public, ill health and malnutrition, drain of forest resources and financial liability of the household, denied rights over land, the existence child marriage, polygamy.

Introduction

The tribal women, constitute like any other social group, about half of the total population. The tribal women, as women in all social groups, are more illiterate than men. Like others social groups, the tribal women share problems related to reproductive health. When primary and secondary subsistence activities are counted, women work more than men. Status of women varies in different societies. The conceptual framework to analyse women's status comprise the seven roles women play in life and work: - parental, conjugal, domestic, kin, occupational, community and as an individual. In order to appraise the social status of women in these diverse ecological areas, the findings have been divided in to subsequent categories: - (a) a girl; daughter; a unmarried woman; (b) a married woman; (c) a widow; (d) divorcee; and (e) a barren woman. Role of women is not only of importance in economic activities, but her role in non-economic activities is equally important. The tribal women work very hard, in some cases even more than the men.

The Malai Pandaram or otherwise termed as Hill Pandaram is a scheduled tribe. They are mainly distributed in the high range areas of Kollam and Pathanamthitta Districts. The 2011 Census recorded their population as 2,422. In the Travancore region they have a patios referred by others as Pandaram Basha. With others they converse in Malayalam and educated use the Malayalam script for writing. The Malai Pandaram's economic life is overwhelmingly forest based. They are landless as well as seminomadics in nature. Presently, the government has allotted plots to groups in which they have erected their huts. The mean sof life of these people is gathering of forest products. Some of them have traditional knowledge in herbal medicines. Satha or Ayyappan is their principal deity and their settlements are located near the Sastha temples like Aryankavu, Achankovil and Sabarimala.

Statement of the Problem

The present article unfurls the problems encountered by the Malapandaram tribe of Kerala. Malapandaram is one of the semi- nomadic tribes located mainly in the premises of Periyar Tiger Reserve, to the south of it and in the vicinity of the Kollam district. The study highlights the problems encountered by this tribal community. The particular problems extracted from the study were, problems in finding employment for a minimum standard of living, lack of education, lack of stable income, threat of displacement, distance to educational, medical institutions, rules and regulations of the government, exploitation by the agents and public, ill health and malnutrition, drain of forest resources and financial liability of the household, denied rights over land, the existence child marriage, polygamy.

Women empowerment is the buzzword now-a-days. Nocountry can afford development without considering women who constituteabout half of its stock of human resource. So, development has bypassedwomen in India despite worshiping and paying respect to women in mythologyand historical texts. Gender disparities vary vastly across cultural, geographicaland historical context.Gender disparity is comparatively less in tribal societies, but because of the backwardness of the community itself lead to the backwardness women, especially tribal women. Malapandaram as nomadic tribes in Kerala suffering from lot problems, sometimes it seemed as unique in nature.

Objectives of the study

1. to study the status of Malapandaram women in Pathanamthitta District
2. To find out the different dimension of development of tribal women
3. to find out the factors responsible for the backwardness of Malapandaram women in Pathanamthitta District

Area of study

Two blocks from Pathanamthitta were selected for the present study, in which Malapandaram families used to live in.

Unit and Universe of the study

Universe will be the total families living in the two blocks in Pathanamthitta. Only 300 families were there. There are only One woman from one family will constitute unit of study.

Method of data collection

Focus group discussion and participant observation were adopted for data collection. They are residing as groups of 4-12 families.

Findings of the study

Compared to other tribal groups, status of women among Malapandaram is seen as vulnerable. Status of Malapandaram women can be analysed with the help of the factors such as, **Cultural dimension**-status of rights of indigenous people, participation in local resources management, inclusion of indigenous knowledge; **Legal Issues**-awareness of rights, decentralization, Mainstreaming gender perspective, Decision making;

Political Aspects -Gender justice, elimination of all forms of gender discrimination; **Economic aspects and Social Dimension** -poverty eradication, micro credit, women and economy, women and agriculture, women and industry, support service, globalization; **Social dimension** – education, Health, Nutrition, drinking water, sanitation, housing and shelter, environment.

Cultural dimension

• ***Status of rights of indigenous people***

It is observed that, the rights of indigenous people can be assessed with the help of their ownership on land, control over ethnic medicine and forest products , control over religious practice are getting reduced day by day. Malapandaram people are land less and they are considered as nomadic in government records. They own the right to collect medicinal plants, materials and forest products for the intermediaries only. They are not getting the actual price for these commodities. Women along with men and children participating in collection of forest products, but they can't make it for income or means of life. So we can find they are exploited as whole, especially as women too.

• ***Participation in local resources management***

The 249 families among 300 residing in Sabarimala forest region. The Malapandaram owns the right of "viri", (during Sabarimala pilgrim season the Eco Development Committee allotted places on way side for commercial purpose, there they can have shops, facilitation centers for the pilgrimers etc.) But now a days the non tribes from rest of the district as well as from other places capturing this places by giving them a nominal amount. Every family has the right to set "viri" along the way side, but the intermediaries will influence the tribal people and the "viri" will be occupied by non-tribes. The malapandaram family will remain in poverty. It directly affects the women and children more.

• ***Inclusion of indigenous knowledge***

Inclusion indigenous knowledge, basically on ethnic medicine can be tested here. But the people those who know the name, utility and sources are deprived of its commercial aspect. The labour power of women is also questioned here.

Legal Issues

• *Awareness of rights*

Type of Right	*Frequency of positive response*	*Percentage*
Forest Right	194	64. 7
Right to Education	35	11.67
rights of women	16	5.33
Atrocity prevention act	23	7.7
Constitutional rights	30	10

It is found surprising that, the 64% of women is aware about forest right act, but when we move on to the next items, it ranges between 11.67% and 5.33%. Only 11.67% were aware about right to education and 10% were aware about constitutional rights. Only 5.33% were about rights of women and 7.7% were aware about atrocity prevention act. It shows the pathetic condition of Malapandaram women and it is because of their social backwardness. It should be getting serious attention from the government and public to get rid of this backwardness.

Mainstreaming gender perspective

There is no difference in between the role played by women and men in family affairs. They are participating equally in cooking, collecting firewood, rearing children, engaging in their means of life etc.

They are equally enjoying right to discarding of marriage, but after separation the responsibility of the children will be with mother after their. It is found that, they are providing equal opportunities to their children in engaging in domestic affairs, in their means of life. Both boys and girls seen as discontinued from their studies. Rate of child marriage is high among Malapandaram group; both boys and girls are not exempted from this social evil.

• *Decision making*

In decision making process with regard to the domestic affairs, engaging in forest product collection, educating children, or in any social sphere women get equal chance to put their choice forward.

• *Decentralization*

The Malapandaram family is not autocratic in their nature; they are organizing their family, their job, decision making in a decentralized manner.

Everybody is getting equal importance in conveying their opinion; even the child itself has the right to combat with their parents too.

Political Aspects

• ***Gender justice***

Women specific and women related legislations have been enacted to safeguard the rights and interest of women, besides protecting against discrimination, violence, and atrocities and also to prevent socially undesirable practices.Malapandaram women playing equal role with their men and most of the indicators in gender perspectives are equally circulated among men and women. Among Malapandaram women they exercising equal rights with man and at the same time discriminated by non tribes.

• ***Elimination of all forms of gender discrimination***

Normal forms of gender discrimination are not found among Malapandaram.From the focused group discussion it is found that, the majority (94.67%) women are not aware about rights of women or women specific legislations. But there are cases registered under women specific legislations, only one case was reported under Domestic violence among 300 women.

Economic aspects and Social Dimension

• ***Poverty eradication***

Poverty eradication programmes under government of Kerala is not beneficial for the malapandaram women. Only15 (5%) women are members of Kudumbasree. Malapandaram women are not getting benefits from other state sponsored programmes. One of the women has shown an intimation letter from panchayath to pay the beneficiary contribution of 4500/- to avail the goat rearing programme by Seethathodu panchayath. As she is separated, getting only nominal income from her job and she was not able to pay the amount.

• ***Micro credit***

Nobody is a member of micro credit units and, not availed any loans, because of their lower wages.

• ***Women and economy***

Both men and women engaging in job equally and earn equally for family. But nobody have either separate saving or common assets.

• ***Women and agriculture***

Malapandaram are not agricultural laborers and they are not sharing role of agriculture laborers.

• ***Women and industry***

Malapandaram women are not industrial laborers and are not equipped with technical education too.

• ***Support service***

Support programmes for social development only applicable to Malapandaram women, they are not getting support from authorities to sell their collection too.

• ***Globalization***

Even though they are leading isolated life from non tribes, they are also influenced with globalization. In the foremost scene they are exploited by the intermediaries, in selling collected materials, they are not paid fairly by cash. Sometimes they will get price of their product as liquor, saree, food itemsetc. They are living in huts made out of plastic sheet and most of the families have music system and solar panel for generating power. 112 families have mobile phones both men and women using same phone. For travelling to other parts apart from forest they are using jeep, bus, auto riksha etc.

Social dimension

• ***Education***

Particulars	***Frequency of negative response***	***Percentage***
Enrolment Ratio of children	0	0
Gender Parity Index in Education	0	0
Dropout rate	295	5

In spite of education initiatives, there is disparity between the states in the case of tribal literacy rates. Low enrolment coupled with soaring drop-out rates in primary schools increase the problem, which has its origin in a gamut of inter-related cultural and socio -economic variables. Malapandaram people are associated with a certain stigma and behavior, which can be partially tackled through a change in mindset among non-tribes. Enrolment Ratio of ST student's Gross enrolment ratio of ST Boys is more than ST girls in all classes.

From the focus group discussion it is found that, even though not at exact age every child is enrolled in school. Both boys and girls are entrusted to get admission at school, but only 1.6% has continued their education till higher secondary level. 99% women are illiterate like Malapandaram men. Only one woman has completed her high school level. 85% have discontinued from studies from their primary level itself. It also leads to discontinuation in studies of their child too.

As they are exercising nomadic life, they are not able to avail the school or anganwadi services and it will result in discontinuation of studies.

- ***Health***

To review health status of the following dimensions: sex ratio, age at marriage, fertility and mortality, life expectancy, nutritional status, maternal mortality, mother and child health care practices, family welfare programmes and sexually transmitted diseases.

It is found that, among the total population of Malapandaram is only 38.8% are men and 61.22% are women. Number of female is greater than number of men and among children 67.56% are girls and 32.5% is boys.

With regard to maternal mortality rate, there is 100% death reported in 2018, and the mothers were under 20 years of age; one girl was a survivor of POCSO too. Maternal mortality rate among adult women found zero. For Maternal care90% depending hospitals, interesting thing is that, 80% of them have gone to hospital only for delivery. No caesarian sections were found. It is observed that, birth control measures are poor in practice most of families have minimum three children. Above 45% of women have more than 5 children. Sexually transmitted diseases are also found negative.

- ***Nutrition***

Children below 18 years and women are also found malnourished and according to a field study conducted by district Child Protection Office, that 59% female children found malnourished. Only 10% families are getting regular nutritional food from anganwadies.

- ***Drinking water***

300 families depending on traditional water resources for drinking water; and during drought season they used to settle besides the river side for availing river water. Pamba and Kakkattaaru are the main rivers they are usually depend upon. Pampa appears one of the most polluted rivers in Kerala;and the people tribal in Pathanamthitta has to depend on Pamba for drinking water throughout the year.

- ***Housing / sanitation facilities***

Malapandaram are semi nomadic in nature and they used to live plastic covered huts. Single room huts with kitchen inside is seen everywhere. 90% women have temporary housing facilities. They are living inside forest and permanent housing is not possible for their nomadic nature of life. With regard to sanitation facilities, ODF campaign is not benefitted for 90% of Malapandaram families. Lack of sanitation facilities also result in pollution of river water and land at the same time.

- ***Environment***

They are born in forest, live in forest; depend on forest for their lively hood; dies in forest. Their identity is constructed with forest; their uniqueness is result of their forest life. Conservation of forest and environment if their way of life, because they will be faded away without forest. They treat forest animals as their counterparts in forest. They give respect to them and take respect from them.

Implication

The present study confirms some of the existing views on problems faced by tribes in India, especially malapandaram women. The social fabric of our society is not conducive to the sustainable development of the weaker sections of the society – Malapandaram in this case. Malapandaram girls are not provided with adequate opportunities to have education. The highest frequency of the term education itself is very important. Gainful employment which can bring social upliftment can only be achieved through inclusive education system based on a policy sensitive to cultural factors. The work domain is also not supportive for the tribal women to have their rights accepted and granted by the society. The role of women in economic and social spheres is yet to be accepted for its real value. Health has not been found among the frequent themes, even though health problem is an important issue concerning women in general. This study is explorative in nature, which aims to act as a starting point to further –and deeper- analyses of the issue in question. The associations found out through such explorative studies can also be helpful in formulating survey questions and questionnaire items in similar studies. The findings suggest that some core areas where thrust has to be given in addressing problems of tribal women are education, social roles, child rights, etc. Welfare measures designed for tribal population in general and women in particular, should keep these areas in focus. (Chinchu C, JRF, Dept. of Psychology, Periyar University, Salem).

Conclusion

Status of Malapandaram women is found vulnerable with compared to other tribal women. Obviously improvement in the status of Malapndaram women will be possible only with socio-economic development of the community as a whole. Government and concerned department have to plan, implement and monitor the developmental activities for Malapndam in Pathanamthitta district.

References

1. Basu, Sarah. Mental Health Concerns for Indian Women. *Indian Journal of Gender Studies* 2012 19: 127.
2. Chandramouli, C. (2013). *Scheduled Tribes in India As Revealed in Census 2011*. Ministry of Home Affairs, New Delhi.
3. Panda, P. (1988), "Barriers to Educational Development in Tribal Areas", *Indian Journal of Adult Education*, vol. 49, no.3, pp. 79-83.
4. Pradhan, S. K (2011), "Problems of Tribal Education in India", *Kurukshetra*, vol.59, no.7, pp. 26-31.
5. Rajyalakshmi, (2010), *Study of Indian Society,* Jawahar Publishers and Distributers, New delhi.
6. VIP 'human safari' organized by top cop tasked with ending scandal. (2012). Survival International Retrieved from http://www.survivalinternational.org/news/8157.

Chapter - 23

Educational Status of Scheduled Tribes-A Gender Perspective

Dr. Sivasankar, V and Premkumar, A

Introduction

India has one the most illiterate in the world and among the total population the level of literary was 80.33 percent in 2011 (Census, 2011). Over the periods the level of literacy had improved, and 36.39 percent in 1961, 45.4 percent in 1971, 54.9 per cent in 1981, 62.66 percent in 1991 and 73.44 percent in 2001. However, Indian society divided in to different religion and caste system and the economic status is determined by the level of caste strata. On the basis, Scheduled Castes and Scheduled Tribes are the lowest level in the caste system. This level of caste disclose the level of literacy and hence, level of literacy is not a economic problems than social problems. In the context, the present study examines the level of literacy of tribal in rural and urban areas. This study also explores the gender gap of literacy of tribes. The methodology of the study is based on Census reports of various years.

Level of Literacy of Scheduled Tribes in India

Over the decades, the proportion of scheduled tribe literacy has increased (NUEPA, 2014). In 1961, the proportion of literate was only 8.51 percent, and it increased nearly 60 percent in 2011 (see table 1). Gender analysis, the female proportion was less than male. In 1961, the male literacy was 13.83 percent and female was only 3.16 per cent. In 2011, the male literacy rate was 68.53 percent and female was nearly 50 percent. The increasing proportion of literacy of female was very slow than male for scheduled tribes. The highest increasing proportion of literacy in the decades of 1991 to 2001. In 1991, the level of literacy was 29.60 percent and it increased 17.5 percent in 2001, which was 47.10 percent. During 1961 to 1991, the gender gap between male and female has increased and the period of 2001 to 2011, indicates the trend of decline.

Table - 23.1: Scheduled Tribes Literacy Rate

Year	*Male*	*Female*	*Gap*	*Total*
1961	13.83	3.16	10.67	8.53
1971	17.63	4.85	12.78	11.30
1981	24.52	8.04	16.48	16.35
1991	40.65	18.19	22.46	29.60
2001	59.17	34.76	24.41	47.10
2011	68.53	49.35	19.18	58.96

Source: Various Years of Census of India

Scheduled Tribe Literacy Rate in Rural Areas

Generally, majority of tribes are located in the rural and hill areas. In 1961, the proportion of rural tribal literacy rate was 8.16 percent and among these, male was 13.37 percent and female was 2.90 percent (ESAG, 2018). The level of literacy rate has increased and it was nearly 57 percent in 2011. During 2011, the male literacy rate was 67 percent and female was 47 percent. The gender gap in rural area has increased from 1961 to 2001 and during 2001 to 2011, it declined.

Table - 23.2 : Scheduled Tribes Literacy Rate in Rural India

Census Year	*Male*	*Female*	*Gap*	*Total*
1961	13.37	2.90	10.47	8.16
1971	16.92	4.36	12.56	10.68
1981	22.94	6.81	16.13	14.92
1991	38.45	16.02	22.43	27.38
2001	57.39	32.44	24.95	45.02
2011	66.80	46.90	19.90	56.90

Source: Census of India

Scheduled Tribe Literacy Rate in Urban India

Generally, the level of literacy rate in urban areas has higher than rural areas and this same tendency also replicated scheduled tribes also. The urban scheduled tribes' literacy rate was higher than rural scheduled tribes. In 1961, the scheduled tribe literacy rate was 22.41 percent and for male was 37.09 percent and female was 13.45 percent. During 2011, the level of literacy of scheduled tribe was 76.0 percent; male was 83.20 percent and female was 70.30 percent. The gender gap in urban areas has declined since 1991 Census.

Table - 23.3: Scheduled Tribes Literacy Rate in Urban India

Census Year	*Male*	*Female*	*Gap*	*Total*
1961	37.09	13.45	23.64	22.41
1971	37.09	19.64	17.45	28.84
1981	47.60	27.32	20.28	37.93
1991	66.56	45.66	20.90	56.60
2001	77.77	59.87	17.90	69.09
2011	83.20	70.30	12.90	76.80

Source: Census of India

Conclusion

The major finding of the study as follows; the scheduled tribe literacy rate had lower than scheduled castes and other general groups both in rural and urban areas. The female scheduled tribe literacy rate had very wretched level than any other social groups in India. This clearly indicated that the constitutional right failed to provide right to education for scheduled tribes. Hence, both union and state government think to reframe their policy to encourage tribal education.

References

Department of Educational Management Information System. Educational Development Index (EDI) 2014, National University of Educational Planning and Administration (NUEPA). 1–21.

Government of India (2011). Census of India 2011.New Delhi: Registrar General and Census Commissioner of India, Ministry of Home Affairs.

Government of India. (2018). Educational Statistics at a Glance (Annual Report 2018). New Delhi: Department of School Education & Literacy Statistics Division.

Ministry of Statistics and Programme Implementation, G. of I. (2017). Selected Socio-Economic Statistics India 2017 (Annual Report). Central Statistics Office Social Statistics Division.

Ministry of Tribal Affairs, Government of India. Annual Report 2016-17 (Annual Report). New Delhi: Ministry of Tribal Affairs.

Chapter - 24

Health Status of Paliyan Tribal Women in Sirumalai Hills: A Sociological Perspective

Dr. K. Seenivasan

Abstract

In Sirumalai hills, Paliyan tribes are illiterate and highly ignorant and gullible. They are heterogeneous group; most of them remain at the lowest stratum of the society due to various factors like geographical and cultural isolation, primitive occupations and extreme levels of poverty. They are short in nature and black in colour with curly hair, thick lips, broad and flat nose. Tamil is their mother language. This paper attempts to study the socio - demographic characteristic of Paliyan tribal women, to access the level of awareness of public health services undertaken by Government/NGO and to study the health problems of Paliyan tribal women in four settlement areas of Sirumalai hills at Dindigul District, Tamil nadu. A majority of them had health problems such as visual sight problems, malnutrition, diabetes, arthritis, hypertension, anemia etc., The result of the study shows that there is a need for a Health mobile van with health personnel that can take care of their Physical health and Psychological needs on a regular basis and to conduct an awareness programme about personal hygiene and health education, and Govt. welfare schemes for tribal community at Sirumalai hills, Dindigul District, Tamil nadu.

Keywords: *Health status, Paliyan tribal women*

1. Introduction

The tribal population is identified as the aboriginal inhabitants of our country. For Centuries, they have been living a simple life based on the natural environment and have developed cultural patterns congenial to their Physical and social environment. According to *L.P. Vidyarthi* (1981) tribe is a social group with definite territory, common name, common descent, and common culture behaviour of an Endogamous group, common taboos, and existence of distinctive social and political system with full faith in leaders. According to India's recent *Census in 2011*, Scheduled Tribes comprise 8.6 per cent of the population. The distribution of Scheduled Tribes population varies widely across India's States and Territories. In Mizoram and Lakshadweep, Scheduled Tribes represent close to 95 per cent of the population whereas in Kerala and Tamil Nadu Scheduled Tribes represent only 1 per cent of the population. The total number of Tribal population in Dindigul District is 4580 comprising 2325 males and 2255 females.

Paliyan tribes

The word *'tribe'* has not been defined anywhere in the constitution of India. But it states in Article 324 that the Scheduled Tribes are '*tribes or the tribal communities*'. As these communities are presumed to constitute the oldest ethnological segment of the Indian Society, the term *'Adivasi'* ('*Adi*' means oldest and '*vasi*' means inhabitation) is commonly used to designate them. The aboriginal tribes, Paliyans live in the clad of Western Ghats falling in the Districts of *Dindigul, Madurai, Theni, Tiruppur, Virudhunagar and Tirunelveli*. Paliyans lives as isolated groups. *Poolavadi puliyampatti* in Palani hills of Western Ghats is considered to be the origin of this tribe. They used to live in rock crevices and caves like structures called *Kalazhais* and later on constructed a small hut in the forest.

Statement of the problem

The Paliyan tribes are illiterate and highly ignorant and gullible. They are short in nature and black in colour with curly hair, thick lips, broad and flat nose. Tamil is their mother language. Scheduled tribes are special status under five year plans of the Indian constitution, their status on the whole; especially their health still remains unsatisfactory. The health problems need special attention in the context of tribal in India. Available research studies point out that the tribal population has distinctive health problems which are mainly governed by their habitat, difficult terrains and ecologically variable niches. The health, nutrition and medico-genetic problems of diverse tribal groups have been found to be unique and present a formidable challenge for which appropriate solutions have to be found out the planning and evolving relevant research studies. Primitive tribal groups have special health problems and genetic abnormalities like sickle cell anemia, red cell enzyme deficiency, and insanitary conditions, ignorance lack of personal hygiene and health education are the main factors responsible for their ill health (Basu, 2000).

A Scientific method of study is necessary to gain knowledge of the health problems of Paliyan tribal women. In order to make the present study is an attempt to analyze what are the problems existing among the tribal women. It also explores the accessibility and availability of public health services to these disadvantaged women in the Paliyan tribes in Sirumalai hill areas at Dindigul District, Tamil Nadu.

Objectives

The objectives of the study are:

1. To analyze the Socio – demographic characteristics of the Paliyan Women.
2. To identify the Health problems of the Paliyan Women.
3. To find out the problems faced in accessibility of Health services.
4. To highlight the role of supporting system for the welfare of Paliyan Women.

Methodology

The present study is an explorative research and the survey method has been used for collection of data. For the purpose of survey, structured pre-tested interview schedules were prepared and administered to the Paliyan tribal women in Sirumalai Hills. Purposive sampling procedure has been adopted. Observation method was also employed as a tool for data collection. The identification of villages with Paliyan tribes was done with the help of secondary data available with Sirumalai Panchayet office at Sirumalai in Dindigul District; there were a total of 43 Paliyan families in all the settlements during the year 2018-2019. The study has been conducted in four settlements of Sirumalai Hills. The data have been collected from the heads of the tribal families or any adult members in the family who is knowledgeable in providing data. The purpose of this research design is to describe the problems and other units under investigation like Socio - demographic characteristics of the Paliyan Women and elicit new information about the Paliyan tribal Women in the study area through the above objectives.

Study area

The areas under study, the Sirumalai hills is located in Dindigul District of Tamil nadu between 10°07′ - 10°18′ N latitude and 77°55′- 78°12′ E longitude. It covers 52 km^2 hill ranges, with an average temperature of 28° c in summer and 10° c in winter. Paliyans usually live at an altitude of 900-

1350 m in isolated settlements on the hill slopes. The study was conducted *four* Paliyan settlements in Sirumalai village panchayat. Namely, *Ponnuruki, Paliyankadu, Vellan pannai and Tholukadu*. All the four areas have similar Socio-demographic backgrounds. These settlements belong to the Paliyan community. In the study area, 28 Paliyan families with 124 populations (39 males, 64 females and 21 children) were noticed.

Data Processing

After completing the data collection, the filled schedules were cross checked for reliability and validity; then they were edited and finalized for analysis. The data have been processed and tabulated. The simple percentage frequency tables were drawn and interpreted. The analysis has been attempted with a view to find out factors responsible for the health of Paliyan tribal women in Sirumalai Hills.

***Paliyan families in Ponnuruki*, Sirumalai**

Major Findings

Demographic characteristics of Paliyan tribal women

A vast majority of the respondents (70.4 percent) were Females. A majority (60.2 percent) of the respondents were aged between 41-60 years. A majority (88.9 percent) of the respondents were married ie. They were living with their spouses and a majority of the respondents (66.7 percent) came from nuclear families.

Social Characteristics of Paliyan tribal women

A majority of the head of (86.0 percent) family (males) had not reached the primary level education, while a majority of the women (97.1 percent) were illiterates. A majority of the respondents (96.5 percent) were Hindus, and the percentage of school going children was found to be low (11.1 percent) in paliyan tribal groups.

Economic background of Paliyan tribal women

A majority of them (69.4 percent) were living in hut type of houses, 69.4 percent of the houses of the respondents had thatched or tin sheet roofing, more than four-fifth of the respondents (84.8 percent) were living in their own houses, more than three-fifth of them (62.6 percent) were in a dilapidated condition and nearly one-third of the houses (31.7 percent) were kerosene lanterns. Majority of the fathers (62.0 percent) and mothers (58.1 percent) were agricultural Coolies.Income of the majority of these tribal families (49.1 percent) falls between Rs. 1501-2000/- per month. Monthly expenditure of a majority of the respondent families (47.2 percent) was Rs. 2001-2500 per month.

Basic Amenities

Safe shelter was not available for the majority of the families. They do not have a separate kitchen; they use the space outside their living room or a corner inside their living room for cooking purpose. Out of these 4 settlements, 2 settlements constituting (46.4 percent of families) had road facility up to Sirumalai palaiyur.

In Ponnurukki village, people reported that there is no electricity facility. Mostly, all the families in Thazhakadai and Velampannai villages on Sirumalai hills, in Dindigul district, have been living under darkness since independence. A few of them are having kerosene lanterns for their work after sunset. They get kerosene in the ration shop. They are supplied with 3 to 5 liters per month. It is not sufficient because, they languish in darkness for several days in a month. Some houses had solar panel but after some time, it did not function.

It is very clear that basic need of drinking water was not available for Paliyan settlements. Mostly they collected drinking water from private well and stream. Ration card was possessed by 90 percent which can be used for their livelihood ie. Free rice, Kerosene, Dhal and Oil. Mostly they used Government provided free rice from fair price shop, once in every month. More than 50 percent were facilitate with tribal ID card issued by Forest department.

The entire Sirumalai hills neither private nor Government hospital. The nearest hospital is 40 km away from their settlements. Government hospital is only source for their health. Recently Non Governmental agencies established a health care centre at Sirumalai palaiyur through video conferencing, but Paliyan showed little interest as they believe in Government hospital at Dindigul city.

Health problems of the women

The health problems need special attention in the context of tribal communities of India. The tribal population has distinctive health problems which are mainly governed by their habitat, difficult terrains and ecologically variable riches. The tribal groups continue to carry high burdens of diseases of the poor' namely under nutrition and infectious diseases high levels of chronic under nutrition have been observed among child and adult population (Bone et.al.2006). Micronutrient malnutrition is also major problems among ST's including anemia and iodine deficiency disorders (Ghosh & Bharathi, 2003: Artappa et. al. 2009.)

The poor tribals do not get healthy food regularly so they fall sick. Due to mosquitos' bites, skin diseases, natural calamities they suffer and do not get any treatment on time. Hygiene problem is very common in tribal areas. Due to unhygienic conditions their children suffer from many diseases like measles, mumps, polio, tetanus and whooping cough. This is in tune with the study conducted by Deka (2011). Prevention of diseases is an important part of medical care.

In the Paliyan settlement villages, people reported that Forty three percent of Paliyan women complained of one or more problems as shown in the table. Digestive complaint was the most common problem. Loss of appetite, gas formation indigestion and constipation were the specific problems reported. Difficultly to move around, loss of vision, body ache, and decayed and loss of teeth were predominant discomforts of tribal women. Delivery was assisted by an old lady (Pappammal) of 90 years, for the last 50 years. Now, she is very old and unable to do the delivery. Pregnant women usually approach to the Government hospital at Dindigul city for their delivery.

Delivery was assisted by 90 years old lady (Pappammal) for Paliyan women in Ponnuruki, Sirumalai

Table - 24.1: Health problems of the Paliyan women

Sl.No.	*Health Problems*	*Percentage of Women*
A.	Physical Disabilities	
1	Physical Disabilities	58
2	Digestive disturbances	49
3	Loss of vision	44
4	Body ache	27
5	Sleeplessness	17
6	Tiredness	11
7	Decayed,& Loss of teeth	17
8	Loss of hearing	37
B.	Diseases	
1	Asthma	18
2	Diabetes	22
3	Blood Pressure	05
4	Arthritis	05
5	Whooping cough	15
6	typhoid	46
7	Chicken pox	02

As far as health problems is concerned, majority of the women were affected with typhoid and fifteen percent were suffered from whooping cough. Twenty two percent of them were diabetic and eighteen percent asthmatic. A good number of women complained arthritis or high blood pressure and a few of them were infected with chicken pox. The proportion of women complaining of disability to move around without support increased with advancement of their age. This condition indicates that they need for considering their needs of the aged while building a house.

The findings shows that majority of the husbands of them have bad habits like smoking and drug addiction. As far as the medical treatment was concerned, nearly half of them took treatment from Government hospital at Dindigul and above one fourth of them took traditional way of treatment.

The result of the study shows that there is a need for a Health mobile van with health personnel that can take care of their Physical health and Psychological needs on a regular basis and to conduct an awareness programme about personal hygiene and health education, and Government welfare schemes for tribal community at Sirumalai hills.

Conclusion

Tribal isolation remains the main cause of social, economic and moral exploitation of tribal by non tribal, poverty, illiteracy, health problems, exploitation by middle man and traders, land alleviation and forest policies etc., are major experience by the Paliyan tribals in Sirumalai Hills. Thus need of money, attention and motivation along with, there is an urgent need to launch income generating, education and health awareness programmes to make them aware and help them to take opportunities given by the Government and Non Government Organizations.

References

Books

1. Arulappa, N.et.al.,(2009).*Prealence of anaemia among rural pre-school children of West Bengal,* India. Ann Hum Biol, Pp. 1-12.
2. Basu, A.M.,(1992). *Culture, the status of women and demographic behavior: Illustrated with the case of India*. Oxford: Clarendon Press.
3. Bose, K.et.al.,(2006).*High prevalence of undernutrition among adult Kora Mudi tribals of Bankura District,* West Bengal, India. Anthropological Science, 114, Pp. 65-68.
4. Behura, N.K. (1996). *Planned Development and Quality of Life among Indian Tribes. Tribes of India on goingchallenges,* NewDelhi: M D Publications.
5. Dipak K. et.al., (2003). *Demography and Health Profile of the Tribal,* Anmol Publications, New Delhi.
6. Ghosh, R., & Bharati, P. (2003). *Haemoglobin status of adult women of two ethnic groups living in a peri-urbanarea of a Kolkata city, India: a micro-level study.* Asia Pacific J Clin Nutr,12, Pp.451-59.
7. Kulamani Padhi, (2005). *Tribal Development in India - A Study in Human Development*. Orissa Review, Pp. 72-78.
8. Ministry of Tribal Affair, (2010). *Statistical Profile of Schedule Tribes in India.* Ministry of Tribal Affairs Statistical Division Government of India. www. Tibal. nic. in.
9. Singh N, et.al., (2003). *Forest malaria in Chhindwara, Madhya Pradesh, Central India: A case study in a tribalcommunity.* Am J Trop Med Hyg, Vol. 68, Pp.602-607.
10. Salil Basu, (2000). *Dimensions of Tribal Health in India. Health and Population-Perspectives,* 23(2), Pp. 61-70.
11. Vidyarthi, L. P, (1981). *Tribal Development and its Administration*, Concept Publishing Company, New Delhi, Pp 12 -14.

Journals

1. India Ministry of Tribal Affairs, (2004). *The National Tribal Policy: A Policy for the Scheduled Tribes of India* New Delhi: Ministry of Tribal Affair.
2. Prakash Chandra Mehta, (2000). *Tribal Development in 20th Century,* Durga Taldar Shiva Publishers,Udaipur, Pp. 7.
3. Sundara Rao, M., & Lakshmana Rao, B. (2010). *Factors Influencing Socio-Economic Status of the Primitive Tribal Groups (PTGs) and Plain Tribes in Andhra Pradesh,* World Applied Sciences Journal 11 (2): 235-244.

4. Shankar. R., & Manimaran, S., (2013). *Socio – economic conditions of Pachamalai tribes,* Cognitive Discourses International Multidisciplinary Journal, Vol.1, July, Pp.112-117.

Chapter - 25

Education and Empowerment of Tribal Women: Empirical and Theoretical Dialogues

Vinayakan S B, & Dr. Sukumaran M

Abstract

Tribal women everywhere are the most under privileged and marginalised segments of the society. Historically they are backward and prone to exploitation. Educational backwardness of the tribal women is seems to be one of the significant factor which contribute and accelerate the backwardness of the tribal women rather than development. They most often encounter lack of freedom in life and decision making as well. Everywhere they have been excluded and denied the entitlements which are enjoyed by others. This is a form of exclusion that the tribal woman undergoes. In this context this paper is an attempt to articulate the relationship between education and empowerment of tribal women in Kerala, Kollam district. The primary and secondary data were used in the study and analysed with simple statistical techniques. The study found out that, the educational status of the tribal women is very poor and they are facing a sort of enslaving not with in the tribe but outside the tribe.

Key Words: *Education, Empowerment, Tribal women*

1. Introduction

Education plays a significant role in the socio-economic development of the individual and society. It is invariably articulated by different researchers about the relationship between education and socio economic wellbeing of the individual and the society as a whole. Education plays an important role in human development. Human development encompasses development in several dimensions of human wellbeing (Venkatraja, B and Indira, M). There exists a positive relationship between education standard and the socio-economic wellbeing. It tells us that, higher the level of education higher will be the level of socio-economic development. It is a fact that the educational standards of tribal population is comparatively poor than the non tribal population. It is also true in the case of tribal women also. The poor educational standards of the tribal women cause to various issues related to women empowerment. It leads them to keep away from the mainstream socio-economic and political activities and prone to social exclusion. It is also observed that, social exclusion among the tribal women is highly prevalent among the less educated compared to educated. This paper discusses the educational status of tribal women and empowerment of tribal women.

2. Significance of the study

Numbers of policies and programmes have been implemented in India particularly intended to mainstream the tribal population in general and tribal women in particular. But it is very emphatic that, most of the policies and programmes were least effected to the tribal population including tribal women. The Tribals have been given numerous rights and concessions under various statutes of central as well as State Governments but they remain deprived of the benefits arising out of such statutory provisions due to their ignorance and apathy of enforcing agencies (D. Muni Swamy, 2015). It is felt that, educational backwardness is one of the significant factors which exclude them from the access of many of the policies and programmes. It is a fact that development of the nation also demands the empowerment of women. Hence it is very urgent to ensure adequate education to the tribal women to ensure all the entitlements and privileges enjoyed by other women in the society. This paper tries to relate the education and empowerment status of tribal women in Kerala. Hence the result of the present study will have a strong impetus on policy makers and planners when the formulate policies and programmes exclusively meant for tribal women.

3. Methodology of the Study

The study has been used both primary and secondary data. The primary data were collected from 30 respondents in Piravathoor village of Pathanapuram block in Kollam district. The data were gathered using a semi structure questionnaire and rating scale. The data were collected, organized, classified and analysed using statistical software. The simple statistical techniques like averages were used to analyse and interpret the data. The empowerment status of the tribal women has been done on the basis of arbitrary mathematical operations. Arithmetic Mean and Standard Deviation has been used to classify the empowerment status as below average, average and above average. The results of the studies were explained with the help of existing body of knowledge in the related area.

4. Objectives of the Study

The present study has the following objectives

1. To examine the educational status of tribal women in the study area.
2. To find out the women empowerment status of the tribal women in the study area.
3. To theoretically explain the relationship between education and women empowerment.

5. Results and Discussion

This part of the paper gives detailed presentation of the results followed by discussions. In this section details of the tribal communities taken for study, educational standards of the parents of the respondents, educational standards of the respondents an empowerment status of the women were presented.

5.1. Tribal groups in the study

The details of the tribal communities taken for the present study are presented in Table. 25.1. From the table it is evident that, majority of the tribal groups come under study are Malapandaram, and it is followed by Malavedar. The percentage of other three tribal groups is comparatively very meagre.

Table - 25.1: Tribal groups come under the study

Name of the Tribal Group	*Frequency*	*Percent*
Malavedar	7	23.3
Malapandaram	18	60.0
Ulader	2	6.7
Kanikar	1	3.3
Malakuravar	2	6.7
Total	30	100.0

Source: Field Survey, 2020

4.2. Education Standards of the Parents

It is very significant to note that, the educational standards of the tribal parents are comparatively meager. When the educational status of the parent is low, that will also affect the educational standards of the next generation.

It would be equally effective to the tribal women. When the parents are less concern about the need and significance of education the same thought will transmit to the next generation. There exists a significant positive effect of the parent's income and educational levels on the academic achievement of primary school students based on a Longitudinal Survey of Families and Children in Gansu province (Sun et al. 2009).

Table-25.2: Highest Education Standards of Parents

Education Standards	*Frequency*	*Percent*
Illiterate	27	90.0
Secondary	1	3.3
Higher Secondary	1	3.3
Higher Education	1	3.3
Total	30	100.0

Source: Field Survey, 2020

From the data furnished in Table. 25.2, it is pertinent that, majority of the tribal parents are illiterate. This shows the educational backwardness of the tribal parents and their inability to guide their girl child to direct towards empowerment. Here 90 percent of the parents are illitereate. Only very meagre percent of the tribal parents were secured secondary and higher education. This data itself is a portrayal of the educational backwardness of tribal parents. Currently, the tribes lag behind not only the generalpopulation but also the Scheduled Caste population in literacy and education. This disparity is even moremarked among Scheduled Tribe women, who have the lowest literacy rates in the country (Maharatna, 2005). It is very pathetic to see that, about 90 percent of the tribal parents are illiterate even with respect highest education acquired by the parents.

4. 3. Education Standards of the Women

The educational status of the women in the study area is presented in Table. 25.3. From the figures it is evident that, even among the tribal women about 40 percent of the women are illiterate followed by 20 percent primary or literate women. About 17 percent of the tribal women are secured secondary education and higher education. The percentage of women who are secured higher secondary education is only 6.7 percent. A bird's eye view of the data presented gives us a detailed picture of the educational status of the tribal women in the study area. It describes the educational backwardness of the tribal women and they have to go miles to par with the non-tribal women. We know that education enables individual to think rationally and act purposefully according to different circumstances. Women education inIndia plays a very important role in the overall development of the country. It not only helps in the developmentof half of the human resources, but in improving the quality of life at home and outside. It necessitates concerted effort from the part of the government to supply adequate educational opportunities to the tribal women which are very fit to the socio-economic and psychological conditions of the tribal women.

Table - 25.3: Education standards of the Respondent

Education standards	*Frequency*	*Percent*
Illiterare	12	40.0
Literate/Primary	6	20.0
Secondary	5	16.7
Higher Secondary	2	6.7
Higher Education	5	16.7
Total	30	100.0

Source: Field Survey, 2020

4. Tribal Women Empowerment Status Field Based Analysis

Tribal women empowerment status has been estimated based on some arbitrary mathematical operations. Here the Arithmetic mean of the women empowerment status of tribal women is measured and found out as 13 and the Standard deviation is 3. Here the below average, average and above average measurement has been made on the basis of Arithmetic Mean and Standard Deviation. The result of the arbitrary calculation has been presented in Table. 25.4. From the measurement it is evident that, 20 percent of the tribal women in the study area are still having below average empowerment, a large majority of the tribal women lies in the average empowerment status that is 63.3 percent and around 17 percent of the tribal women are having above average empowerment status. It tells us that, a lion portion of the tribal women are lagging behind the lack of appropriate women empowerment status. It further demands the strategic planning and policy making in tune with the felt in need of the tribal women.

Table - 25. 4: Tribal Women Empowerment Status

Class	*Frequency*	*Percentage*	*Status*
0-4	0	0	
5-10	06	20.0	Below Average
11-15	19	63.3	Average
16-17	05	16.7	Above Average
Total		100	

Source: Field Survey, 2020

6. Major Findings of the Study

1. Educational status of the tribal women is very poor. However, a 60 percent comprises literate, primary education, secondary education and higher education is a cape of good hope.
2. Still 20 percent of the tribal women are having below average empowerment, more than 63 percent having average women empowerment status an only 16.7 percent of the tribal women have above average of women empowerment.

Conclusions

Based on the analysis and discussions the study can be concluded that, the tribal women in the study area are not well empowered. This is more emphatic from the empirical data as well as the qualitative interacation with the tribal women in the study area revealed that, they are feeling empowered with in the tribal community and their tribal settings. What makes them unconfortable and powerless is in the outside of the tribal settings. Some of the students felt powerlessness during the time of their higher education. They are saying that when they interact with the non-tribal students some time some of the students trying to cornerthem by ridiculing and excluding them form interactions. This is one instance in which they lacking freedom. In fact empowerment is not more than freedom and capability to functioning. The capability approach is a theoretical frame work that entails two core normative claims: first, the claim that the freedom to achieve well-being is of primary moral importance, and second, that freedom to achieve well-being is to be understood in terms of people's capabilities, that is, their real opportunities to do and be what they have reason to value (Robeyns, Ingrid, 2016). Actually the tribal women lack the capability to functioning along with freedom when they feel the problem of powerlessness and capability deprivation. It necessitates adequate supply of education to the tribal women that enable them to develop freedom and choice of their life.

References

Muni Swamy, D. (2015). Impact of tribal welfare and development programmes on the scheduled tribes: A Study of Ananthapuramu district. International Journal of Applied Research; 1(13): 512-517. Retrieved from. http://www. all research journal. com. Role of Education in Social Development: An Empirical Analysis

By Venkatraja, B and Indira, M. (2011). Role of Education in Social Development: An Empirical Analysis Madhya Pradesh Journal of Social Sciences. Retrieved from. https://www. questia. com.

Sun, Zhijun, Zeyun Liu, and Baicai Sun. 2009. Family, school, and children's academic achievements—based on the study of rural areas in Gansu Province. Journal of Beijing Normal University (Social Science Edition) 37 (5): 103–115.

Maharatna, A. (2005), Demographics Perspectives on India's Tribes, Oxford University Press.

Suguna M. (2011). Education and Women Empowerment in India. International journal of Multidisciplinary, Research: 1(8). Retrieved from. http://www. zenith research. org. in.

Robeyns, Ingrid, "The Capability Approach", The Stanford Encyclopedia of Philosophy (Winter 2016 Edition), Edward N. Zalta (ed.), URL = <https://plato.stanford.edu/archives/win2016/entries/capability-approach/>.

Index

A

Abolition of Slavery, 172
Aboriginal tribes, 218
Accredited social health activists, 149
Action from UNICEF, 33
Additional Commissioner of Police, 173
Adiyam, 83
Administrative hurdles, 59
Adolescent empowerment scheme, 150
Affordable financial services, 50
African continent, 103
Agrarian background, 133
Agricultural Census report, 14
Agricultural loan, 54
Agricultural operations, 183
Agricultural production, 16
Agriculture Census, 14, 16, 17
Ajay Saraogi, 155
All Forms of Discrimination Against Women 103, 172
Allopathy medicines, 118
Analysis and Interpretations of Data, 53
Anamala Tribal colony, 43
Andaman Nicobar Islands, 90
Andhra Pradesh, 90, 172
Andhra Pradesh Devadasis, 172
Andhra Pradesh, 83
Animal Sciences University, 43
Anti-social activities, 105
Arithmetic Mean, 228
Arunachal Pradesh, 68
Ashok Kumar, 155
Assets as Goats and Hens, 118
Attapady area, 185
Awareness on Banking Services, 130

B

B.R. Hills, 163
Backwardness of women, 104
Bagalkot, 31, 35, 37
Balanced diet, 59
Bank Linkage Programmes, 70
Banking and Non-Banking Finance Corporation, 154
Barren woman, 204
Barriers to entry, 142, 143
Beda, 29
Begalkot district, 74
Behaviour of health care providers, 193
Beijing Conference, 161
Beijing Declaration, 103
Belagavi, 37
Below poverty line, 69
Beneficiary of the Father's Property, 159
Beti Bachao Beti Padhao Scheme, 69
Bettakuruba women, 156
Bhagyalaxmi scheme, 69
Bhil, 83
Bidar District, 176, 179
Bihar, 184
Biological process, 148
Biological relation, 186
Bombay Devadasis Protection Act, 172
Born in forest, 211
Brahamanandan and Babu, 52

Bride price, 177, 184
Bringing Health Services, 99
Burkha system, 142
Byadaghi, 65

C

Chenchu, 83
Chhattisgarh, 86, 90, 91, 184
Chicken pox, 223
Child birth, 178
Child malnutrition, 190
Child marriage, 28
Child Marriage Act, 37
Child Marriage Prevention Officers, 39
Child Marriages, 30
Child Protection Office, 210
Child rearing, 42, 159
Chinna Melam, 169
Chintana Foundation, 163
Chola times, 169
Cholanaickan tribe group, 84
Cholanaikkan, 83
Chota Nagpur and Santal Paragana region, 25
Christian missionaries, 171
Christine Bradley, 142
Chronic energy deficiency, 98
Coastal regions, 95
Collaborative Water Supply and Sanitation Council, 149
Collection of forest products, 206
Communicable diseases, 120
Community mobilization, 34
Community participation, 192
Concept of Health, 96
Conclusion and Suggestion, 38
Consumption of alcoholic drinks, 176
Coorg Organisation of Rural Development, 163
Corruption, 142, 143
Crimes against Tribes, 88
Crop growing area, 71
Cultural background, 65
Current Scenario, 173

D

Dadra and Nagar Haveli, 90, 176
Dancing female, 171
Davanagere, 36
Decision making, 76
Demographic characteristics, 220
Demographic Profile of Tribes, 82
Department of Social Welfare, 69
Department of Tribal Welfare, 69
Depend on forest, 211
Determinants of Financial Inclusion, 54
Devadasi community, 169
Devadasi families, 174
Devadasi system, 172
Devadasi tradition, 174
Devadasis, 142
Devadasis Rehabilitation Programme, 66
Development Through Education, 163
Dharmapuri, 136
Dharwad, 37
Dies in forest, 211
Digital Financial Inclusion, 48
Digital India, 47, 48
Dindigul city, 222
Dindigul District, 115, 121, 218, 219, 221
Disposal of used sanitary napkin, 150
Domestic violence, 143, 208
Dr. D. M. Nanjundappa, 67
Dr. Sunitha Krishnan, 173
Drinking water, 64, 86, 210
Drinking water facilities, 86

E

Eco Development Committee, 206
Ecological factors, 190
Economic background, 65, 221

Economic Factors, 52
Economic Growth, 51
Economic status of Women, 77
Economic Survey of Karnataka, 66
Education Standards of the Women, 230
Education, electricity, 64
Educational status, 118
Educational status of the tribal women, 232
Educational status of tribal community, 196
Educationally backward classes, 106
Effects of Social Exclusion, 144
Elder women of Mannan community, 185
Electrical Facilities, 117
Emergency Transportation, 99
Emergency transportation for expectant mothers, 193
Empirical review of Literature, 66
Empowering Tribal Women through Sports, 23
Empowerment of tribal women, 132, 142, 157
Epigraphical and literary sources, 170
Evaluation of Ashram Schools, 24
Expectant Mothers, 99

F

Family welfare programmes, 210
Female scheduled tribe, 215
Fertility and mortality, 210
Fifth Five-Year Plan, 69, 107
Financial assistance, 60, 70, 71
Financial challenges, 48
Financial Exclusion, 52
Financial facilities, 54
Financial illiteracy, 49
Financial Inclusion, 52
Financial indiscipline act, 49
Financial literacy, 47
Financial Practices, 51, 55
Financial services, 48
First Five Year Plan Period, 200
Food gathering and hunting, 182
Former President Dr. APJ Abdul Kalam, 96
Foundation for Educational Innovations in Asia, 163
Fourth Five Year Plan, 200
France, 141
Free residential schools, 162
Free rice, 221
Freedom of movement, 164
Frequency of Attending Gramasabha, 131
Fuel and fodder, 177
Functions of Social Exclusion, 142
Fundamental Rights, 81
Funeral feast, 178

G

Gadag district, 31
Gaddi family, 161
Gaddis and Bhutias, 160
Gadhika ceremony, 183
Ganga Kalyana Scheme, 67
Garo and Khasi Tribal communities, 182
Gender wise distribution, 17
Genetic disorders, 98
Geo-climatic conditions, 95
Geographical boundaries, 142
Geographical location, 107
Geographical Segregation, 142
Ghetto Mentality, 145
Ghokale Vasudha, 44
Girl Child, 159
Girls' empowerment, 34
Gods Rejoice, 68
Gond, 83
Good hygiene practices, 147
Goud, 83
Government and civil society, 107
Government tribal welfare programmes, 119

Gross Enrolment Ratio, 84, 85
Gujarat, 83, 176

H

Hanagal, 65
Haveri, 65
Haveri district, 64, 65, 66, 70, 71
Health and Family Welfare, 149
Health care, 64
Health care and transportation, 64
Health Care Providers, 99
Health Challenges, 99
Health Department, 163
Health education, 87
Health index, 173
Health Issues, 98, 99, 192
Health problems, 223
Health problems of the women, 222
Health services to remote populations, 193
Health status, 96
Health Status of Tribal Women in India, 96
Health worker from tribal communities, 193
Health Workers, 99
Heath Status, 99
High Power Committee, 67
Higher literacy levels, 108
Hill areas of Kodaikanal, 121
Hill Pandaram, 204
Himachal Pradesh, 184
Hindu society, 171
Hirekerur, 65
Human Resources, 148
Hygiene problem, 222
Hypertension, 98

I

Idukki district, 185
Importance of Women Education, 104
Important demographic factor, 60
India Population Project, 163
Indian tribal population, 97
Indian tribal societies, 155
Indian tribal women, 96
Indira Gandhi Matritva Sahyog Yojana, 69
Infant mortality rate, 190
Infections of the reproductive tract, 148
Institute for Development Studies, 149
Integrated Child Development Scheme, 150
Integrated Child Development Services, 66
International market, 133
International publications on tribal women, 115
Iodine deficiency disorders, 222
Irular Tribal Women, 25

J

J. Jayalalilthaa, 172
Janashikshana Trust, 163
Jharkand, 83
Jharkhand, 25, 86, 176
Joint families, 116

K

Kadar, 83
Kamakhya temple in Assam, 149
Kammrar, 83
Kancheepuram District, 25
Kannur district, 50, 55
Kannur- Mysore highway, 50
Karnataka, 29, 36, 64, 74, 154, 164, 172, 179
Karnataka census data, 154
Karnataka Devadasis, 172
Karnataka Mahila Abhivrudhi Yojana, 66
Karnataka State Commission, 37
Karnataka State Women s Development Corporation, 66
Kattunayakan, 83
Kerala, 49, 50, 83, 84, 87, 124, 196

Kerala State, 190
Kerala State Backward Classes Development Corporat, 200
Kerosene, 221
Kinnauri society, 186
Kinnauri tribal group, 184
Kinnauri Women, 184
Kishori Shakti Yojana, 150
Kollam district, 204, 228
Kondakapus, 83
Kondas, 83
Kondkappus, 83
Koppal, 31
Koraga, 83
Kota, 83
Koya, 83
Kozhikode districts, 75
Kudumbashree, 124
Kuruba, 83
Kurumba, 83
Kurumbar communities, 185

L

Lack of awareness, 99
Lack of health, 192
Lack of physical activity, 87
Lactating women, 69
Lakshadweep, 87
Lambadis, 83
Land holdings, 13
Land ownership, 18
Land Purchase Scheme, 67
Language problems, 55
Large size of land, 54
Latrine facilities, 87
Latrine Facility, 86, 87
Law and Order, 173
Law enforcement, 34
Leadership qualities, 109
Legal rights, 18
Level of Literacy, 213
Life expectancy, 210
Literacy Rate, 104
Live in forest, 211
Local Tribal Education in Kerala, 197
Low educational status, 124

M

Madhya Pradesh, 83, 86, 88, 89, 90, 176
Madras Devadasis, 172
Madras state, 137
Mahalingapur Soratur, 31
Maharashtra, 83, 86, 89, 90, 172, 176
Maharashtra Devadasi, 172
Maharashtra State, 24
Mahila Abhivrudhi, 173
Mahila Mandal, 151
Major tribal groups, 83
Malai Pandaram, 204
Malais, 83
Malapandaram families, 207, 211
Malapandaram men, 210
Malapandaram women, 207, 208, 212
Malaria strain, 88
Malarial deaths, 88
Malayali, 136
Male female gap, 196
Male-biased ideology, 162
Malnutrition, 59, 87, 97
Marital status, 118
Marketing Assistance Scheme, 66
Marriage by elopement, 176
Marriage rituals, 177
Married Women, 159
Maternal mortality, 97, 98, 210
Mathamma temple, 172
Matrilineal communities, 184
Matrilineal Societies, 182
Matrilineal system, 182
Mattu Samrakshana Samsthe, 173
Medical clinics, 87
Medical expenses, 21

Medical institutions, 204
Medicine plant, 118
Medico-genetic problems, 218
Melakkarars, 169
Melghat in Maharashtra, 190
Membership in Kudumbashree, 131
Membership of tribal women, 125
Menstrual hygiene, 150
Mental and emotional development, 28
Mental illness, 98
Mexico, 105
Mexico City, 162, 165
Mexico Plan of Action, 103
Micro credit units, 208
Micro finance institutions, 70
Micro financing, 71
Middle School Level of Education, 116
Miller and Lester, 30
Ministry of Tribal Affairs, 82
Modern facilities, 64
Modern society women, 74
Morbidity, 97
Mortality, 97
Mota Naik, 29
Mrs. Indira Gandhi, 105
Mughals women, 142
Multipurpose Tribal Development Projects, 200
Munda tribal group, 185
Mutual fund, 60
Mysore, 163
Mysore district, 155

N

Nairobi Forward Looking Strategies, 103
Nana Naik, 29
National Agricultural Policy, 14
National and international levels, 158
National Commission for Women, 172
National Committee Reports of Tribals, 82
National Crime Records Bureau, 36, 82, 89, 90
National Family Health Survey, 35, 88, 190
National Fifth Five Year Plan, 69
National Fifth Five-Year Plan, 162
National Human Rights Commission, 172, 173
National Tribal Plan, 99
Natural hazards, 44
Nature of Habitation, 52
Navratri festival, 178
Negotiated marriage, 176
Non Government Organizations, 224
Non Governmental agencies, 221
Non-Banking Finance Corporation, 30
Non-Government Organisations, 163
Non-tribal merchants, 59
Non-vegetarian in nature, 176
Non-Vegetarian type of food, 119
North Chennai, 173
North East India, 182
North Karnataka, 35
North Kerala, 41
Northeastern region, 83
Northern States, 83
Number of earning members, 59
Nutritional problems, 114
Nutritional status, 98, 210

O

Olympic gold, 23
Open defecation, 87
Orissa, 83, 86, 172, 184

P

Palakkad district, 185
Palani hills, 218
Paliyan settlement villages, 222
Paliyan tribal Women, 219, 220
Paliyan Women, 219
Paliyar tribal women, 114, 116

Palliyar, 83
Panchayat Raj Institutions, 124
Pandaram Basha, 204
Pandit Jawaharlal Nehru, 96
Paniya Community, 55, 125
Paramedical health professional, 150
Parental perception of education, 159
Parivara, 29
Participation of Tribal Women, 127
Partilineal and matrilineal societies, 186
Pathanamthitta, 210
Pathanamthitta Districts, 204, 212
Pathanapuram block, 228
Pathetic position of women, 102
Patrilocal family, 184
Peria Melam, 169
Periyar Tiger Reserve, 204
Periyar University, 211
Personal lustful benefits, 171
Personal Survey, 70
Physical Violence, 142, 143
Political Aspects, 76, 208
Political awareness, 65
Political environment, 157
Political Relation of Tribal Women, 130
Poor health condition, 124
Poorest Area Civil Society programme, 143
Post offices, 50
Post-Independence period, 196
Poverty and indebtedness, 192
Poverty eradication programmes, 208
Pre-metric hostels, 162
President Pranab Mukherjee, 37
Primary data, 65
Primary education, 70
Primitive tribal area, 135
Primitive Tribal Groups, 67, 82, 83
Primitive tribes, 87
Private Moneylender, 54
Production of sanitary napkins, 150
Professional women, 38
Progress of tribal women, 68
Prohibition of Child Marriage Act, 34
Promoting convergence, 34
Protection of tribal culture, 69
Pudukottai, 136

Q

Qualified doctors, 106
Qualitative improvement, 109

R

Raising awareness of health issues, 193
Rajasthan, 83, 90, 176
Ranibennur, 65
Regular educational programs, 106
Rehabilitation camps, 44
Rehabilitation schemes, 44
Remote places like hills, 105
Remote Populations, 99
Remote rural areas, 99
Reproductive health issues, 98
Reproductive tract infections, 147
Research Methodology, 52
Rural areas, 64, 72
Rural communities, 105
Rural Development, 148
Rural women empowerment, 68

S

Sacred thread, 169
Salem, 136, 211
Samagra Grameena Ashrama, 163
Sample blocks, 65
Sanitary facilities, 149
Sanitation facilities, 211
Sastha temples, 204
Satha or Ayyappan, 204
Savanur, 65
Savings Bank Account, 59
Schedule tribe women, 68, 71
Scheduled Areas, 200
Scheduled Tribe Literacy Rate, 214
Scheduled Tribes, 58, 59

Scheduled Tribes Welfare Department, 197
Seethathodu panchayath, 208
Self Confidence of Tribal Women, 127
Self Help Group, 70, 124
Senior Devadasis, 170
Sexual attacks, 93
Sexually transmitted diseases, 98, 210
Shifting cultivation, 184
Shiggaon, 65
Shiva temple, 170
Sickle cell anemia, 98
Sirumalai Hills, 118, 219, 221, 223, 224
Social background, 65
Social Characteristics, 220
Social Status of the Tribal Women, 128
Social Welfare, 200
Social Welfare Department, 162
Socio-economic factors, 54
Socioeconomic status, 134
Socio-familial problems, 51
South Tamil Nadu, 121
Special Component Plan, 69, 162
Special Development Programmes, 67
Sports as a Social Tool, 21
State Poverty Eradication Mission, 124
Statement of the Problem, 113
Statistical profile of scheduled tribes, 14
Status of Tribal women, 157
Status of women, 102
Status of Women in Tribal Societies, 184
Strategic developments of women, 103
Stratified sampling techniques, 53
Stree Shakthi Programme, 66
Stri-Sabha, 151
Sugalis, 83
Supreme Court of India, 104
Swachh Bharat Mission, 148
Swami Vivekananda Youth Movement, 163

T

Talwars, 29
Tamil Nadu, 115, 136, 137, 172, 176
Tamil Nadu Scheduled Tribes, 218
Tamilnadu, 83, 89
Tatra Ramanthe Devatha, 68
Telangana, 176
Temple authorities, 169
Tendulkar Methodology, 86
Teradal in Bagalkot, 36
Thenmalai, 115
Theoretical review of Literature, 66
Third Five Year Plan Period, 200
Thiruvallur District, 172
Tiruchirapalli, 136
Tiruvannamalai, 136
Toda, 83
Township Colony, 50, 55
Traditional leather working castes, 133
Transport facilities, 192
Transportation, 64
Tribal communities, 47, 99, 113
Tribal community in India, 22
Tribal cultivators, 88
Tribal Development, 148
Tribal Development Blocks, 200
Tribal economy, 113
Tribal education, 196
Tribal farmers, 88
Tribal Health, 99
Tribal societies, 165
Tribal Sub-Plan, 69, 107, 162
Tribal Sub Plan Strategy, 200
Tribal women, 103, 123, 164
Tribal women and empowerment, 228
Tribal Women and Social Exclusion, 144
Tribal Women Empowerment Status, 231
Tribal women in India, 96, 98, 99
Tribal women in Karnataka, 157
Tribal women in Kudmbashree, 125

Tribal's Sub-Plan, 69
Tuberculosis, 88

U

U N Women's Conference, 105
UN Agencies, 201
Undernourished, 191
United Nation Declaration, 112
United Nations, 34
United Nations Children's Fund, 149
United Nations Conferences, 165
United Nations Conferences on women, 162
Urban areas, 28
Uttar Pradesh, 30, 154

V

Valmikis, 29
Vanavasi Kalyana Ashrama, 163
Vegetarian type of food, 119
Vellore, 136
Vellore City, 137
Vellore district, 137
Village in Sirumalai, 115
Village Panchayats, 71
Violence against women, 143
Vishnu temple, 170
Vivekanada Girijana Kalyan Kendra, 163
Vivekananda Foundation, 163
Voting rights, 108, 161
Vulnerable Tribal Groups, 82, 183

W

Wayanad, 44, 88, 185, 190
Wayanad District, 43, 125, 183
Welfare Programmes for Scheduled Tribe, 67
West Bengal, 91, 176, 184
Western Ghats, 218
Western medieval mind-set, 171
Widow remarriage, 184
Woman's Work, 159
Women and Child Development, 34, 36, 68
Women and Children, 148
Women complained arthritis, 223
Women Empowerment, 64, 67, 74, 126, 144, 205
Women entrepreneurship, 96
Women in tribal population, 53
Women in Tribal Societies, 182
Women of reproductive age, 148
Women Skill Training Programme, 66
Women Entrepreneurs and Adolescent Girls, 68
Women's economic empowerment, 73
Women's Health and Rights, 99
Women's Role in Disaster Manangement, 44
Women's Role in Political Sphere, 161
Women's Role in Social Sphere, 160

Y

Yatra Naryantu Poojanthe, 68

Z

Zero balance accounts, 60
Zero Child Marriage, 39